Two week loan

Please return on or before the last
date stamped below.
Charges are made for late return.

IS 239/0799

INFORMATION SERVICES P

PARTICIPATION, NEGOTIATION AND POVERTY: ENCOUNTERING THE POWER OF IMAGES

To my dad,
for his unwavering tough stance on education,
and my mum,
for her patience and care

Participation, Negotiation and Poverty: Encountering the Power of Images

Designing Pro-Poor Development Programmes

FLETCHER TEMBO
University of Reading, UK

HN
49
.C6
.T3

The author has asserted his moral right under the Copyright, Designs and Patents Act, 1988, to be identified as the author of this work.

Published by
Ashgate Publishing Limited
Gower House
Croft Road
Aldershot
Hampshire GU11 3HR
England

Ashgate Publishing Company
Suite 420
101 Cherry Street
Burlington, VT 05401-4405
USA

Ashgate website: http://www.ashgate.com

British Library Cataloguing in Publication Data
Tembo, Fletcher
    Participation, negotiation and poverty : encountering the
    power of images : designing pro-poor development
    programmes. - (King's SOAS studies in development
    geography)
    1. Non-governmental organizations 2. Economic development
    I. Title II. King's College, London III. University of London.
    School of Oriental and African Studies
    338.9'1

Library of Congress Cataloging-in-Publication Data
Tembo, Fletcher, 1964-
    Participation, negotiation, and poverty : encountering the power of images : designing
pro-poor development programmes / Fletcher Tembo.
        p.cm.– (King's SOAS studies in development geography)
    Includes biographical references and index.
    ISBN 0-7546-3377-2 (alk. paper)
    1. Rural development projects. 2. Non-governmental organizations. I. Title. II.
    Series.

HN49.C6 T447 2003
307.1'412–dc2

2002034502

ISBN 0 7546 3377 2

Printed in Great Britain by Antony Rowe Ltd, Chippenham, Wiltshire

Contents

List of Figures

List of Tables

Preface

Development NGOs have long been recognized as viable co-players with the state and the market in addressing rural poverty. With a strong presence in civil society, NGOs focus not only on 'eradication' or 'reduction' of poverty but also on transformation of the structural configurations that constrain poor people's livelihoods. At the grassroots level, this agenda has largely been pursued through participatory practice, in the context of external resources being channeled to selected communities via projects.

In this fascinating study, however, Fletcher Tembo has shown that the nature of agency, which encompasses people's ability to decide and take appropriate action, has never been properly explored. He showed that, where desired transformational outcomes have failed to be achieved, the common recourse in recommendations is to call for 'more participation'.

Tembo argues that projects create relationships where the negotiation of the different stakeholders' 'images' of the role and purpose of external assistance affects the nature of their decisions and actions. This is of great interest, since currently popular development concepts such as participation, capacity building and empowerment carry powerful images of emancipation of the poor. In essence, Tembo argues, these are the popular currency of good intentions that every development agency now uses in order to describe its purposes for being involved in development.

The seriousness of this global currency of development is becoming more intense as both the state and the large institutional donors such as the World Bank, make 'empowerment' the central tenet of their development philosophy and field operations. Since the essential product of development, as suggested through use of such concepts as 'empowerment', is non-tangible, it has become all too easy for the agencies to allude to development without specifying the quality of delivery of their outputs.

In such a context, a great deal depends on who it is that is able to effectively position themselves and to use the expected development 'language' to their particular advantage. This then becomes the rural people's major strategy for accessing external assistance, a kind of 'weapon of the weak', even though it often fails to relate to their own images of reality. Unfortunately, many people in these communities are unable to use even this strategy effectively, because of the different forms of gate keeping and exclusions occurring within their particular social settings. As a result, despite 'good' participatory practice, not much actually happens beyond the 'naming of the poor' in development practice. Tembo thus proposes that adopting an 'image-sensitive' approach in the design of pro-poor development programs and projects merits serious consideration amongst both researchers and practitioners in development.

Tembo's work is based on a careful and thought provoking research carried out in rural Malawi for a PhD thesis of the University of Reading. Although the book is based on selected case studies from just one country, the sophistication and depth of the ethnographic methodology makes it sufficiently rich for broader theoretical generalizations to be drawn. Tembo has struggled to bring together the critical questions of 'agency' and 'power', as experienced by the different key stakeholders in the project-based development process. He has shown that these questions are critical for any genuine commitment to empowerment of the poor, the creation of space for their authentic participation in development cooperation. As research supervisor I am indeed privileged to commend this book, the work of a young, thoughtful and ardent researcher from Malawi, to all those development researchers and practitioners who are anxious to see genuine and fundamental progress being made in the livelihoods of the truly poor. Its depth of analysis clearly provides a basis for further study and practical application in other contexts.

Ian Wallace
International and Rural Development Department
The University of Reading

Acknowledgements

On the meandering road that has led to the production of this book I am deeply indebted to many people who helped me in various ways. First and foremost, I acknowledge the encouragement from Dr. Janet Townsend of Durham University, who examined my PhD thesis. Her insights will always be useful as I attempt to explore further some of these complex debates in development. For the thesis itself to be produced, however, it was the capable supervision of Ian Wallace of the Department of International and Rural Development at The University of Reading. He had a consistent commitment to providing quick feedback on the many drafts and field reports, which was very helpful to my planning of the research process. In the same vein, I would also like to acknowledge the input of Dr. Wycliffe Chilowa of the Center for Social Research, University of Malawi, for his help during my fieldwork in Malawi. His experience in research logistics and networking with important offices in Malawi was an excellent resource.

I am also grateful to the people of Zabwe and Mpira (not real names) who were open to me and provided the substance on which the arguments in this thesis have focused. While I am grateful to all, the ones who provided a place for me to sleep in the village, often in their already small houses, are always on my mind. Staying in these villages in order to observe and listen to people in their daily life ups and downs was a great inspiration for the research. I thoroughly enjoyed watching *'malipenga'* a traditional dance in some of these communities. Although at first I thought these dances were for fun and socializing, I later on discovered that they were interlinked with fundamental principles of society and culture to which any participation in development was related albeit in indirect ways. Alongside this acknowledgement, I need to extend my thanks to the field staff of World Vision International, Malawi Red Cross Society, Malawi Rural Finance and MASAF, with whom I spent a lot of time in generating data for this research. Dickens Thunde, the National Director, and the senior management team of World Vision Malawi deserve special thanks. Many were the times when they came to my rescue on some difficult research logistics while I was in the various parts of the country.

A number of people also made significant contributions to this research from Reading and other Universities. In this connection, I am grateful to Dr. Peter Oakley, who helped me to develop the initial research argument and the important literature sources. Unfortunately, I will have no chance to share with him this product because he passed away just weeks before finalizing the thesis. May his soul rest in peace! I am also thankful to Dr. Alberto Arce of the University of Wageningen, The Netherlands, for his useful comments on my research arguments. He is a long time professional researcher and writer on the actor-oriented paradigm, which formed the theoretical foundation for this work. I also need to thank Anne Lewis of the University of Surrey for help on the use of NUD*IST, a computer software, which I used in the managing and analysis of data. I am also indebted to thank all my colleagues and lecturers who commented on my research project. Dr. Kevin Waldie's support, mostly during student's research seminars, were particularly constructive and helpful. Similarly, Ulela Kaferawanthu, a friend of mine, was a good sounding board and encourager in times of my vagueness, boredom and tiredness.

Furthermore, the process itself would not have been easy if it were not for the commendable secretarial services of Jane Thompson, Janet Curran and Margaret Keen in the Department of International and Rural Development (DIRD). They deserve my profound thanks. Even after successfully gaining acceptance for the Higher Degree studies, however, it would not have possible if it were not for financial support from the University of Reading. I am particularly grateful to Mrs. Sylvia Stirring who at the start of my studies was the Senior Assistant Registrar and committed herself to make this funding a success. My heartfelt thanks are due to my work colleagues at World Vision UK, especially Jill Gasson, Ian Gray, Clive Bacon and Chris Webster, for the friendliness with which they supported the different aspects of this work. This work has of course received high quality advice from Ashgate Publishers, especially Rosalind Ebdon on editorial techniques. She deserves my sincere thanks.

Lastly, but by no means least important, I extend my sincere thanks to my wife Peggy and my children Chimwemwe and Temwa who untiringly provided the needed family support. They carried on waiting for some uncertain future date when the PhD, whatever it meant, would be obtained. Peggy worked hard throughout the research period in order to keep the family financially healthy, beyond the stipend from The University of Reading. She deserves my most profound thanks. Most of all, I thank God who, by His grace through faith in Christ Jesus, saved me and gave me immeasurable grace to carry on. From my humble beginnings, He has perfected that which concerns me!

List of Abbreviations

ADMARC	Agricultural Development and Marketing Corporation
ADP	Area Development Programme
CDP	Community Development Project
CONGOMA	Council for Non-Governmental Organisations in Malawi
DANIDA	Danish Agency for International Development
DSA	Development Studies Association
GOM	Government of Malawi
GTZ	Deutsche Gesellschaft fur Technische Zusammenarbeit
IEC	Information Education and Communication
LFA	Logical Framework Analysis
MASAF	Malawi Social Action Fund
MIS	Management Information System
MRCS	Malawi Red Cross Society
MRFC	Malawi Rural Finance Company
NGDOs	Non-Governmental Development Organisations
NGO	Non-Governmental Organisation
NUDI*ST	Non-Numerical Unstructured Data Indexing, Searching and Theorising
PCT	Personal Construct Theory
PDAs	Popular Development Agencies
PRA	Participatory Rural Appraisal
PRSP	Poverty Reduction Paper
QUANGOs	Quasi-Governmental Non-Governmental Organisations
SEDP	Small Enterprise Development Programmes
VHC	Village Health Committee

Glossary

Actor-oriented Approach: An analytical approach used for studying the different ways in which social actors (people in a local community, political leaders, NGO staff, market dealers, policy makers etc) respond to similar circumstances. The argument is that social actors actively and different work with their new experiences, whether from their immediate society or from outside, within the limits of the knowledge and information that they have. The best way, therefore, is to study what meaning social actors themselves make of any situation, in that particular context (Long and van der Ploeg, 1994).

Agency: The process of social actors doing something about what they have made of a life situation, which they are facing. These actions relate to the meanings they form of the situation and the motivation they draw from such meanings. As a result, the nature of this agency shows where particular actors stand in a particular 'meaning-making' and acting process, based on the situation they are concerned about (Long, 2000; Kabeer, 1999).

Construing/Construction: The meaning-making process through which social actors perceive a given life situation as one thing and not the other, based on what they know from their past experience. Although they might not say all of what they are considering in their interpretations of an experience, the two sides of something being 'this' rather than 'the other' (bipolar constructs), are always there in meaning-making (Dalton and Dunnett, 1992; Pope and Denicolo, 1993).

Fieldworker/people/community: These are social actor categories that are mostly used in the book. Fieldworkers are employees of NGOs who have direct contact with people in a community where a development project is being implemented. My emphasis is on 'direct contact with people' rather than to a special staff level in the organisational structure. It is possible for a staff member located at the NGO headquarters to be in constant and direct contact with people in a particular community, as a fieldworker. The term 'people' refers to the various social actors in a given community, either as individuals or groups, who might form a 'community' when they live together in a geographical locality.

Image-conflicts: An active engagement or struggle among social actors whose images or understanding of an object or issue are opposed to each other. The struggle is about one social actor attempting to override the meanings the other social actors make of a given situation, with their own meanings (see also the definition of power).

Images: The meanings that social actors make of the life situation that they are facing so that they are able to decide, relate and act in a certain way towards that situation (tangible or non-tangible). In essence, with such images, they form a structure within which they interpret or construe whatever is happening with the object in view. The structure of meaning, however, should be understood as relatively dynamic. This is because it can change as the social actor obtains more or contrary information about the object, or they think about the object/issue from other angles (Hamlyn, 1969).

Interface: The imaginary area of interaction where differences in meanings/values that interacting social actors form/have of a given situation emerge or are likely to emerge. This understanding is drawn from Long (1989), for whom 'interface' is 'a critical point of intersection or linkage between social systems, fields or levels of social order where structural discontinuities, based on differences of normative value and social interest, are most likely to occur' (pp.1-2). In this definition, 'interface' is not limited to face-to-face encounters.

Non-Governmental Organisations (NGOs): Non-profit distributing organisations, which are institutionally independent from the state (while operating within its legal framework), channelling social development aid to the poor, from donors who are largely situated in the developed countries. In this context, they can also be referred to as Non-Governmental Development Organisations (NGDOs) (Fowler, 1997) or Popular Development Agencies (PDAs) (Clark, 1991). In this book, the term NGO is used to stand for NGDOs.

Power: The ability of social actors to effectively influence the meaning-making processes of other actors towards their construction of a particular life situation. It is 'the ability to get other people to accept your definition of reality' so that your reality poses as their reality (Rowe, cited in Epting, et al., 1996; Willlutzki and Duda, 1996). This implies that the 'powerless' actors would have processed and dealt with the life situation in question differently if they were not facing the imposition of the reality of the 'powerful'.

Social Actor: An individual, group of people or organisation, capable of making decisions and acting upon them, while drawing from a common social base, which could be culture or some fundamentally shared values (organisational core values). In which case, 'social actor' is not the same as 'an individual' who is pursuing his/her self-based interests, without relating to other people (Long and van der Ploeg, 1994).

Social Transformation: The process of change, as development, that is based on fundamental changes in the way individuals or groups perceive their lives, the lives of other people and their environment. It involves changes in people's motivations, behaviour and relationships, as products of 'intrinsically-driven' processes of change, which means that it can only be externally supported but not imposed (Korten, 1990; Burkey, 1993).

Use-Values: The values of goods and services in association with the meaning people of the uses of these goods or services in their livelihoods. This is different from the technical value, which depends on the chemical composition of goods. In this case, any good or service acquires value in relation to other cultural or social beliefs of the society in which it is presented or found. This implies that the same good or service could have different 'use-values' in different social contexts and sometimes seen differently by different social actors in the same society (e.g. differences between the youths and the elders) (Ingold, 1992).

Chapter 1

Introduction: the Difficult Question

Suppose a rural Malawian man, woman or a group of people pursuing the same livelihood cause, purposefully or suddenly encountered an NGO (or vice-versa) in their community, how would he/she/they accommodate the NGO and how would the NGO accommodate them?

This question depicts my initial struggle with the designing of projects for social transformation in the context of development NGOs. This is not fantasy, such as imagining or dreaming of a river looking like an ocean. It emanates from my engagement with literature on social transformation and NGO projects and a reflection on my seven years of grassroots experience with some of the rural communities in Malawi. I worked for an international NGO whose primary development philosophy was 'transformational development'. From this experience and literature review, it became apparent that NGOs' development intentions are very promising for the poor. This promise is not just to alleviate or eradicate poverty for a moment in time but also to change the power configurations in the various livelihood spheres that cause and sustain poverty. The results coming from evaluations and my own field experience, of the extent and nature of such transformational change in these projects, however, have not been clear. This made me question the nature of accommodation[1] that takes place when NGOs and people, operating from different 'life-worlds' meet in a project relationship. This book discusses these issues, based on empirical research results, with a view to contribute to the improvement of project interventions aimed at social transformation.[2] This chapter provides the overall framework of the book, showing how the difficult question stated above was pursued in an actor-oriented study.

The chapter starts with a research background, based on the literature review, reflecting on the changes in the understanding of the place of NGOs in development. This then forms the basis for the rationale of the study, answering the broad question of why I was interested in NGO projects in this research. The main research questions that formed the basis for this study are then stipulated followed by the contribution that the book makes to knowledge and practice. The contextual situation of the communities and NGOs in the areas where the study was conducted in Malawi is briefly presented. Although these discussions are based on real people and areas in Malawi, the names used are not real. This is done in order to guide the reader to issues and theories that were pursued and developed in the study. Furthermore, it protects the confidentiality of the people that provided the sensitive information, as I promised them during my fieldwork. Therefore, the book is based on people and areas that exist somewhere in Malawi. I conclude this chapter with a brief outline of the rest of the chapters in the book.

Research Background

In the post-cold war era, development theorists have taken the challenge to inform development practice towards managing diversity, learning processes and relationship between the macro and micro (Schuurman, 1993; Booth, 1994). This represents a change from the earlier theories that tended to focus on the wider picture while looking for grand explanations to the 'supposedly' homogenous life situations. Both modernization and structural dependency theories were part of this reality. The former was based on assumptions of external technological supremacy meant to improve homogenous traditional societies while the latter was based on assumptions of similarities of the structural causes of underdevelopment (Long and van der Ploeg, 1994). With their linear conceptualization of causes of poverty and the means to counteract it, these theories could not explain the different responses and results in societies to similar poverty approaches. Instead, poverty and disparities between the rich and the poor continued to worsen.

At the heart of this interrelationship between theory and practice, in search for better ways of 'reducing' or 'eradicating' poverty in the post cold war era, is the debate about the role relationship among the State, Market and Civil Society. Here too there have been significant changes. The immediate aftermath of the cold war was seen to involve theories that shifted practice from centralized state planning to those that favored market liberalism, with the withdrawal of the State. However, at the beginning of the 21st century, this has changed towards bringing back the State. This of course, is a different State, a decentralized one, which can work well with the Market and enable civil participation (Turner and Hulme, 1997; Schneider, 1999; Mohan and Stokke, 2000). It is within the context of this withdrawal and restructuring of the State, and the recognition of civil society organizations, that the importance of NGO participation has come to the fore.

Seen from the perspective of the withdrawal of the State, also conceptualized as a 'state failure', NGOs were in the 1980s the favored channel for development assistance (Fowler, 1997; Hulme and Edwards, 1997). Concomitant with theories of diversity and learning process characterizing new explanations of poverty, NGOs were seen to have distinct comparative advantages over the state. Their structural and voluntary orientations meant that NGOs were more flexible, better attuned to learning through experience and experimentation, innovative, participatory, low cost and efficient, and responsive to the needs of the poor (Fowler, 1988, 1997; Clark, 1991). In a conceptual analogue of the State, the Market and Civil Society, Korten, (1990) likens their relationship to 'The Prince', 'The Merchant' and 'The Citizen', respectively. In this analogy, NGOs, as working for the interests of citizens, are attributed the intrinsic potential for facilitating a people-centered development agenda in civil society. This is because of their voluntary characteristics, which are unique to civil society organizations and not the State nor the Market. In other words, NGOs were regarded as institutions, which could genuinely promote and protect interests of the poor.

With this interpretation of the NGO role in development, the challenge was seen as one of scaling up their small-scale practice in order to bring about a significant impact on the rampant poverty situations in the Third World (Edwards and Hulme, 1992; Chambers, 1993; Farrington and Bebbington, 1993). However, as more funding came through NGOs from official sources, multilateral organizations and governments, at the close of the decade, NGO analysts pointed to the danger of co-optation into the official system (Fowler, 1997; Hulme and Edwards, 1997). There was a sensing of threats of NGOs becoming more of 'Public Service Contractors' (PSC) and in the process, losing their unique capacity for achieving people-centered development. In this case, since the government or multilateral donors contract NGOs to carry out development activities, NGOs can neither function as a pure civil society actor nor its promoter. This would mean acting against their contractors in some cases in order to protect the interests of the poor, which is difficult because it also means acting against their growth in funding. The alternative theory offered in this situation was that of NGOs working towards strategic planning and negotiation with the state, markets and donors (Fowler, 1997; Hulme and Edwards, 1997). Fowler, further conceptualizes a kind of 'learning for leverage' NGDO role, with new tactics noting,

> ...the key tactical change is to move away from the notion of manning the barricades against political imperialism and market exploitation, be it local or international. Instead, what is needed are tactics which draw on principles of martial arts – such as judo and jujitsu – using the momentum and energy of the opponent to knock them off balance and throw them in the direction wanted (Fowler, 1997, p. 227).

With the recent upsurge of globalization, where market capitalism shapes the structure of the State, the danger is seen as not only that of NGO incorporation into public agendas but also NGOs losing on their civic roots (Edwards, Hulme and Wallace. 2000; Fowler, 2000a). The growth of market capitalism suggests profits coming before relationships and hence threatening the central thread of civil society where the poor compose their livelihood security. This is especially the case in developing countries where the market is imperfect and the State does not offer the alternative livelihood security for the poor.[3] The alternative NGO practice suggested in this context is that of 'innovation' (Lewis and Wallace, 2000). Other writers have pointed to the need for NGOs to develop their *'development as leverage'* with new ways of handling relationships, new capacities, and ensuring legitimacy and accountability (Edwards et al. 2000). The NGO position in the third sector has also been re-visited for a 'fourth position', with their behavior resembling the state, markets and civil society. This is in recognition of the new, conceptualized roles of 'negotiator', 'validator', 'watchdog' and 'innovator or demonstrator' (Fowler 2000a, p.599).

These changes in development theory and practice and how NGOs are located in them represent an NGO reality that is also changing. Ultimately, these changes get translated in various representations in rural communities, via project assistance. This is where the product of NGO bargaining and negotiation with the State and the Market along these changes finally emerge, in the form of development. When we look at development theories meant to inform this practice at grassroots level, we find that people, in their diversities, are involved through participation. Although there is also 'conscientization' theory (Freire, 1972), which is a more radical form of participation, most development NGOs do not actively pursue it. This is because 'conscientization' is easily translated into antagonism with the State, which is often counter-productive (Turner and Hulme, 1997).

Participation from a populist theory and practice, however, is consensus based or at least consensus is methodologically assumed in methods such as PRA (Mosse, 1995; Bevan, 2000; Cleaver, 2001). The politics of the local is undermined or at best disguised through the 'publicly' staged conflict resolution methods in this methodological orientation. In order to draw attention to alternative thinking, some writers have now gone outright to refer to participation as 'the new tyranny' (Cooke and Kothari, 2001). My opinion is that whereas these contentions are genuine, they cannot theoretically amount to saying that there is no social transformation with participatory practice, such as in the use of PRA. As Chambers (1997a) rightly points out, people analyzing their life situations together and presenting their findings to others can build their confidence. This confidence could result in transformational changes in their livelihoods. What these arguments show, instead, is that the way NGOs engage and influence a given project (their nature of agency) and the way people engage and influence the same project (also people's nature of agency) at the interface through participation, is not clear. PRAs, for instance, might provide the environment for this agency, but they do not show us the actual agency and hence managing the effects of political behavior in PRA practice becomes difficult. In the final analysis, this translates into problems in the processes of project designing and implementation and the achievement transformational outcomes and impacts.

Research Justification

The conceptual argument in the discussion above is that populist theory and practice, as participation, does not provide for analytical ability for the local politics implicit in participation and hence the way 'agency' is constructed in a project. In other words, NGO performance does not have an analytical approach for political conflicts on the local and wider interactions and how they affect the way poor people decide and act in development processes. This is the context in which people in a local community accommodate external relationships, including the incoming NGO and similarly the context in which the incoming NGO accommodates the people. Therefore, I perceived the need for an empirical research to deconstruct the nature of 'agency' people and NGOs have at the project interface. In other words, I aimed at understanding how both people and NGO actors make their decisions and actions while managing each other's perceptions and actions in a given programme or project. The thinking was that decisions and actions (or non-actions) that people take are dependent on their ability to find or create the necessary socio-political space to negotiate from their understanding of reality in relation to other actors.

The relevance of this research position was further justified considering the fact that the people in the rural contexts are not isolated from the wider and local transformations but interface with them in different and unpredictable ways (Long, 2000). This, according to Long (2000), implies that we have to contend with their differing perceptions and the images they form of these changes. In this case, the NGO involvement constitutes another of the many encounters that people in a rural community have with their external worlds. Additionally, Long (2000) alerts us to the 'meaning construction' process that people go through in these encounters. To this effect, he argues that they anticipate actions of other actors, which then shape their behavior towards those actors. In other words, people in a Malawian community are as engaged with the NGO as the NGO itself, even outside of face-to-face encounters. This affects people's behavior towards NGOs as they accommodate them into various aspects of their livelihoods. The same situation should hold for how NGOs behave towards the people, also operating within their encounters with their own forms of local and wider transformations. It is these various accommodation processes that involve 'agency'.

The concept of agency, besides observable actions, includes 'meaning, motivation and purpose' that social actors draw upon in conceiving their actions (Kabeer, 1999, p.3). Kabeer (1999) goes on to explain that whereas agency has often been limited to 'decision-making', it has other forms, including bargaining and negotiation, deception and manipulation, subversion and resistance, and reflection and analysis. This implies that there are various forms of agency that social actors could be associated with in a particular project; in this case where NGOs and the people are together involved. In their definition of agency, Long and van der Ploeg (1994) add the phrase 'coping with life, even under the most extreme forms of coercion' (p.66). This means that in other forms of agency, actors, out of the necessity of living, have to bear under negative life situations, including the agency of others as they accommodate them into their livelihoods. Therefore, in thinking about the accommodation processes characterizing a rural community and an NGO, we need to be thinking about the nature of their agency at the interface. This makes even more sense when we consider political relationships at this interface.

The need for understanding political relationships was drawn from the conceptualization of relationships between NGOs, states and donors that Hulme and Edwards (1997) have constructed. In this respect, they perceive two-dimensional relationships, enacted in various forms of 'bargaining' and 'negotiation' taking place among these actors, which are forms of agency. The first dimension encompasses 'the stated' and 'the hidden' objectives that actors pursue in engaging in the relationship, while the second refers to the use of leverage to persuade or coerce the other actors towards given objectives. It is possible, therefore, for NGOs to similarly deploy subtle political tactics, some of the so-called 'martial arts', using the 'state, and market-influenced' realities to drive the people towards particular directions. Similarly, people are liable to use their bargaining and negotiation strategies entailing different tactics, the kind of 'weapons of the weak' (Scott, 1985), to influence projects towards certain unintended directions. The problem with these NGO and people's tactics, however, is that we do not know how the poor people are affected in this process. Political tactics could negatively affect the achievement of transformative outcomes. Therefore, it is important to develop a theoretical understanding of the nature of the 'participation' interactions between NGOs and rural people in projects. As Cornwall has recently argued,

> Understanding how and why people participate, in turn, requires that we take a closer look at how would be participants *or participants* are constructed in discourses of participation, and how they construct their own engagement and entitlements: what spaces they are given, and what spaces they occupy as theirs (Cornwall, 2002, p.51, italics mine).

This discussion shows how the need for an empirical research with a conceptual focus on the nature of agency of NGOs and the people in social transformation projects emerged. Various forms of research have been conducted from this premise to empirically show such interface realities in government projects, for example, Arce and Long (1993), and Villarreal (1992). However, it is difficult to apply the lessons learnt to NGO contexts because governments relate to people differently. Porter, Allen and Thompson (1991) conducted a study in this direction, in which the accommodation of NGO interventions in people's cultural livelihoods was discussed. However, they did not compare these accommodation processes to NGO philosophical and operational realities. As a result, their conclusions reflect mostly on the failure of NGOs without giving much attention to the realities that the NGOs they studied faced in their environments. In my opinion, realities that NGOs face, such as donor influences, are important to consider if we are concerned with the practical application of lessons from these studies.

Research Focus

In the light of the aforesaid research issues, this research was focused on gaining an understanding into the accommodation of NGO assistance in peoples' livelihoods and NGO frameworks of meanings, using cases from rural Malawi. This was done with an interest in finding out how this accommodation process can show the nature of agency of the people and NGOs. This is with regard to the various aspects of the processes of project design and implementation. Two specific research aims or objectives were constructed from this general focus of the research. These are:

- To compose a comparative view of the interface between NGOs and people, in a given project community, in terms of images they form of the different aspects and forms of NGO assistance.

- To derive a theory from this comparative analysis of image interactions, which could assist project managers in improving the design and implementation of projects that are meant for social transformation.

Research Questions

- How does the way NGOs define the livelihood situation of the people compare to the way people themselves understand their livelihoods?
- How do images that people form of the role of NGO assistance in their livelihoods compare to those that NGOs form of the same?
- How do the images that these people form of change in their livelihoods, resulting from implementation of the project, compare to those that NGOs form of the same?

Contribution to Knowledge and Practice

As a product of an empirical study based on research questions and arguments discussed above, this book contributes to the current body of knowledge in three ways. These include, the role of development NGOs in grassroots development under the current influences on development practice, the search for better ways of strategizing NGO negotiations with the State, Market and Civil Society for pro-poor development. Lastly, the book contributes to improving research practice.

In terms of grassroots development, understanding the nature of agency of different stakeholders can be used to understand the political dimensions of stakeholder interactions. This will strengthen the use of participatory or anthropological techniques in project designing and implementation in that fieldworkers will gain better understanding of the position of the poor in the different aspects of their involvement. This is a significant contribution in the current context when 'empowerment', 'capacity building' and 'participation' are the key words for effective development practice. These concepts have permeated popular development dialogue as well as international development policy. The focus of the World Development Report on 'opportunity', 'empowerment' and 'security' is evidence of such a context (Squire, 2001). The World Bank has also developed a framework for conceptualizing and implementing 'empowerment' (Nayaran, 2002). Related concepts, such as 'strengthening civil society', 'participatory governance' and 'rights-based development' have also gained privileged momentum. Poverty Reduction Strategy Papers (PRSPs) and Country Strategy Papers (CSPs) make these concepts their basic framework. On the whole, such a focus suggests that the poor have become the subjects rather than objects of development. This focus, however, does not say much about what these concepts mean in practice, for both people and development agencies, apart from playing the familiar tune of 'people's participation'.

This is a cause for concern because, as Mohan and Stokke (2000) have rightly warned, there is a danger of reinforcing a 'revised neo-liberal position' meant to achieve institutional reform and efficiency without challenging the structures and processes that underline poverty. In this model, these authors argue, is a construction of participation and empowerment of the poor and their organizations (civil society) based on a 'harmony model of power' (ibid. 2000, p. 249). Without a strategic analysis of empirical realities, NGOs are likely to be co-opted into this 'harmony' while the poor they serve in their development programmes and projects remain locked in chronic poverty. This book makes a specific contribution in developing principles for engaging NGOs into a 'meaning-revealing' process at the grassroots, to inform pro-poor development programming, advocacy and implementation.

The conceptualization of the interface negotiations, as discussed in this book, can also be used for understanding the politics of negotiation in different interface situations rather than with the people in a rural community. As a result, it will contribute to improving the quality of NGO negotiations with other actors in development. This makes it potentially useful for contributing to improving strategies for strengthening civil society and advocacy. As argued elsewhere, and also later in this book, strategic negotiation provides NGO political leverage at the different stakeholder interfaces (Tembo, 2001b). Otherwise, advocacy as such at these different interfaces is difficult for NGOs because they are in many cases too 'small players' to effectively influence state policies. This is in comparison with the bilateral and multilateral donors (Edwards and Hulme, 1992). The grassroots interface 'meanings' understanding that NGOs can develop through this analytical approach, feeding into implications of wider policy, is what large institutions such as the World Bank and the European Union do not have (Edwards, 2002).

Finally, the research design that was used in this study was developed from a grounded thinking about interfacing images of reality, which could be applied to the general qualitative research practice. As indicated above, interface analysis that brings meanings of different actors into question has been done in government programs but not in other contexts. Additionally, the study incorporated more cases by using Personal Construct Theory as a tool for strengthening interviews and participant observations. This enabled avoidance of pre-emptive judgments on the people's accounts and actions, and thus adding rigor to the findings. Other researchers exploring interface interactions could benefit from the methodology as discussed in this book.

The Area of Study: Somewhere in Malawi

In this section, I will discuss the contextual issues pertaining to Malawi and the areas in Malawi where the study was conducted. This is to provide a contextual background to the study, based on which the research was designed.

NGOs in a Malawian Context

Malawi is in sub-Saharan Africa with a population estimated at 11 million. It is rated in literature as one of the poorest countries in the world (GOM, 1994; World Bank, 1995). Schroeder (2000) observed that Malawi has an average *per capita* income of US$220 and *gini coefficient* of 0.62, which is among the highest in African countries for which data was recorded. This has been the situation despite experiencing phenomenal economic growth between 1964 (year of independence) and 1979.[4] This growth was as a result of investments made in agriculture, from a bimodal economic development policy. The policy had an engine of economic growth located in the estate sector, producing mainly tobacco, while food self-sufficiency was situated in the smallholder sector. However, this economic growth could neither trickle down to the majority of the population nor sustain itself under external shocks (Chilowa and Chirwa, 1997). These shocks, including the rise in interest rates on the international market, droughts and refugees of war from Mozambique, led to a drastic decline in economic growth indices. The situation forced Malawi to get loans from the World Bank and IMF, under the Structural Adjustment Programs in the 1980s (Chilowa and Chirwa, 1997; World Bank, 1995).

However, the social exclusion of the rural population as seen in their insecurities: food, human rights, health, employment and so forth continued, largely because of lack of a proper social policy[5] (Chilowa and Apthorpe, 1997). NGOs (estimated at more than 200) are seen in this context as helping the state where it is not capable, due to financial constraints and lack of personnel (Kutengule, 1997; Kalemba, 1997). This means that they are part of the policy response to social problems through provision of social services as 'demanded' in the rural sector. Following the change from one party to multiparty system of politics in 1994, state functions have been decentralizing towards participatory governance. In this context, NGOs are seen as complementing the government in its poverty alleviation programme.

> The NGOs have specially important role of complementing government efforts in all sectors of poverty alleviation, particularly in the implementation of micro-projects focusing on domestic demand creation, productivity improvements and marketing and community mobilization (GOM, 1995, p.40).

The general picture of NGOs in Malawi, as from independent commentators and NGOs, is that of a marked difference between the period of the single party and the multiparty government. In this case, there was a celebration of the move from very sensitive operations in a single party government to a 'supportive' environment for civic action in development or human rights (CONGOMA, 1996; Glagow, Lohmann et al. 1997). In the single party era, NGOs limited their operations to relief, mainly as a result of Mozambican refugees, rehabilitation of the environment, following floods and humanitarian assistance (Rogge, 1997). The transition to multiparty democracy was hence seen as if they were 'pushed out of the development shadows, thrust front-stage-center' to take many previously neglected or hidden roles in civil society (ibid. 1997, p.2). The secretariat for CONGOMA, the coordinating body for NGOs in Malawi openly stated,

> A weak civil society poses a threat to any sound democratic government and militates against any sustainable development initiative. The NGO community in Malawi has an urgent task of developing strong institutional and social capacities that are supportive of greater local control, accountability, initiative and self-reliance by grassroots (CONGOMA, 1996, p.1).

However, in practice, NGOs found that besides dealing with problems of their own capacities to do development, they had to face questions of the extent of self-regulation, relationship with the state and the necessary codes of conduct.[6] These were not clearly defined in the laws of Malawi (CONGOMA/NDI, 1997). Against a background of the politics of ethnicity that characterized the first multi-party general elections (Kaspin, 1995), the lack of clear guidelines and protection by law, most development NGOs have continued with an 'apolitical' image in their operations. Their operational image is that of 'helping' the state in 'poverty alleviation',[7] as discussed above. In other words, they are forced by the nature of the interface with the state to move towards a neo-liberal type of participation, where participation serves interests of the market (Mohan and Stokke, 2000). This is the context in which the NGOs studied in Zabwe and Mpira communities in Malawi were situated. In the following sections, I briefly reflect on the general background situation of these communities.

Zabwe and Mpira: a Descriptive Area Analysis

Zabwe and Mpira communities are both in Malawi, approximately 44 miles from each other. Since the area is among those parts of the country with the poorest road networks in the country 44 miles would take an average of 3 hours of travel between them. Travel time is even longer in the wet season because of gullies on most parts of the road. As I interacted with people in both communities, there was no evidence of interactions between people of Zabwe and those of Mpira. There were several development agencies, which were working in these communities during that period, while some had already phased out their programs. I begin the reflection with community descriptions.

Community descriptions and observations   Zabwe and Mpira were said to be among the poorest communities in the district, looking at social-economic indicators, such as health, communication and agricultural productivity (District Commissioner, personal interview communication). They had populations of 12,000 and 20,000 people, respectively. Their socio-economic livelihoods are based on agriculture with maize, rice, cotton and cassava as the major crops. They comprise of people of various ethnic groups (there were up to eight groups in Zabwe and twelve in Mpira), which have links with other groups in the neighboring districts and even countries. This multicultural societal configuration meant that there was already cross-fertilization or 'mutational' effect from the various encounters that people had in their livelihoods (Arce and Long, 2000).

Historical accounts from these communities showed that in Mpira, the other ethnic groups migrated to the area following the rich alluvial soils along the river and the Mpira Rice Scheme. The rice scheme was supported by the Chinese government since the 1970s and was handed over to the Malawi government in the 1990s. In the scheme were people from all regions of the country, because the government used it to train youths in agriculture, under the Malawi Young Pioneers (MYP). Most of them never went back to their original districts but intermarried with the traditional tribes in the area. Other ethnic groups, however, migrated to Mpira because they were displaced from the neighboring plateau when the government turned the forest area into a National Park. This was not the case in Zabwe, where migration was on a very small scale because there was not much agricultural land except along the river. This showed that there was more cross-cultural activity in Mpira than in Zabwe.

Despite all these different ethnic migrations to Mpira and Zabwe, the village headmen were of the tribes that came to these areas earlier. Their leadership pattern was customary where sons of the chief became village headmen and hence gave no room to other incoming tribes to participate in those positions, except as advisers. This had implications on resource endowments and entitlements, especially land. With the customary land ownership, it was the chief who delegated the sharing of land to the village headmen, who then could share it to the different households. They were not owners, in private ownership sense, because the chief had the prerogative to take it back when dissatisfied with the household. In both Zabwe and Mpira, the major issue that would lead to eviction of certain households from farming land was witchcraft. Ultimately, it showed that the traditional leadership had enormous ascribed power on the affairs of the village, which were linked to the implementation of development activities. In this context, women could also become village headmen if they happened to fall in the clan that was in that position, but they could not become advisers or chiefs. In this way, when it was a woman who was in leadership, the advisers, who were men, made the decisions.

NGO descriptions and observations   Although the research was focused on the involvement of NGOs, I took note of all the external agencies, which were working or worked in these communities in the past. As will be further explained in the methodology chapter, projects supported by other agencies, rather than those bearing the label NGO provided a basis for comparison and therefore, easier understanding of images people formed of NGOs. At the time of this research, development agencies working in Mpira included World Vision International (WVI), Malawi Social Action Fund (MASAF), Malawi Rural Finance Company (MRFC), European Union, Malawi Council for the Handicapped (MACOHA) and GTZ. In Zabwe, on the other hand, it was WVI, MASAF, Malawi Red Cross Society (MRCS) and MRFC, which were working there. The southern part of Zabwe and the whole of Mpira also benefited from provision of safe water, under an Integrated Rural Ground Water Project. This project was supported by DANIDA and phased out in 1994.

The common observation that I made from all these development agencies was that they emphasized community ownership of projects, participation, capacity building, empowerment of the people and project sustainability. As explained further in the methodology chapter, I kept my analysis open to these agencies as a group among which NGOs existed, but focused more on people's images of assistance. Since forms of assistance were often specific, I traced them to specific agencies that provided the assistance. This was done with assistance from my research guides/assistants who came from the same communities and from my initial access to information about all these agencies. I, however, looked more on the work of WVI, MRCS, MASAF and MRFC. The first two were NGOs in the sense of Popular Development Agencies (PDAs) while the later two were government agencies in the sense of Quasi NGOs (QUANGOs). These agencies had the common orientation of emphasis on capacity building and empowerment of the people, an important attribute when classifying NGOs (Vakil, 1997). As a matter of observation, people also looked at all these organizations as NGOs, or institutions other than the government. In the following sections, I briefly present a general overview of the organizations involved in the study from this understanding.

WORLD VISION INTERNATIONAL (WVI)

> World Vision is an international community of Christians seeking to empower people by God's grace to transform their lives and their world (WVI, 1991, p.1).

Having started from a relief and evangelism ministry in the 1950s, World Vision moved on to development in the 1970s, with a development position paper drafted in 1973 (WVM, 1988). The organization has since embraced a multidimensional mission in humanitarian relief, evangelism and development. World Vision started operating in Malawi in 1982. Most projects started during this period were in response to applications for assistance from the various churches in Malawi. A typical CDP covered an area of 5 to 10 villages, with an average population of 3,000 people and for a period of 5 to 8 years. The project documents, which I reviewed during the research, clearly showed that assistance in CDPs was rendered mainly for the building of primary school infrastructures. There were also provisions for revolving loans for agriculture, roads, boreholes, homecraft training programs for women and child immunization programs. It was in the early 1990s that World Vision changed the development approach from CDPs to Area Development Programs arguing that, 'they encompass large areas as opposed to community projects that have less impact' (Kapambwe, 1995, p.2).

In this case, ADPs were meant to cover large geographical areas, of populations of at least more than 15,000 for a period of 10 to 15 years (WVM, 1991). Furthermore, professional staff would live closer or in the community rather than in the central cities in order to facilitate transformational development. This was the context in which ADPs were started in Zabwe and Mpira communities. Adding the phrase 'enhancing the capacity of the people to', notably changed the goals of the projects in ADPs, in order to emphasize the transformational focus.[8] This also changed the naming of certain forms of assistance. For example, there was a change from Revolving Loans to Small Enterprise Development and from Agriculture to Food Security. Ultimately, ADPs for WVI reflect an organizational paradigm shift towards better ways of achieving transformational development. This is seen as possible through better understanding of concepts of human development, improving financial management, relationships with sponsors/donors and communities, and staff development (WVSA, 2000).

MALAWI RED CROSS SOCIETY (MRCS)

Malawi Red Cross Society has been working in co-operation with the Danish Red Cross Society in addressing primary health care concerns in the country since 1979. A Community Based Health Care programme (CBHC) was formed for this purpose in 1994, an intensive baseline was conducted and report done in 1996 based on which, Karonga, Dedza and Machinga districts were chosen. According to MRCS, CBHC is

> ...a philosophy, approach and strategy for community development based on the identification of priority problems and their solutions by the villagers themselves in collaboration with other agencies such as government departments and NGOs (MRCS, 1996, p.6).

It is in this respect that MRCS puts emphasis on participation in micro-planning and budgeting processes by project communities through committees and volunteers. It is believed that, through such a process, MRC will build the capacity of people to plan and implement their own development.

MALAWI SOCIAL ACTION FUND (MASAF)

Having started in 1995, following the change of the system of government, MASAF has become a household name on poverty alleviation by the government, especially in rural areas. MASAF was launched with a loan from the World Bank of US$ 56 million, which was repeated in 1998, as a second phase. Institutionally, MASAF has a Management Unit with professional staff and conducts its operations as 'an autonomous body' (MASAF, 1999). It has a board with representatives from selected government ministries, CONGOMA, the Center for Social Research, Traditional leadership and independent experts in management.

The Community sub-projects division, where projects such as those in Zabwe and Mpira were managed, is structured with the community at the top, signifying the bottom-up approach, in institutional design terms. This institutional set-up is expected to relate with the decentralizing of local government, which has Village Development Committees, Area Development Committees and Area Executive Committees, at the community level. They are responsible for project identification, 'marshalling' participation, contribution and implementation of projects (GOM/UNDP, n.d). In other words, these committees were meant to create the 'demand' for MASAF support in communities. According to Schroeder's (2000) analysis, MASAF assistance was largely on public infrastructures, with other development programs including enterprising forming only 0.8% of the budget. In my own analysis of MASAF funding trends, out of all projects funded by July 1998, infrastructures in education, water, accessibility and health took 98% of the budget (MASAF, 1998).

It is in this context that, in terms of development philosophy and operations, MASAF is based on principles of 'community participation'. In this case, people are involved in making decisions at all stages of the project cycle, and in managing their projects independently, through community-elected committees. This follows a development policy change made in 1995 meant to enable people to participate in project management as a means for empowerment (Kishindo, 2001). Communities are meant to implement projects in a transparent and accountable manner, and through ensuring 'self-help' activities at all stages of the project because they own the projects. In essence, MASAF revitalizes the community development policy of the government, which is focused at integrating people, economically, culturally and socially into national progress through self help work (Malawi, 1987). In the second phase, which started in 1999, MASAF incorporated a special project for enabling participation of the disadvantaged and vulnerable groups of people thus broadening its areas of focus (MASAF, 1999). MASAF programs in the communities studied were hence similar in nature to those of development NGOs.

MALAWI RURAL FINANCE COMPANY (MRFC)

This organization came out of the Ministry of Agriculture in 1994, as part of the privatization programme undertaken by the government of Malawi under the structural adjustment conditions (World Bank, 1995). It originally was the Small Holder Agriculture Credit Administration (SACA) through which the Ministry of Agriculture was providing loans to smallholder farmers for agricultural inputs in order to improve smallholder agricultural production. The rationale was that by improving agricultural productivity in the smallholder sector, which forms 84% of the farming population in Malawi, food security would be ensured and family incomes would improve. However, due to gross inefficiencies, SACA had to be privatized and hence it became an autonomous enterprise institution, but with the government mandate of handling smallholder agricultural credit. The privatization was meant to improve efficiency of the institution and making it a sustainable organization, which is able to survive from its own business. The name changed to MRFC, seen as the Rural Bank with the objective that was stipulated as,

> ...to ensure that the near-landless rural poor are given the opportunity to borrow and invest in income generating activities (GOM, 1994, p.16).

According to the MRFC field officers interviewed, MRFC is committed to providing access to credit for the poor, and hence uses the same field extension workers to organize groups for accessing credit. This is meant to increase accessibility to the loan facilities for the smallholder farmers, as different from commercial banks. Unlike SACA, MRFC has a special programme for the poor, called *Mudzi* business, which allows the poor to get access to small amounts of loan as a start up for growing into bigger borrowers at no collateral in the first year. This strategy is meant to encourage the poor in the rural and urban societies of Malawi so that they are empowered economically. These characteristics are similar to those of Small Enterprise Development NGOs, including World Vision, as explained above. They only differ in some of the logistical systems, such as loan repayment periods and sizes of groups.

Ultimately, this book focuses on analysis of the accommodation process in the interaction that occurs between people of different cultures and development agencies that assist them. Case studies of people of different cultures of Zabwe and Mpira interacting with NGO of different 'cultures' with philosophical positions focused on transformational outcomes will be used to develop emerging issues and theory. It should be noted that any generic category used in the discussions in this book, such as 'the community', 'NGOs' and 'the poor', are used with the author's awareness of problems of using such theoretical categorizations. Throughout the book, emphasis is put on issues rather than categories with which these issues emerged or were understood. This is done so as to give room to any future research or NGO-Community interactions in contexts that are different from Malawi (even within Malawi) to emerge with any other characterization of the social actors involved. This makes the issues raised in book, although based on a single country study and within one area of that country, amenable to analysis in other community and country contexts (Yin, 1994).

Presentation of the Book

This book has been divided into ten chapters. The following are the major highlights of discussions in each chapter.

Chapter One

Provides the framework of the problem, research aims and questions, and the conceptualization of what needed to be done to conduct an empirical research in order to address the problem. The context in which the study was conducted is also discussed in general terms in this chapter.

Chapter Two

This chapter deals with the conceptual framework of social transformation as was understood in this study. The main aim is to locate the understanding of the involvement of the people in NGO projects. These are the people who are the primary group to experience transformation as a result of NGO interventions. Therefore, how we conceptualize the way they come into the social transformation agenda is important.

Chapter Three

The conceptual framework of NGOs involvement in the social transformation agenda via projects is discussed in this chapter. The aim is to bring out a conceptual picture of how the realities of NGOs and 'the project' as an instrument for managing the NGO interventions influence the conceptualization of the social transformation agenda. In essence, this chapter also justifies the nature of research questions raised in chapter one so that they relate to these realities.

Chapter Four

In this chapter, the research design that was used in generating data necessary to answer research questions is discussed. The main focus is on the logical thought process that characterized the major steps towards data generation and not necessarily the logistical steps followed.

Chapter Five

I discuss the findings from the analysis of data on the comparison of the people's and NGOs' construction of livelihoods in the two communities studied. The focus on the differences in constructions of livelihoods between people and NGOs studied.

Chapter Six

This is where conflicts in images that people and NGOs formed of the role of NGO assistance in people's livelihoods are presented. The presentation focuses on these conflicts as identified at the interface with NGOs and within the community. The understanding that emerges from this presentation is that of different aspects of NGO assistance relating to conflicts in different aspects of people's livelihoods and different characteristics of these people.

Chapter Seven

Presents the nature of conflicts in images that were observed with regard to the understanding of change resulting from different aspects of NGO assistance, whether positive or negative. In this case too, the presentation shows how different aspects of NGO assistance were construed in relation to different aspects of people's livelihoods.

Chapter Eight

This is where the image conflicts that were observed in connection with the definition of people's livelihoods, role of NGO assistance and change, are discussed. The discussion takes the form of analyzing the nature of negotiations in which both NGOs and the people were engaged in the context of these image conflicts. It was realized that projects were being implemented despite these conflicts because of the various forms of 'strategic' negotiations as enacted by both NGO fieldworkers and the people.

Chapter Nine

This chapter discusses the image sensitive approach, which is presented in this book as a possible theory that could assist project managers to understand the nature of engagement that different people have with the project.

Chapter Ten

In this last chapter of the book, I discuss the conclusions that can be drawn from the study. This is in terms of the extent to which research questions are answered, implications on NGO development policy and practice, lessons that I learnt in conducting the study and recommendations for future research.

Notes

[1] Thinking in terms of 'accommodation' meant understanding social relationships as not mere encounters or interactions but influenced by the interacting actors' worldviews.

[2] The book is a revised version of my PhD thesis submitted at the University of Reading (Tembo, 2001a).

[3] Wood (2001) argues that the developing country state is part of the unequal power structures of the society and hence cannot act independently in order to protect those disadvantaged by these structures.

[4] Kalemba (1997) observes that during this period domestic savings increased from 0.3% to 17.7% as a proportion of GDP while industrial output grew at the rate of 8.2% per annum.

[5] For example, despite food problems in the country, food security never reflected in the development policies until as an attachment to the main policies in 1990 (Devereux, 1997).

[6] A written code of conduct for NGOs in Malawi was only first ratified by the general assembly of NGOs in Malawi on 25th April 1997 (CONGOMA, 1997).

[7] Wood (2001) draws an interesting distinction between poverty eradication and alleviation noting that poverty eradication 'is about cohorts confronting power and inequality, whereas poverty alleviation is about reducing the incidences of poverty via processes of graduation and successful incorporation into existing social arrangements and patterns of distribution' (p. 12).

[8] The CDP goals were stated in terms of 'reduction' of deprivations or 'increasing' assets. For example, 'By FY92, at least 200 poor families in community x will have their incomes increased from an average of US$75 to US$250 per annum per family'.

Chapter 2

Social Transformation, NGOs and Development

Introduction

This chapter, recollects on the theory of social transformation, in its historical context, and conceptualizes its meaning in the context of the different interpretations that have emerged in the post cold-war era. It is such an analysis that will illuminate the major practical questions that arise when theory is translated into practice. For purposes of this book, this debate is centered on aspects that are relevant for NGO contexts. This is achieved by firstly, conceptualizing social transformation and social development, where the position of external interventions is located. The chapter ends with a conceptual framework that shows how people and NGOs are brought together into a transformational development agenda. In doing this, I am able to define how people through participation, are theoretically seen as involved in an agenda that is meant to improve the quality of their livelihoods.

Conceptual Analysis of Social Transformation

The changes in development theory and practice into the post cold-war period, as introduced in chapter one, have been in terms of both the way poverty is defined and ways of dealing with it. In the manner of defining poverty there has been a change from targeting the specifically defined conditions of life of the people to the more 'holistic' sustainable livelihoods thinking. The social targeting approaches, developed as an aftermath of the inadequacies of economic 'big-push' theories of the 1950s, were meant to focus of specific social problems in communities (Rondinelli, 1993). This meant that some authorities or development experts had to define what these problems or needs were and who had them. The 'Sustainable Livelihoods' approach, on the other hand, accommodates all aspects of what it means to make a living (Chambers and Conway, 1992; Carney, 1998; Scoones, 1998; Bebbington, 1999). Since no one can define what living means for another, the approach is centered on the people's definition of poverty.

Accordingly, in terms of how to deal with poverty, the previous approaches were centered on 'injection of capital inputs', including technology, and dealing with obstacles of development found on the way to people's participation (Oakley and Marsden, 1984). This practice also included the blueprint and linear interventions, based on accurate management capacity (Rondinelli, 1993). In more theoretical terms, people and their social systems were seen as homogeneous groups with common poverty characteristics. These kinds of definitions were hence associated with corresponding deterministic and linear views of the path of change. The sustainable livelihoods thinking has, instead, focused on expanding people's assets and capabilities, of both material and social nature, so as to improve quality of life and reduce its vulnerability to external shocks (Scoones, 1998; Carney, 1998; Rakodi, 1999; Bebbington, 1999). The central idea of the approach is to start from the existing assets and capabilities of the people and move on to better assets and capabilities, using various strategies that are in line with people's aspirations. Since livelihoods are diverse, there cannot be a common antidote to poverty in this regard.

In terms of social transformation, therefore, these changes are concomitant with the shift from the large 'improvement' and 'transformational' models (Long, 1977) to a more 'micro-informed' people-centered impetus. Taking the modernization stance of Wilbert Moore, for example, social transformation was seen as,

> A total transformation of a traditional or pre-modern society into types of technology and associated social organizations that characterizes the 'advanced' economically and relatively politically stable nations of the western world (cited in Long, 1977, p.9).

In the current development thinking, on the other hand, with a people-centered thinking, social transformation is conceptualized in terms of participation, empowerment and capacity building (Korten, 1990; Burkey, 1993). These are the theories that are in tune with the idea of expanding people's capabilities and assets. For example, Bebbington (1999) conceptualizes the expansion of capabilities and assets through transformation of existing assets and access to resources from markets, civil society and states. In this case, increasing capabilities is meant to 'enhance people's ability to be agents of change' (p.2034). Access, in this context, is meant to increase the amount and command over resources, seen herein in both material and non-material forms. In which case, the social transformation agenda is a people's agenda.

These changes represent a significant shift in the theory of development. The question of how much of this theory has translated into practice, however, is different and often a debatable one. Literature suggests that the discursiveness of the language of development is able to disguise the actual practice, which still carries the traits of the old, with external legitimacy (Hobart, 1993; Escobar, 1999; White, 1999; Arce, 2000). Drinkwater (1994) actually makes it clear that, 'in practice, ingrained habits die hard and old rigidities are far from being demolished' (p.35). In this chapter, however, I will show that there is more to the business of development than just the rigidity of habits.

In my view, there are three major theoretical interpretations of social change, which inform the current understanding of social transformation, from which NGOs also draw their practice. These are the evolutionary, structural and theological interpretations. Their theoretical relationship is particularly relevant to the identification of the main characteristics of social transformation. Establishing these characteristics is important if we are to conceptualize its application in the NGO context. Although some of these theories were developed as early as 1950s and 1960s, they find particular emphasis in the current explanations of social transformation. In the following sections, I briefly discuss these theories and bring out their relationship and relevance to the conceptual understanding of NGOs at the end.

Evolutionary Interpretations

Evolutionary interpretations focus on the processes of social change that are intrinsically part of societies, as a characteristic of being human. Learning, based on the intrinsic capacities of people as individuals and corporately in a social system to creatively effect change, according to their aspirations and goals, characterizes these processes (Dunn, 1984). According to Dunn (1984), this learning occurs because people are engaged in a process of 'evolutionary experimentation' as they adapt to changes in the environment in order to meet their objectives. In this connection, Dunn asserts that a misunderstanding of this process of social change has led interventions to focus on 'instrumental goals', which are productivity-centered. This undermines goals, which fit the system together, resulting into a tragic failure of the system. Only people themselves, therefore, have the capacity to determine what is instrumental to them. The people's understanding of this 'instrumentality' may be quite different from how external agents understand instrumentality.

However, the evolutionary interpretation of social change does not make social interaction issues clear, and hence tends to lean on functionalist[1] understanding of societies (Cohen, 1968; So, 1990). A focus on social interaction in a society brings out structural issues, which underlie differential achievement of individual and societal goals. Individuals having particular motivations, capacities and experiences, have their options for action affected by structural issues prevailing in their social systems (Giddens, 1990; New, 1994). How these structures affect action, however, is a subject, which is very debatable but it constitutes a significant theoretical basis for interpreting social change, and hence transformation.

Structural Interpretations

There is an ongoing debate in social theory on the concepts of agency and structure, and therefore, the resulting process of change. In this case, some writers on social theory emphasize agency whilst others emphasize structure. There could be foundational reasons for both of these positions, though that is not of much relevance at this point. What is important, however, is to note that in both cases, structure is seen in terms of conditions created along social positions that enable individuals to act in certain ways and not others, which could be in their interest. The condition in question is said to be the rules and resources in a society, which individuals draw upon in order to pursue their interests (New, 1994).

In this context, an emphasis on agency advances the argument that although there are pre-existing structures, individuals are actively engaged with them and hence are able to make any structural condition relate to their interests in some way (Giddens, 1990). This ability to engage with structures in different ways is the basis for transformation. In this connection, Long and van der Ploeg (1994) propose a more dynamic understanding of social change, which focuses on the central role of human action and consciousness in social transformation rather than structure. Social transformation, in this case, is a process of change that results from continuous action by agents on the different forms of structures that they face, within and outside their societies.

However, Wilmott (1997) argues that conceptualizing structure as 'enabling and constraining' does not properly explain the fact that certain actors occupy positions in a society to which they have no free control. Position in society is also associated with authority and power, which are the key resources for social action. In this case, the social-cultural constraints, which surround the individual in a certain position in society, will affect which actions they are to take amongst the different options available to them. Therefore, pursuing of goals in a society, in this case, is shaped by what is possible within a social setting. In essence, this interpretation reflects more of the 'situatedness' of agency, giving importance to what structure can do to different members of a particular society.

Ultimately, the question of agency and structure in relation to social change from these arguments brings out the understanding that we cannot reduce the actions or possibilities of actions of individuals to limiting conditions that surround them. At the same time, however, we cannot conceptualize actions in terms of 'voluntarism', where individuals pursue actions according to their individual motivations (Schuurman, 1993; Long and van der Ploeg, 1994). Therefore, my position on this debate, in relation to understanding social transformation, is the view that people, as social actors, are agents of change, within circumstantial limitations. This is the understanding with which I interpret Long and van der Ploeg's (1994) argument that people are 'knowledgeable and capable' under certain conditions. This means that there are conditions or circumstances under which human agency can be constrained but not muted because people will still find ways of functioning within constraints. Wilmont's (1997), however, argues certain people face consistent constraints in situations where others progress. This means that these people are continually disadvantaged and rightly so, it becomes a justice issue.

Theological Interpretations

Theological interpretations are centered on matters of the heart in the understanding that poverty is a result of sin, which perpetuates the unjust structures in societies. In an elaborate conceptual framework or liberation theology, Gutie'rrez indicates that

> Sin is a breach of friendship with God and others ...the ultimate cause of poverty, injustice, and oppression in which persons live... Things do not happen by chance and that behind an unjust structure there is a personal or collective will responsible – a willingness to reject God and neighbor (Gutie'rrez, 1988, p.24).

The main argument is that transformed hearts will lead to transformed people in their attitudes and values, which then lead to transformation of the unjust structures. This transformation leads to freedom not only for people as the individuals concerned, but also their relationship with others in a social setting. Liberated people are not expected to pursue goals by sustaining structures that are a hindrance to other people but to advocate for transformation of unjust structures. They are to pursue just and peaceful relationships with other people and the environment (Hope and Timmel, 1984, Myers, 1999). Byrant Myers (1999) further explains that transformation starts with changed people, people who have discovered who they are, 'their identity' and value, 'their vocation'. He goes on to articulate that it is this 'rediscovery' of identity and vocation empowers them 'to live out these values in search for their new vision' (p.117), which includes building just and peaceful relationships.

The emphasis on liberation is based on the centrality of the people's own capacity in the process of creating a better world, a more human world. To this effect, Gutie'rrez (1988) explains the fact that the poor in whatever state they are, find their livelihood, which includes their thinking, loving, struggles for justice and peace and seeking their freedom from unjust structures, in that poverty situation. Being poor does not equal being incapacitated to see think and have a worldview, or being helpless in the way of making personal or corporate initiatives. This interpretation, therefore, also has a clear focus on agency as a mechanism for dealing with constraining societal structures, as explained above. The difference with the structural interpretations is in the understanding of the nature of 'agency' and hence ways of dealing with constraining structures, where theological approaches emphasize value change.

In this context, although not appearing in terms of liberation theology, I would argue that other forms of explaining social change, that emphasize on moral transformation and commitment of actors, also reflect this interpretation. For example, Edwards and Sen (2000) allude to the need for changes in the 'subjective states that constitute our inner being – our personal feelings and intuitions in the deepest sense' (p.606). In different ways, Chambers (1995, 1997a) has referred to the 'primacy of the personal' or 'responsible well-being' for genuine development. This framework of understanding might not directly refer to religion, although Edwards and Sen (2000) do so, but demonstrates the aspect of social change that occurs from personal convictions. In this position, the powerless might not need to challenge the structures at all because the powerful might, out of conviction (or 'new vision', according to Myers, above) let go of their exercise of power. There is a subtle cause for debate here, with regard to how this approach could be put into explicit project goals, beyond moral or evangelical appeal to the assurance of identifiable outcomes within a set timeframe. We can also argue that there is power available also for the giving by the powerful and the taking by the powerless rather than only for contesting as espoused in most empowerment projects. I do not go into this debate in this book but relate to it later in the discussion about NGOs' understanding and managing image-conflicts in favor of the poor.

The three interpretations of social change, therefore, are centered on the structure and agency debate. In other words, it is the interpretation of agency and structure, and hence the resulting social change, that differentiates them. In the evolutionary interpretation, agency is in terms of the learning, based on people's intrinsic capacities to create a better environment for their livelihoods. The concept of structure does not come out clearly in this context because any impediment to achieving livelihood objectives would be seen as subject to learning better ways of tackling them. In the case of structural interpretations, agency is in form of engaging and challenging the social or cultural impediments to better living. The concept of power helps to explain the nature of this engagement in the context of the actor's relationship with other actors who are strategically pursuing their objectives. Finally, in the position of theological interpretations, agency is seen in similar patterns as in the structural interpretations. However, structure is seen beyond the behavior of some actors in the social system to the cause of this behavioral orientation. As a result, agency is as much an agenda of those who perpetuate structures as to those who are disadvantaged. In Table 2.1 below, I summarize these conceptual differences and similarities.

Table 2.1 Framework of agency and structure under different interpretations

	Agency	Structure
Evolutionary	Learning and adapting	Life problems in various dimensions
Structural	Challenging structures, finding room for manoeuvre	Oppressive rules and norms of the social system
Theological	Self-recognition of justified living, changing values and structures in which they are expressed	Oppressive rules of the social system as a result of sin or greed

Despite the differences in the interpretation of agency and structure, these theories face a common challenge of failure to determine the nature of agency or structure that is in a particular livelihood situation. Even when structural factors are generally similar, agency actions tend to be diverse thus making transferability of impact to other societies and circumstances difficult (Long and van der Ploeg, 1994; Pottier, 1999). Therefore, each situation and outcome has to be taken as unique to the context rather than a logical linear progression amenable to exact replication. According to Long and van der Ploeg (1994), this is where past theories of development, modernization and structural dependency, failed both to account and design interventions for the desired social transformation. Therefore, theories meant for understanding social change have shifted from those of grand explanations for all situations to a process of 'deconstruction' (Booth, 1994).

The deconstruction process seeks to focus on specific local or micro contexts and understand their links with the wider sphere. In essence, the question of diverse outcomes in different contexts has caused theories to focus on understanding change from the people involved in the change. Similarly, any desired change in a social situation has to be conceptualized as from the people and the influence they have in the process. This is because they are the primary agents, whether through learning or the challenging of structures or through change in self-identification. This realization has been embraced in the language of, among others, participation, empowerment, capacity building, equity, and sustainable development. It is therefore, important to explore how the concepts of agency and structure reflect in these concepts, which are discussed as social development theory. This reflection will provide a clear understanding of how these theories inform practice in the NGO contexts.

Social Development

This section is not meant to explore all dimensions of participation, empowerment, capacity building, equity and sustainable development. Instead, the discussion is meant to establish an understanding of how social development, with a transformation focus, accommodates agency and structure, as discussed above. These social development concepts provide the link between theory and practice.

Participation

The concept of participation in literature is defined in different ways but with the central tenet of involving people in decisions that affect their lives (Eyben and Ladbury, 1995; Eade, 1997). In essence, these should be decisions that reflect their interests. Interests can range from control over or access to material resources, access to power, prestige, self-esteem to maintenance of cultural goals for social relationships (Cohen, 1968). Different people in diverse environments pursue these interests in different ways, as part of their learning processes that lead to different forms of change. From this thinking we find that participation seeks to build on these processes and enhance people's decision-making, based upon their knowledge and systems (Scoones and Thompson, 1994). In this context, participation has to form part of the people's learning process, not only to adjust to change, but to determine the process of change as well; thus an issue of agency. Most participatory practices in social development reflect this view with an underlying premise that,

> Greater involvement of local people in defining local problems, identifying solutions and implementing them, ensures that the resulting programmes are more effective and sustainable.... A process whereby local people are given the capacity and power to make their own analysis, direct the process, grow in confidence and take their own decisions (Gueye, 1999, p. 1).

However, it has also long been learnt that not all individuals influence or take their share in making decisions concerning a desired change because of the actions of other social actors in the process. As a result, various observers of participation in practice have tended to put it into categories according to different levels of control over decision-making and resources between the beneficiaries and the external agents (Guijt and Shah, 1998). For instance, it is seen as a 'means' or an 'end' (Oakley and Marsden, 1991), while White (1996) has categorized participation as ranging from instrumental to transformative forms. In which case, participation has to involve a shift of power, if those people denied of the opportunity to have a share in influencing change have to be genuine participants (Nelson and Wright, 1995). This interpretative analysis of participation recognizes the constraining aspects of structure and the differential ways in which agency is possible. At this point, however, there is an override with the concept of empowerment.

Empowerment

Empowerment has been defined in literature in different ways but generally focusing on issues of addressing power imbalances in social systems. The most comprehensive definition that I have come across, however, is the one where McWhirter defines empowerment as,

> The process by which people, organizations or groups who are powerless (a) become aware of the power dynamics at work in their life context, (b) develop the skills and capacity for gaining some reasonable control over their lives, (c) exercise this control without infringing upon the rights of others and (d) support the empowerment of others in the community (cited in Rowlands, 1995, p.103).

The understanding of empowerment, as in the definition above, has a structural transformation focus. This is evident in the mention of power for gaining control, which has connotations of people's lives controlled in some ways from external sources. However, it starts from 'power within' (ibid.1995, Townsend, 1999). This orientation reflects the evolutionary interpretation, based on learning, 'becoming aware of the power dynamics at work in their life contexts'. Similarly, Eade (1997) puts it in terms of 'gaining the strength, confidence and vision to work for positive changes in their lives...' (p.4). The aspect of 'without infringing upon the rights of others, and supporting the empowerment of others' in McWhirter's definition above has a theological interpretation in my view. This is because it reflects the individual's 'personal' commitment to the good life of others. Ultimately, this suggests that these interpretations can be interwoven in order to bring about structural transformation, as an agenda for empowerment.

It is structural transformation that is at stake here because even the awareness aspect, where we can identify the aspect of learning, is geared towards power dynamics. This assumes that power is the aspect of life on which people in a particular situation need to focus in order to effect change. Essentially, this emphasis shifts the evolutionary interpretation to structural interpretation because in the former, the aspect of power dynamics is not emphasized. In this case, 'power to', 'power with' and 'power within' are all seen in terms of their ability to tackle and change 'power over' relationships and hence give chance to the powerless to pursue their interests (Rowlands, 1995; Mayoux, 2001). In other words, the agenda is one of turning 'social power' (productive capacity) into 'political power' (expanding control) (Friedmann, 1992). In this connection, Friedman clearly states,

> Poverty is a condition of systematic disempowerment whereby implied structural conditions keep the poor and confine their needs to social power, to the level of day to day survival. ..., therefore, calls for the transformation of social to political power and a politics capable of turning political claims into legitimate entitlements (Friedman, 1992, p.70-71).

There are interesting variants of the understanding of empowerment from this picture. For example, we find concepts of 'conscientization', and 'awareness creation', which focus on the power dynamics in a particular situation deemed as working to the disadvantage of some of the agents (Freire, 1972; Hope, 1984). The sustainable livelihoods framework is also centered on transformation through claiming and challenging spheres of power over assets, the 'structures' and 'processes' that are institutionally located in the state, market and civil society (Carney, 1998; Bebbington, 1999). I find the explanation of 'situated agency' in social transformation, as discussed above, relevant here. It is in this context of turning outcome or social power to political power that the understanding of empowerment frames the conceptualization of 'capacity building'.

Capacity Building

In its basic sense, 'capacity building' is about enabling people both to determine and achieve their objectives (Eade, 1997). In this form it suggests evolutionary social change, based on learning but where that learning is enhanced through some form of interventions. This enhancement of learning can be through provision of more or better information, for instance because information reduces uncertainty and widens options for decision-making (Fuglesang, 1982). This is a form of better agency in the evolutionary kind of change, that is enhanced through gaining new skills by active practice or gaining access to externally generated scientific information relevant for their objectives. This relates to the process of finding alternative explanations to their life situations, which cannot be directly attributed to action of oppressors in a social system. Otherwise, it is an increase in social power through access to productive information, knowledge and skills.

However, capacity building, with a structural interpretation, emerges when the conceptual framework of capacity building shifts to dealing with 'power over' in a social setting. In this case, capacity building becomes the way of enhancing not just learning but the agency located in an asymmetric power relationship. It then takes on the 'political' agenda where agency is about challenging structures and gaining better access to resources. In this context, there is a deliberate emphasis on the enhancement of those capacities that relate to gaining more control and access to resources by a certain category of people. Therefore, empowerment also provides the theoretical framework for capacity building in this context. The interpretation of agency and structure takes the form of structural and theological interpretations.

Equity and Justice

The argument has often been made that through the process of 'authentic participation' the inequalities and imbalances in the access and distribution of resources for development in a given social setting will be addressed. The re-organization of power, based on agency, should result in transformation towards equitable distribution of resources in such a context. In essence, this also reflects the structural interpretation of agency because some of the agents within a social relationship under consideration are seen as monopolizing available resources.

Similarly, the question of rights and therefore, justice depend on power rather than knowledge alone. The rules and norms can contain provisions that discriminate against certain categories of people because they are made by people in a society, who themselves share in its biased cultural inclinations and myths (Mushota, 1995; Middleton and O'Keefe, 2001). The empowerment process, as Mushota explains, is based on the complex issues involving culture, substance of the law and structures of the society at micro and macro levels, which interact with each other in the process of transformation. However, the questions of rights and justice in this context would also be associated with theological interpretations, requiring some moral obligations on the part of both the oppressed and the non-oppressed. The moral obligation will affect the setting of societal rules and the judgment of what and whose rights are concerned and strengthen responsibilities.

Sustainable Development

The common interpretation of sustainable development arises from a concern with the environment and its natural resources within which people's livelihoods are located. In this case, it focuses on accounting for the ability of future generations to meet their needs based on the ability of the current generation's development practice to provide that insurance (Croll and Parkin, 1992). The International Institute for Sustainable Development (ISSD) has constructed a definition, which is clearer in terms of the specific aspects of this sustainability. They define sustainable development as,

> A process of change in which the utilisation of resources, the direction of investments, the orientation of technological innovation and exchange, and institutional change reflect both future and present needs' (Titi and Singh, 1995, p. 8).

Such definitions, however, have been criticized for their emphasis on ecology and economic concerns, whilst neglecting the social dimensions (Middleton and O'Keefe, 2001). This criticism is laudable in the context of social development; hence a more socially focused definition could be better. Croll and Parkin (1992) have argued against theories that separate the ecological from the social livelihoods. Such a separation, they argue, creates 'imaginative dichotomy' that could reflect negatively in the nature of interventions for change. They argue that we can only understand the ecological in the context of the social because the environment does not exist for itself but for the people in their social systems.

In this context, sustainability is a more embracing theory that defines the nature of transformational development that should take place under the framework of participation, empowerment, capacity building and equity. This implies that any form of transformation has to be undertaken with consideration of needs of the future and not just the present. In which case, interventions should generate improvements in people's livelihoods, both for the present and for the future, going beyond the period of the intervention itself. In terms of sustainable livelihoods, this assurance is built on increasing capital assets, so that future shocks are contained (Carney, 1998). To this extent, it reflects both deliberate and moral commitments of the agents to the nature of transformation, the structural and theological interpretations of social transformation.

The foregoing analysis of the nature of agency and structure in social development, as understood in the context of the concepts of participation, empowerment, capacity building and equity, is centered on empowerment. In essence, this is the theoretical position through which external interventions come into people's livelihoods. In this case, social power is the starting point for the relevance of priorities and learning processes, but much attention is given to political power, where access and control over resources can increase for those disadvantaged in a given social system. The social system, in this case, goes beyond the immediate locality to include the interactions that people have with the wider sphere. Ultimately, therefore, an empowerment-based social development, with a transformational focus brings together concepts of participation and capacity building towards practice in different contexts and by different external development agencies (cf. Oakley, 2001). My conceptual research interest, however, was on how this empowerment-based agenda is underpinned by agency and structure in these different contexts and different discourse domains of interacting project actors.

Figure 2.1 below shows how under the concept of 'empowerment', the agendas of the external agents and the people, 'internal agents' are brought together. In this case, the concepts of interventions and participation are the forms in which external agencies and the people respectively, are brought together to an empowerment agenda, for transformational development. Therefore, there is an ongoing interplay between empowerment and capacity building as people and NGOs work together in a development project. Finally, the figure shows that transformational development has to be sustainable, as an outcome of people's empowerment.

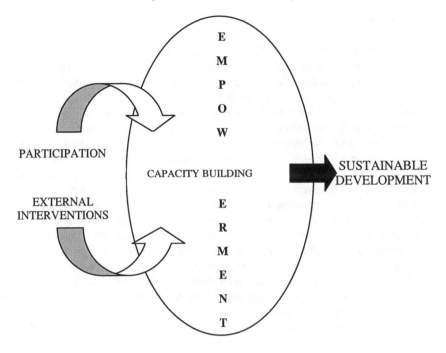

**Figure 2.1 Framework of an empowerment-based social transformation
process**

Empowerment-based Transformation

As indicated above, participation is the mechanism through which people, in their
diverse livelihoods, are brought into the empowerment agenda that is formed
jointly with the external agents. The differences in the nature of this involvement
of the people brings out the different typologies of participation that various writers
have expounded on, as discussed above. An agenda for social transformation has to
be based on 'authentic' participation,[2] it is argued (Oakley, 1995; Fowler, 1997).
Accordingly, the concept of external intervention is, in this case, a deconstructed
one because it is based on the understanding of agency, learning and diversity. In
this context, an intervention has to be understood as 'an ongoing, socially
constructed and negotiated process, not simply the execution of an already
specified plan of action with expected outcomes' (Long and van der Ploeg, 1989,
p.228).

Conclusion

The shift in the understanding of social transformation has meant a change from the deterministic, linear and homogenizing interpretations to focus on human agency, learning and diversity. These new interpretations have provoked the need for new operational frameworks, in order to bring the theory to practice. In this chapter, this framework has been conceptualized through an analysis of agency and structure under the evolutionary, structural and theological interpretations of social change. The operational framework for social transformation has been established as people's empowerment in their own different social contexts. This is where people's participation and the external agencies' interventions are mediated in order to bring about transformational and sustainable improvements in people's livelihoods. It has been argued, however, that in the interest of understanding the nature of accommodation between NGOs and the people in such a context, we need to question how empowerment is underpinned by agency. This is how the decision-making capabilities and actions of the people that are meant to benefit from projects (normally stated in every project or programme design as the poor) vis-à-vis that of actors could be understood (Kabeer, 1999, Long and van der Ploeg, 1994). Otherwise the social development concepts being used here are so abstract that it is very easy for development agencies to lay claims on them without the poor identifying with experiences of empowerment. Long and van der Ploegs' (1994) construction of intervention analysis compels us to follow through how the intervention practices of NGOs are shaped in the social contexts of the people. I, however, take the stand that we need to firstly understand interventions as part of the NGOs' realities before they are analyzed as part of any particular social intervention. This forms the central discussion in the following chapter.

Notes

[1]   Functionalist approaches draw on the work of Durkheim, which perceives societies as organisms with each part contributing to the total achievement of socially agreed goals (Cohen, 1968; So, 1990). Conflict is therefore seen as alien to the society.

[2]   Authentic participation is defined as 'a process through which stakeholders influence and share control over decisions and resources that affect their lives' (Fowler: 1997, p.16).

Chapter 3

NGO Interventions and Social Transformation

Introduction

In the last chapter, it was established that interventions in a social transformation agenda are shaped in the different social contexts of the people. Instead of conceptualizing strategies for understanding how people accommodate NGO interventions in these life-worlds, I will firstly focus on the NGOs' premise for construction of interventions in this chapter. The argument here is that since NGOs are also social actors, their interventions at the interface with particular communities should not be taken as neutral. Instead, beliefs, ideologies, systems and performance pressures on NGOs shape their interventions even before they decide to work in a particular community. The main objective in this chapter is to bring out a conceptual understanding of how the characterisation of NGOs from this framework could shape the external intervention (see Figure. 2.1). This discussion forms the first part of the chapter. Similarly, NGOs intervene through the project approach, which has its own basic demands of what an intervention should be. Therefore, 'the project' should also be brought into the framework as also being a context that provides for the differential actor influence on the nature of interventions, even before the actual interaction with a particular community.

At the end of this chapter I emerge with a conceptual framework that brings together the interventions as they are shaped in processes external to the community and then in a project, with people's participation. The general conceptual view that comes out from this process supports the understanding of projects as arenas of continuous negotiation among the actors for meanings and space (Elwert and Bierschenk, 1988; Long and van der Ploeg, 1994). I then link this understanding to the characterization of NGO realities and develop a conceptual framework that provided the theoretical basis for the main research questions for the empirical study. Essentially, the conceptual framework reveals the necessary aspects of the NGO interventions, in project contexts, that needed to be understood through empirical data.

Where are NGOs in Development Theory and Assistance?

From the general overview of changes in development theory and practice provided in chapter one, it was argued that NGOs' prominence followed a theoretical position that accorded them the ability to involve people in their own development. The conceptualization of 'involvement of the people' was based on the underlying NGO characteristic of 'voluntarism' (Korten, 1990). It was explained that the 'voluntary' characteristic confers on NGOs the value-based relationship with the poor and hence having a natural orientation to properly respond to the priorities of the poor. This implies that NGOs are well placed for facilitating 'authentic participation' of the people in development, for improvement of their livelihoods, on a people-centered agenda. However, as discussed in the next three sections, the changing nature of development assistance over the past two decades has affected the relationship of NGOs with the other development actors. This has hence affected the nature of their operations at the grassroots level, rendering the theory of voluntarism inadequate for determining NGO performance. In this chapter, I consider demands on performance and the associated evaluations and the wider political and economic influences in order to explain this new reality.

Demands on NGO Performance

The rise in funding from public sources has resulted in tightened standards for transparency on NGOs regarding the real cost of their business, evaluation and quality control on the development process and accountability (Fowler, 1997; Smillie, 1997). Donors require evidence that shows that the development funds they give actually reach the poor and have an impact on their lives; the notion of 'value for money'. The major challenge for NGOs in this situation is to achieve professional performance while maintaining administrative costs low, so that the money value is reflected. In this context, accountability implies that NGOs have to reconcile their legitimacy and objectivity to the different constituencies (Edwards and Hulme, 1995; Najam, 1996; Smillie, 1997). Najam (1996) provides a typology of this form of accountability by categorizing forms of accountability as to 'the patrons', 'the client' and to 'themselves'.

It is through financial accountability (the actual management of funds) and policy (the use to which money is put) control that the relationship that NGOs have with their donors, as patrons, is maintained. Donors require that funds be used with integrity and for the intended objectives and are able to sanction NGOs through 'punishments', which can include the withdrawal of funding. NGOs in such a context tend to 'mirror' donor requirements rather than fostering true bottom up approaches. On the other hand, Najam further argues, NGOs have to be accountable to 'themselves' by continually reconciling their actions to their missions. In which case, missions dictate the nature of actions in the field and not the other way round. Finally, NGOs relate to the people through development objectives and not funds, which then weakens their accountability to the people (Fowler, 1996). This is because there are no clear forms of actions by which communities can directly evoke accountability on NGOs, especially in the context of NGOs having the money and people having the needs.

Since the action point, in terms of delivery of assistance, is in the community, where there is a weak and informal accountability, it implies that NGOs' performance and accountability can only be objectively analyzed through evaluations. Evaluations enable assessment of performance against objectives and benefits against the costs of NGO projects (Marsden, Oakley et al. 1994; Gosling and Edwards, 1995). In this way, evaluation reflects on the accountability questions. Furthermore, these evaluations could be made jointly with the community, with reports shared to all stakeholders for scrutiny, and hence achieve transparency and accountability. However, evaluations in NGO contexts have not been able to provide this accountability efficiently. This has been due to the conceptual problems associated with social transformation objectives and practical difficulties with the conduct of evaluations.

NGO Evaluations

Conceptually, the ideological load in the objectives, which are largely non-material, has not been effectively translated into conceptual terms that can be interpreted in objective terms (Brown, 1991). The cognitive stance in objectives, such as empowerment, participation, capacity building, solidarity and cohesion, does not lend itself to the use of conventional evaluation techniques, which have been developed based on quantitative measures. At best, authors on social development have argued that such normative objectives can be understood based on observation and interpretation (Marsden, Oakley et al. 1994). The other way has been through participatory monitoring and evaluation so that perspectives of the people who are involved in the development processes are accommodated. In this direction, there has been a growing theoretical move towards 'process' and involvement of the people in conducting evaluations (Mosse, 1998; Cracknell, 2000). These theories, however, do not provide for understanding how the people and NGOs' values are negotiated.

Otherwise, evaluations are still conducted as linked to funding and as part of NGO accountability to donors, hence they conjure fear of withdraw of funding, where project impacts are not apparent (Smillie, 1997). This shows that evaluation is still perceived as an extra activity that is more for demonstrating accountability to donors than an intrinsic project activity. As a result it represents an external pressure for NGO performance. Therefore, evaluation affects the nature of NGO interventions because they have to reflect what is capable of being easily evaluated.

Wider Political and Economic Changes

It was noted in the general overview provided in chapter one that development NGOs came to the open debate following the withdrawal of the state. When looked at from the perspective of implications of these changes on NGO performance we find that political dimensions emerge. As part of the 'New Policy Agenda', NGOs were popular for purposes of enhancing democratization and participation of civil society in market-led development (Bebbington and Riddell, 1995; Hulme and Edwards, 1997). This is understandable because alongside the rise in official funding through NGOs were conditional loans to the state from international donors mainly through the World Bank and IMF (i.e. structural adjustment programs). With this aid there was the need for both the withdrawal of the state and restructuring of its power in favor of 'good governance' or 'participatory governance' (Turner and Hulme, 1997; Schneider, 1999). Hence, the NGO role of strengthening civil society supported the wider political and economic agenda, although they were seen as the 'favored child' in the context of the 'failed state'.

This understanding of the political dimension makes much sense when we consider the decline in foreign aid flows through NGOs in favor of direct foreign investments in the post cold era. If the decline were to do with state failure in the form of bureaucracy, high costs of doing business and other factors, the decrease in development aid should have affected the state but not NGOs. As a result of the new interpretation, NGOs are now seen as requiring to learn new 'rules of the game' rather than just the voluntary activity for development in the poorer communities (Edwards et al. 2000; Fowler, 2000b). The danger for NGOs is seen as that of losing out on the civic values of the people for market values of 'individualism' and 'consumerism' (Korten, 1995; Edwards et al. 2000). In order to counteract these influences, these writers recommend that NGOs develop new relationships that will enable bargaining and negotiation with the state and market. These relationships, however, represent a significant influence on NGO performance at the grassroots level, which is currently not properly conceptualized.

Ultimately, NGOs interventions into various communities are constructed within these demands on performance from their donors and the wider political and economic landscape, besides their defined reasons for existence. Essentially, this constitutes the NGO disposition on the nature of their agency at the interface with communities, forming part of the intervention. The nature of their agency, as discussed in the introduction, implies how they stand for certain ways of doing things and how they defend them against opposing information from the community. For instance, the community might consider the inclusion of women in certain project activities as inappropriate because of certain cultural norms. However, because the donors require inclusion of women in programs they are funding, NGO fieldworkers might use manipulative strategies in order to convince the community to include women in the project, in the name of 'facilitation'. This is a nature of NGO agency that subordinates the agency of the people. In Figure 3.1 below, I map out the conceptual framework for this thinking.

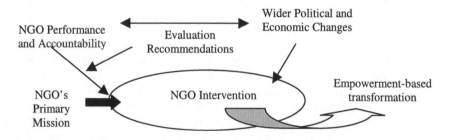

Figure 3.1 A conceptual framework of the wider context of NGO interventions

As shown in Figure 3.1 above, there is an interrelationship between the wider political and economic changes and the performance and accountability demands on NGOs. This is because with more funding from public sources, NGOs are likely to have donors who are also directly or indirectly influencing the political and economic changes on the wider scale. This reduces the influence of evaluations on the nature of NGO interventions, and hence a lower position that works through performance in the framework. This conceptual understanding of the nature of influences, or 'realities' within which NGOs construe interventions before engaging with a particular community, will assist in conceptualizing interventions at the point of engagement with a particular community. On the whole, as Long and van der Ploeg (1994) point out,

> Intervention is an ongoing transformational process that is constantly reshaped by *its own internal organizational and political dynamic* and by the specific conditions it encounters or itself creates, including the responses and strategies of the local and regional groups who may struggle to define and defend their own social spaces, cultural boundaries and positions within the wider power field (Long and van der Ploeg, 1994, p. 79, emphasis mine).

This intervention, however, is constructed in the project context, which also imposes on the intervention its own imperatives, in the form of what is understood to constitute a project. Therefore, it is important that we establish a conceptual understanding of this intervention logic in an NGO project approach. In the following sections, the nature of interaction between the people, through some form of participation, and the NGO, with its own influences, in a social transformation project, will be conceptualized. It is from this process that key issues that characterize this interaction between NGOs and communities were identified, and ultimately research questions were drawn.

The Project Approach in Social Transformation

Projects are being used as the way of intervening into human affairs for development because, it has been argued, they offer a systematic mechanism for bringing together different interest groups to address particular issues identified in communities (Rondinelli, 1983; Dusseldorp, 1990). In this context, these authors argue, projects have the advantage of bringing forward arguments around community issues to be discussed and shared by various partners in the process of strategy formulation. In the process, the project ensures that mechanisms for efficient use of scare resources are built into the intervention. In the process, projects also assist in maintaining accountability of NGOs to their donors and other stakeholders in order to ensure continued supply of resources that are generated external to the community. The project relationship ensures that stakeholders, particularly the donors, who are at a distance from the community, can keep close to that site through specific systems in a project.

However, the social processes in social transformation projects are dynamic and not amenable to external control (Rondinelli, 1983; Brinkerhoff and Ingle, 1989; Dusseldorp, 1990; Cernea, 1991; Fowler, 1996). Projects, by their nature, lend themselves to systematic planning and control in forms, which are not the normal functioning of social systems, especially in 'evolutionary terms'. They are subject to outsider control, and therefore, create a misfit with the normal grassroots initiatives (Lecomte, 1986). Furthermore, the large inflows of funds from outside via projects can easily offset the normal capacity of the communities to handle finances and disrupt their risk aversion mechanisms (Cernea, 1991). This creates more problems for the communities after external funds are withdrawn. Therefore, from this viewpoint, the project approach is not suitable for social transformation objectives. However, others have argued that the problem lies in the users of the project as a tool and not in the project as an approach *per se*; '...we should be careful to separate the baby from the bath water' (Honadle and Rosengard, 1983, p.302). Furthermore, as Charlton and May point out,

> Whether NGOs like it or not, their developmental activities in the Third World will remain substantially defined by the demands of project related work, and that, therefore, such work should be accepted as an opportunity rather than defined as a constraint (Charlton and May, 1995, p.238).

Managing Empowerment in a Project

There has to be a strategic approach to shift the configuration of power in societies if resource flows and control has to benefit the powerless. This is the central tenet of an empowerment and negotiation based transformational agenda, as established in chapter two. This, however, has to be achieved in a project context, where interventions are also shaped by the nature of demands of performance on NGOs and the wider changes in economic and political dimensions. The project approach requires that this process should be conceptualized, in an acceptable structure, in its various versions, in relation to the funding chain (Fowler and Biekart, 1996). In order to meet such requirements, some have advocated a 'structured flexibility' approach, which can also manage the kind of unpredictability involved in social transformation (Brinkeroff and Ingle, 1989). In essence, such innovations represent the framework in which the changed transformational development can be put into practice. Nevertheless, the basic characteristics of a project design still stand.

These characteristics include, a clear means and ends relationship of objectives, a clear analysis of the environment which will both influence and be influenced by the project, indicators of progress and the major assumptions on which the project is based (Gosling and Edwards, 1995). Such a design enables management to execute their key functions of planning, organizing, leading and controlling (Lucey, 1991; Cusworth and Franks, 1993). In the case of NGOs, this is necessary for managing their accountability to donors and other interested constituencies, discussed above. This is done through a management information system (MIS), which provides appropriate information for decision making and reporting to various stakeholders and donor interests (Lucey, 1991). However, given that project objectives are based on an intervention logic that is diffused into unpredictable social transformation processes, the conventional logic of the hierarchy of objectives is challenged. Therefore, the MIS for management is also challenged.

In the following sections, I take a 'deconstruction' approach, revealing these objectives for what they really are in this context, following the understanding of transformational development (Long and van der Ploeg, 1989). From this process I will conceptualize the nature of interventions in the project context, in this case with the participation of people in consideration (see Figure 2.1). The implications that this deconstructed view has on the MIS are not discussed in this book because it would require much attention, which the space in this book cannot allow.

Otherwise, in terms of project objectives, the discussion is centered on the analysis of the cause and effects. I then consider the project environment and progress indicators. These are the major aspects of a project design (Cusworth and Franks, 1993).

Project Objectives: Cause and Effect / Means and Ends Analysis

The causal links for development objectives are in general terms based on the results of the situation analysis, which includes problem analysis, participation analysis and alternative strategies analysis (Gosling and Edwards, 1995; Cracknell, 2000). This process enables planners to identify a set of interrelated problems, based on which the central problem is identified. All problems that are related to the core problem as causes or effects are then logically identified and linked to the core problem. Project objectives are then drawn in a process of turning around problem statements on the problem tree developed in this cause and effect relationship, into objectives linked in a hierarchy on an 'if – then' basis. This implies that by achieving one objective and meeting the assumptions also identified, the project will achieve the objective on the next level of the hierarchy. This process and rationality presents several conceptual mismatches with the social transformation understanding established in the last chapter. These conceptual issues occur in the formulation of project objectives, as purposes, and the treatment of inputs and outputs, on which I briefly reflect in the following sections.

Formulation of project objectives As noted above, in the conventional project appraisal practice, problems are conceptually isolated from their situational context. The core problem, which the project focuses on, is one of these isolated problems. Since this process includes the external agency interested in starting a project, we can also see it as an intervention entry point. Therefore, conceptually, there is potential for the engagement of the external actors to frame the isolation of these problems. This is framing in terms of which problem should be given attention and which one should be put aside. In the case of NGOs, this agency is shaped by the nature of demands on their performance and accountability and the wider political and economic changes (see Figure 3.1). However, the nature of influence on the agency of the 'participating' community by such realities is theoretically difficult to define in the project design process.

From the conceptual framework of the empowerment-based social development model established in the last chapter, identification of social actor problems should entail looking at how people struggle with their social and political contexts in order to make their living. Such a way of problem identification shifts from problems as isolated state of life conditions to the understanding the nature of engagement with these states of life. It is the process of their engagement with life conditions, herein called problems, that relates to the agency and structure interplay in that livelihood context. This is because, as established in the last chapter, empowerment is an agenda of both increasing 'social power', in the form of capacity building, and turning social power to 'political power'. In which case, it is social power that is a basic power, where any problem identification has to start. The construction of this social power, however, is based on the nature of agency, the nature of engagement the actors already have with their situations. These situations could be in terms of poor health, food security, witchcraft and so forth. The important issue for transformation is that this engagement should shape the nature of project objectives.

It should be noted that there have been major attempts to get the people's agency in forming project objectives using PRA and social analysis, which NGOs use in the project practice. In the case of PRA, people analyze their own life situations and problems, and hence their priorities (Chambers, 1997). Such tools as wealth ranking, Venn diagrams, mapping, seasonal calendars, time trends and so forth, have been used by the people in a more inclusive manner. This is because they are built on believing in people's capabilities and using their natural facilities such as crops, stones and the ground, 'democracy of the ground' (ibid. 1997). However, even with use of as many tools as possible in a project appraisal exercise, this would not show the nature of agency with regard to the people's situational contexts. The actual nature of agency depends on how people engage with each of these aspects of livelihood. PRA exercises, in this case, access a map of their isolated occurrences, when yet in real life they are in a whole. Therefore, project objectives, from PRA, are likely to be based on the isolated problems and reflect the agency of a few people in the community and the external agents.

In this connection, Mosse's (1995) advocacy for social analysis emerges as an attractive alternative. Unlike PRA, social analysis is an external activity meant to capture the nature of power dynamics in on-going activities. It is based on participant observation techniques, and hence avoids most of the public representation problems associated with PRA. These attributes relate to seeing agency and structure in action, as their patterns get played and replayed in the process of their engagement with the local and wider world. The nature of agency here would be accessed from the various 'representations' and 'emotional responses' that characterize people's engagement with their life situations (Long, 1997). For example, Mosse (1995) talks about fieldworkers studying a community for patterns of 'participation' and 'non-participation' through categories of 'active' and 'non-active' members. These categories were then traced to a range of social differences in the community including wealth, which helped in designing the project. This shows that targeting of the project, in the form of focusing objectives on known categories of people, could be achieved.

However, the 'externality' of this kind of social analysis serves the analytical purposes of the external agents. As a result, the capability of understanding meanings that people give to their experiences through these representations and reactions is questionable, at least epistemologically. This is because access to meanings entails an elicitation process together with the people during which meanings are also recreated (Pope and Denicolo, 1993; Walker, 1996). This implies that we cannot simply observe and conclude what certain actions mean to the people, unless we actively elicit these meanings with them. I explain more on this thinking in the next chapter. The participation that is reflected in the social analysis quoted above appears as 'the observed participation' but not necessarily meanings that people form of those activities, causing them to 'participate' or 'non-participate'. The resulting project objectives, therefore, will not be clear as to whose agency they reflect. The pressure for performance and the wider changes affecting NGOs could also easily translate into project objectives at this point.

This is especially the case because the meanings and representations of the external agents in this exercise are hidden and yet the intervention has both the participation and external intervention aspects (see Figure 2.1, p.37). There is lack of 'total ethnography' in this kind of social analysis (Garber and Jenden, 1993). This means that we must consider how the agency of the NGO is constructed in that situation in order to fully understand the nature of the empowerment agenda. The nature of influences on NGO performance and those from the wider political and economic arena are such that the influence of the NGO in defining project purposes could override that of the people. I return to this issue at the end. Meanwhile, the two other aspects on the hierarchy of objectives, inputs and outputs, also require deconstruction.

Defining outputs and inputs   The definition of project objectives will both influence and be influenced by the understanding of outputs and inputs. In a project, outputs are defined as those project deliverables which management can guarantee and is responsible for (Coleman, 1993; Wiggins and Shields, 1995). In which case, outputs are also a product of what is possible within the organization's human and financial capacity. These outputs in an empowerment-based social transformation agenda have to relate to the nature of agency of the people in a particular context. In which case, although the social or political needs, as expressed by the people, might be the same for a group or community category, the nature of agency might be different. In other words, there could be people with similar needs but differently positioned, in terms of the meaning of these needs in their lives and what could be done about them. Therefore, the project outputs ought to reflect these differences. Outputs are meant to effectively achieve project 'outcomes' and therefore affect the resultant 'impact' of the intervention, which is a key measure of performance for the stakeholders including the donors (Fowler, 1997; Akroyd, 1999).

It is the nature of these outputs that will determine the relevant project inputs. Inputs are the raw materials, which management uses to produce outputs

(Coleman, 1993; Shields, 1993). These inputs are thought of in terms of materials and personnel, as they exist in the agency's value frameworks, from a technical understanding. For example, in order to embark on a nutrition improvement project, the NGO might consider procuring seeds for green vegetables because they have a higher Vitamin content than other types of vegetables. The exercise then becomes one of defining the quantities of these seeds, budgeting and other logistics, for which management is responsible. However, when we consider that these inputs will be part of the people's social construction of nutrition before people use them, the way they are treated reflects meanings beyond their technical exposition. In this case, we should consider other social factors within which the meaning of that input will be constructed. This, however, introduces the struggle of the agency over meanings between NGOs and the people, into which the conventional project design does not allow us to probe.

Looking at the understanding of objectives, from this conceptual position, the cause and effect rationale shifts from being limited to the state of life condition of the people to focus on the nature of engagement people have with their life situations. It is the nature of engagement that will show us if it is about a shift from 'social power' to 'political power' for increasing 'power to' and 'power over'. In such a social construction view, the necessary project outputs are also based on the nature of agency of both the people and the NGO. Similarly, the required inputs are socially constructed and hence not conceptualized simply as a technical exercise. This understanding, therefore, also affects our conceptualization of the project environment and the assumptions we make about this environment.

The Project Environment

No matter the effort management puts into perfecting the line of intervention, the process of achieving intended objectives will be dependent on the influence exerted on and by factors in other systems with which it interfaces. The factors in question are those which are not directly part of the project but are so related to issues the project is about that whether management influences them or not, they still affect the achievement of the objectives (Shields, 1993; Wiggins and Shields, 1995). These factors can either be known through project appraisal processes or not known before the project is implemented. In cases where they are known, the conventional practice has been to assess their significance to the achievement of objectives based on which they are either put as important assumptions to be observed or used in the design of the project. In cases where they are a serious threat to the success of a project, the whole project might be abandoned.

However, when we consider the case of social transformation projects, this environment should not be conceptualized just as external factors that influence the project in some ways and not in others. Both the people and NGOs engage with the environment in different ways and with successes and failures. In this situation, the nature of their engagement with the environment is also important. For example, the fact that there is inflation in the country might not mean that all people experience it negatively. It might create opportunities for some people while affecting others negatively. In the case of the ecological environment, Croll and

Parkin (1992) cite a case of floods in a village, which were seen as a source of soil fertility by some households and yet for others it was a disaster. Women in particular had their social privacy affected because floods negatively affected their washing and sleeping norms, which in turn was interpreted as a cause of frequent sicknesses of their children. Similar forms of interpretation problems are often also linked to the people's construing of the spiritual occurrences affecting their lives (Bradshaw, 1993; Myers and Bradshaw, 1996). This means that the project environment, despite being out of direct control by project management, is an arena of struggle for meaning and space. This implies that it is also an arena of struggle for agency, as regards the project interventions and social transformation.

Progress Indicators

The concept of progress indicators arises out of the interest of project management to determine the progress of their intervention through some kind of measure, and also reflect on management performance. There are 'process' and 'impact' indicators. The former focuses on the efficiency and effectiveness of the project activities, the achievement of outputs from a set of inputs; while the later focuses on the achievement of the objectives at the purpose and goal level (Gosling and Edwards, 1995). In terms of planning, indicators provide the quantitative and qualitative detail to a set of objectives, reflecting the situation as it is at the point of intervention and the situation that is expected to exist when objectives are reached. This is crucial for NGOs in the current pressure for measurability of their work in order to determine 'value for money', as discussed earlier in the chapter. They might have to demonstrate this in the project proposal before the project is actually implemented. In essence, however, they reflect both the NGO and community perceptions of progress and impact depending on the nature of their construction.

The difficulty in this case is that the merging of NGO and the people's perceptions in defining appropriate indicators does not explain the agency 'black box'. This means that there is room for a kind of agency that could overshadow the other social actor's nature of agency, especially that of the poor. The context of the NGO interventions is such that, with increasing pressures for performance and demonstrating value for money, they would want to enhance certain aspects of people's livelihoods that reflect this orientation. As for the people, they might describe their life changes in certain ways and representations that do not fit the kind of representations that get more money on the donors' side for NGOs. Therefore, the development of 'negotiated indicators' of project progress (Cracknell, 2000) is also an arena of struggle over meanings. In this context, negotiations based on differences of value constructions create room for the privileged agency of some actors, while at the same time constraining that of others. How this occurs, was the subject of the research inquiry discussed in the chapters that follow.

The Case for Conflicting Images of NGO Assistance

In the foregoing discussion, I have attempted to deconstruct an empowerment-based agenda in a project context involving NGOs, with a multidimensional reality, and the people's participation. The underlining basis for pursuing this kind of conceptual analysis has been noted as the nature of engagement that the different actors have with each other in a project. Emerging clearly is the fact that, both theoretically and practically, the nature of the actor's struggle for space (the nature of their agency), for achieving their different purposes via a particular project, is obscure. As a result, it is difficult to understand where the different actors stand in each context of this struggle, and hence the share they take in influencing the agenda. Given that there is potential for some of the social actors to strategically 'enroll' other actors into their agendas, as a form of agency (Long and van der Ploeg, 1994), this is a cause for concern. Apart from showing us the target beneficiaries of a particular intervention, project objectives do not, by themselves, show whose agency and understanding they are reflecting in the processes of design and implementation.

Given that in the discussion above, I have argued that NGO interventions are not neutral but are framed from NGO realities, it is possible for NGOs to be agents of their own realities rather than those of the people, in a project. This should be the case in the context where NGOs are themselves struggling with maintaining their relevance in their own dynamic world of realities, as discussed above. Mawdsley et al. (2002) have ably used the notions of 'the knowledge economy' and the 'new managerialism' to conceptualize the power which such dynamics and realities could have on the NGO practice. Knowledge economy, they argue, pertains to the subtlety with which ideas of certain actors in the development industry are valued over others and become the code words for donor relations, or are otherwise legitimized within such relations. The different structures of partnership, reporting and professionalism account for the new 'managerialism' that produces global similarities in development approaches that makes one wonder 'Whose ideas' they are, these authors contend. In any case, these development dynamics and ideologies find their way to the rural community, through some forms of mediation and become part of the agency of NGOs at the interface with people in the processes of project design and implementation. However, as established above, neither people nor NGOs are homogeneous and hence, we cannot conceptualize one form of agency, in the interactions between people and NGOs via projects. Furthermore, it has been noted that the project approach demands that the inflows of external resources should be based on the isolated needs. This project practice provides room for manipulation of the people's agency in the selection of the needs on which the project should focus.

The task here, therefore, is to conceptualize what happens when an NGO is interacting with people in a rural project community (accommodation process), in the context of these realities, in terms of the nature of agency that is involved. The immediate response could be that of following through how each of these realities, on its own, affects the nature of agency and hence the realization of transformational development in given NGO projects. This is a difficult, if not an impossible, endeavor given that some of the realities that both NGOs and the people encounter might not have been articulated in this discussion. My proposition is that we focus our attention on images that the different actors, in this case NGOs and the people, form of NGO assistance and the processes of its provision. The nature of agency of social actors is likely to be seen through their images of assistance, because images or the way people interpret their world influences how they will act on that world (Freire, 1972). 'Images', in this case, are a perceptive view that entails re-organizing of elements of a situation or object that one is facing and giving it a structure of meaning and applicability to one's life (Hamlyn, 1996).

According to Hamlyn's conceptualization, perceptions as images imply 'seeing as', without claiming that that is the only way the object has to be seen. This means that other people or social actors could see the same object (herein standing for both material and non-material objects) differently. It is this difference, however, which, from a social action position, could politically be used for the advantage of one actor over the other. In which case, those actors that are strategically using image differences for their advantage will deliberately sustain differences or assume 'sharedness' of understanding and goals in order to pursue their gains. Therefore, in the context of social relationships among the different stakeholders in a project, it is by identifying the differences in their images of NGO assistance and how they each deal with them, that we can understand their agency. This is because in the context of difference, images are prone to strategic manipulation by some social actors for their own advantage. Images are a major resource for actor manipulation because, as Goffman argues,

> Sometimes the individual will act in a thoroughly calculating manner, expressing himself in a given way solely in order to give the kind of impression to others that is likely to evoke from them a specific response he is concerned to obtain (Goffman, 1969, p.17).

The indication of 'sometimes', in Goffman's concept above, means that it is also possible that the actor may be acting in the genuine sense of his/her meaningful actions. However, since he/she is not in complete control of the impressions they give, the resulting meaning in the other actor could be the same. In any case, following the 'sociality' principle from personal construct theory, social actors form these images with their assumption of the other actor's interpretations in mind (Dalton and Dunnett, 1992; Walker, 1996). In a project interaction, we can conceptualize some of the actors at the interface attempting to bring other actors into their desired courses of action using their images of reality (Long and Villareal, 1994). As these authors point out, this is 'an essential part of an ongoing struggle over meaning and of strategic relationships and resources' (p.49). Therefore, as argued above, the images that people and NGOs themselves form of NGO assistance is a critical resource in shaping the nature of their agency, as part of their interaction in a project. The aspect of other actors 'deliberately using image differences' for pursuing their goals, however, makes me look at the nature of interactions in a project as one of 'image-conflicts' rather than mere differences in the images that stakeholders form of NGO assistance.

Unlike the concept of 'differences in images', the concept of 'image-conflicts'[1] implies 'active' engagement or struggle among those actors, whose images or understandings of an object or issue are opposed to each other. Through this concept, therefore, the intentional actions involved when some of the actors engage in manipulating the agency of others through their images of NGO assistance, can be analyzed. These intentional actions could either be in terms of actors deliberately hiding their genuine objectives or going forward with an action that involves other actors without properly accounting for their understanding of the action. In the later case, the actor disguising their objectives might have fears of the other actors withdrawing from the 'common' project, if they were to understand their objectives. It could also mean that the actor is deliberately not taking time to properly understand or explain his/her objectives to the other because he/she is worried about the consequences, such as delaying the implementation of the 'common' project. On the whole, this represents the different possibilities of conflicts, which could occur in the images that people form of each other and of the actions that are involved in their interaction. In their book entitled 'Metaphors We Live By', Lakoff and Johnson (1980) discuss the war that takes place in writing and in the use of metaphors, which although not shown in the open, could form a formidable argument among those involved. Similarly, wa Thiong'o (1997) writes on the 'war of images' in literature and society. Therefore, we cannot limit our conceptualization of conflicts to those that take place on the open, during face-to-face encounters in a project context, where external assistance is involved.

Conceptualizing Image-conflicts in the Project Context

The project, with specific goals (assumed herein to be from a shared understanding of those stakeholders involved), offers the context for the possibility of conflicts in the images that NGOs and the people form of assistance. NGOs and the people are involved in a social interaction,[2] where their relationships are shaped within some forms of socially constructed 'role performances'. This means that they both erect an image structure of the 'acceptable' and 'expected' performance of NGO assistance in people's livelihoods (Berger and Luckmann, 1984). In this case, when either the people or NGOs act in ways that are contrary to these performance structures, 'role conflicts' emerge. Related to these role conflicts, are conflicts in the images that both NGOs and the people form of change that is expected or experienced from NGO assistance. This occurs because, as Thompson points out, '...every contradiction is a conflict of value as well as a conflict of interest...' (cited in Scott, 1985, p.1). In other words, underlying role conflicts between NGOs and the people are conflicts of the value of assistance. The value of assistance is seen in the images that people and NGOs form of the change that could result from particular forms of assistance.

In the final analysis, the argument is that if we can study the nature of image-conflicts between NGOs and the people regarding specific forms of NGO assistance and how they are sustained or dealt with, we should gain a good understanding of the nature of their agency at the interface. This should be the case because where conflicts exist, they affect the nature of engagement actors have with each other, with respect to their interests in getting involved in a project. If image-conflicts are sustained while project implementation is continuing, it suggests that one social-actor is taking advantage of the interface image difference to pursue their goals. In other words, they have 'effectively enrolled' the other actors into their project (Long and van der Ploeg, 1994). Otherwise we would expect conflicts to be either resolved or to lead to one of the actors abandoning his/her involvement in the project. The image-conflicts, in this case, are conceptualized as 'role' and 'purpose' conflicts, where the former focuses on conflicts in the role performances of actors and the later on the understanding of change. This conceptual framework has been summarized in Figure 3.2 below.

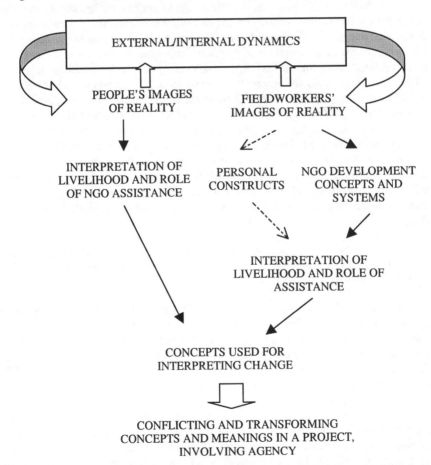

Figure 3.2 Conceptual framework for understanding the nature of agency at the NGO/Community interface

As shown in Figure 3.2 above, interventions in a project context are socially constructed, as the different images of reality interlock and get transformed, within the broader objective of achieving sustainable development. On the side of the people, coming in through the concept of 'participation' (Figure 3.1), they have an ongoing livelihood characterized by various forms of struggle, which in the project design are called 'problems' and are the basis for project objectives. However, in terms of the people, the discussion has shown that the nature of struggles they have in their livelihoods constitutes the framework within which the role of NGO assistance and the resultant change from it is given meaning. These struggles and the images people form of assistance are part of the social processes and engagements they have with their livelihoods. These are livelihoods in interaction with the local and wider spheres, which they both get influenced from and influence in diverse ways, shaping their images of NGO supported projects.

As for NGOs in this position, the discussion in the chapter has shown that they frame their interventions in the context of their ideologies, influences from their donors and the wider political and economic environment. In Figure 3.2 above, this has been shown as a formation of concepts and systems that are relevant to the NGO in question, in the context of the external dynamics. It should be noted that NGOs are also not only influenced by these dynamics in various ways but they also influence them as they interface with other spheres of action, the state, market and donors. The aspect of systems is where project design requirements come in because they relate to how the NGO maintains its accountability to the funding constituencies. The 'fieldworker' is the major interlocutor of NGO images of projects they support because they directly interface with communities. However, whereas they are trained and tuned to perform in a particular fashion in accordance with their organizational missions and objectives, they also bring into the framework their personal constructs. In this connection, Biggs has rightly argued that,

> Projects can be regarded as arenas of social interaction, where development personnel are a group within a whole range of actors who are constantly negotiating for resources, influence and social control (Biggs, 1997, p.101).

This aspect of the fieldworker's reality has been put in dotted lines in Figure 3.2 because it was not directly focused on in this study. In order to deal with it adequately, it required a research designed for fieldworker's personal constructs, using repertory grids, for instance. Owing to time limitations, this was seen as not a feasible endeavor for this study. I refer to it occasionally, however, in the discussion and concluding chapters, based on the information generated while focusing on the project design.

It was from this conceptual thought process that the research questions, presented in chapter one, were construed. It should be noted, however, that in talking about 'assistance', I do not imply mere objects such as money, food and such other material products or forms of NGO involvement in people's livelihoods. Instead, I interpret assistance in these forms but 'personified' (Croll and Parkin, 1992, p.13). In which case, they are assistance as seen in the context of the meaning that they acquire, as part of the people's and the NGO's identity, culture and knowledge (Pottier, 1999). In other words, it is people and NGOs, which attribute to different forms of assistance, their particular meanings. As such, to talk about assistance is to talk about its socially constructed characteristics and values.

Conclusion

This chapter has shown how the pressures for performance and changes in the wider world can conceptually be seen to influence the nature of NGO interventions even before they get to particular communities. In which case, the ongoing process of reshaping the intervention in people's life contexts is fundamentally informed from the agency of the intervention, which is as influenced from NGOs as it is from people themselves. The medium for this influence is provided in projects, as they are used to manage NGO interventions. In such a context, we cannot properly understand the nature of agency of the people, despite indicating that they are participating in a project. In order to achieve this understanding, we need to explore images that both NGOs and the people form of the role of assistance and the change expected or experienced from it, and how they are sustained or resolved. The nature of agency is important to understand, because it relates to the achievement of empowerment-based transformational development, as discussed in chapter two. In the next chapter, I will discuss the research design that made possible the empirical research, based on this conceptual framework.

Notes

[1]   Warner (2001) defines 'conflict' using such words as a dispute, confrontation, argument, disagreement, and so forth. He does not, however, refer to differences in images that those involved in the conflict have of the issue on which the conflict is based. As a result, his debates lend themselves more to managing open conflicts, which could disrupt development programs.

[2]   Bearing in mind that social interaction is 'conventionally restricted to actions which are immediate i.e. carried out either in physical presence of other people or within sight or earshot ...' (Burns, 1992, p.17). In the context of interface analysis, however, we have to be conscious of the distant forms of interaction that have a bearing on the social actor's observable actions (Long, 1989).

Chapter 4

Research Design

Introduction

> A design is the logical sequence that connects the empirical data to a study's initial research questions and, ultimately, to its conclusions. ... In this sense, a research design deals with a *logical* and not a *logistical* problem (Yin, 1998, p.236).

When I reflect on the process that characterised the design of this research inquiry, it is Yin's (1998) conception of a research design that best puts it into picture. The interactions between NGOs and the people, to which the main research questions presented in chapter one pointed, were not amenable to a straightforward design of an empirical research. Looking back at the process, I can trace the strategies and methods that were used, linked together by a thread of logic-based decisions, in order to prepare and generate necessary data from the field. In this chapter, I recollect this logical path.

The process starts with a reflection on how I came to understand the way to deal with perceptions as images, my paradigmatic position, so that I could properly devise a way of studying them in an empirical situation. I then discuss the logic that I used to choose relevant strategies and methods for generating data from the selected sources, including the understanding behind the selection of those sources. I give particular emphasis to the pilot study that was conducted at the beginning of the fieldwork. This is because, on my research path, it marked a major transition from much of theoretical thinking about the research process, to what was practically achievable in the field. The chapter ends with a reflection on the management and analysis of the data and the ethical issues that were considered in the process.

Establishing a Research Paradigm

It became apparent, as I focused on the conceptual framework for the research, that if I were to understand perceptions as images, which NGOs and the people formed of assistance. I needed to establish clearly in my mind how perceptual images occur in the world of knowledge before designing an empirical research focusing on such data (Bryman, 1988; Denzin and Lincoln, 1994). At the start I reckoned that the perceptual images, which I was seeking to understand, occurred as part of the interactive relationship between NGOs and the people. This interaction need not only be limited to face-to-face interactions, but also extended to include those operating at a distance while influencing actions of these actors in some way (Long, 1997). These interactions were based on, but also forming the context for the generation of new meanings, as mediated by the process of 'provision' and 'receiving' of assistance. In other words, NGOs and the people were interacting with each other through assistance. In this connection, I found the work of Sayer (1992) useful for moving from this kind of thinking to the more concrete, and hence practical, ways of understanding image interactions. It was only through this theoretical link that the designing of an empirical research to study such interactions was possible.

Sayer (1992) describes perceptions as having three parts in their development: the object of perception, mechanisms and conceptualisation (p. 31). It is the third factor, he argues, which gives meaning to the object being experienced. We can, therefore, similarly argue that people used their conceptual frameworks to give meaning to project interventions. In this case, project interventions were the object of perception and the various encounters that people had with them were the mechanisms through which they formed their perception of interventions. The interface between the NGO interventions and the people was therefore 'conceptually-saturated' (ibid., 51), in terms of perceptions. According to Sayer, this implies that the ordinary speech that people use to express their point of view, belief or attitude towards something does not completely carry the meaning that they have regarding that experience or object. This is because language is not an efficient mode of transmitting meanings behind concepts; it does not directly relate to perceptual experience (Lyon, 1999). Meanings, and hence images, are linked to the non-verbal communication and the material world in which people live, besides their verbal communication. This also accords to meanings their contextual specificity.

This meant that, although I was looking for data that does not exist in concrete and measurable forms, the non-tangible aspects of people's lived experience; I could still use the language mechanism in the inquiry. In order to do this, however, I needed to relate language use to those other material and non-material aspects that people in a specific context use to form their meaningful concepts. The immediate observation that I made from this was that in the understanding of concepts, language and material objects, I was dealing with qualitative data. This was because I was interested in the meanings that the concepts in the language and material objects would reveal to me, as Miles and Huberman have argued:

> Qualitative data, with their emphasis on people's "lived experience", are fundamentally well suited for locating the *meanings* people place on the events, processes and structures of their lives: their perceptions ... and for connecting these meanings to the social world around them (Miles and Huberman, 1994, p.10).

In identifying this inquiry as qualitative, I was looking at data types and not methods for generating data. This meant that when it came to methods, there was flexibility in the choice of the most appropriate method or a combination of several methods (Silverman, 1997; Hentschel, 1999). The aim in this case was to use the methods that would best generate the data I was looking for; even where necessary, from those conventionally labelled 'quantitative'. However, I still found it difficult to choose the specific research methods at this stage, because I was not sure of how data on image interactions would appear in a given NGO and community project. In other words, there was need for a style of research that would help in getting focused on perceptions as images and their meanings in a given situation. The research interest in meanings behind perceptions drew me to the choice between the style of 'critical research' and 'constructivism' (Denzin and Lincoln, 1994).

Although in both critical research and constructivism meanings of perceptions can be arrived at, in critical research concepts have meaning as seen in the context of structural social relations (of either cultural, political or economic in nature). For instance, Harvey (1990), and Kincheloe and McLaren (1994) argue that a researcher using critical research has to bring out the reality of structures and engage the disadvantaged, perceived in this context as being in a state of 'false consciousness' or of 'oppression'. In this case, meanings appear in the form of expressions of 'false consciousness' or 'oppression'. At the first sight, I found this appealing considering that NGOs, which focus on social transformation, draw heavily on goals that relate to transforming power relations. The difficult question, however, was; how do I escape from projections of my own images on the people I am researching in the exercise of categorising them as in false consciousness or as oppressed? Additionally, I did not think of the study as designed to liberate the poor in the study community, as a direct output of the study in those communities.

On the other hand, I found that operating from constructivism would assist in the elicitation of the images that people and NGOs formed of assistance just with the belief that they are meaning makers of new experience (Dalton and Dunnett, 1992; Stake, 1998). It was from this belief that I found the relevance of the 'Actor-oriented Approach' to data sources so that I could have access to meanings people made of their experience with NGO assistance (Long, 1997). Such a paradigmatic posture still required being 'critical' but of the kind that kept me questioning myself on what I thought I already knew and what I thought I was hearing, so that I could verify it (Drinkwater, 1992; Hammersley, 1995; Strauss and Corbin, 1998). In summary, therefore, the following were the paradigmatic underpinnings of the research design.

- People's perceptions exist in conceptual forms.
- Concepts are products of social interaction and are context-dependent in nature and meaning.
- People are meaning makers of their experience.
- Behaviour is an incomplete indicator of meanings people form of their life situations.
- Language is an incomplete mechanism for understanding meanings of concepts in a social system.
- Understanding of concepts by their meanings is dependent on a holistic, context-based analysis of behaviour, language and material aspects of the social system.

- Constructivism, from an actor-oriented paradigm, is the suitable epistemological position for this research design.

From this position of beliefs about the nature of data and how they occur in the empirical world, I saw that an ethnographic approach within a case study design would be the most suitable for getting to the relevant data sources.

Ethnographic Case Study

According to the established paradigmatic position, images that people formed of NGO assistance, in their interaction with NGOs, could only be understood in a holistic, context-dependent approach. In this case, it implied understanding these images as they occurred in people's cultural, social and environmental settings. This is where an ethnographic approach, which allows us to understand multiple realities in a natural setting, is most suitable (Atkinson and Hammersley, 1998; Fetterman, 1998; Punch, 1998). This, however, was ethnography in an applied sense,[1] in that the conventional, naturalistic principles of ethnography were not followed as required. The quality of data, however, was not compromised because of paying attention to principles of 'reflexivity' and 'reactivity'. Reflexivity refers to the influence of the researcher's own values, from their background orientation, on the interpretation of people's perspectives while 'Reactivity' is the reaction of participants induced by their interpretation of the purpose of the researcher's presence (Hammersley and Atkinson, 1995; Holland, 1999). This was possible through proper access procedures, use of appropriate methods and checking the data for validity, as discussed in other sections below.

The case study approach, in this context, helps us to focus on a few cases, for an in-depth study. The case study design was suitable because of the boundary defined by the project, from the other experiences of people, which is a key consideration for a case study approach (Yin, 1994). In this case, the individual projects, entailing forms of assistance, were the cases, while the various forms of interaction between NGOs and communities were the units of analysis. Given the complexity of issues to consider in the case study design, I found it useful to organise my design work into a logical conceptual framework.

The framework represented the logical progression from the broad conceptual view of the study, to the more specific case study design. It was Maxwell's (1998) theoretical framework of a qualitative research design that was used to map out the broader aspects of the research design. A case study, in this framework, was a methodology for generating data necessary for answering research questions. The specific aspects of the case study design were adapted from Yin (1998) and Stake (1995) on the case study approach. Figures 4.1(a) and (b) and explanations that follow, show how the design was developed in broad and specific terms.

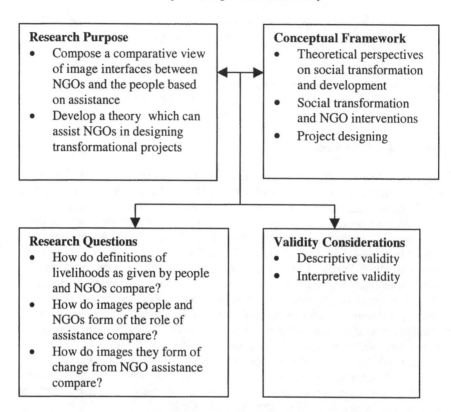

Research Purpose	Conceptual Framework
• Compose a comparative view of image interfaces between NGOs and the people based on assistance • Develop a theory which can assist NGOs in designing transformational projects	• Theoretical perspectives on social transformation and development • Social transformation and NGO interventions • Project designing

Research Questions	Validity Considerations
• How do definitions of livelihoods as given by people and NGOs compare? • How do images people and NGOs form of the role of assistance compare? • How do images they form of change from NGO assistance compare?	• Descriptive validity • Interpretive validity

Figure 4.1(a) Research design process: the broad framework

Figure 4.1(a) above shows how having decided on the purpose of the study, emanating from the broad question discussed in chapter one, the major conceptual underpinnings of the research were developed (see chapters two and three). As Maxwell (1998) rightly explains, the two aspects of the study are interdependent. In this case, it was in the process of developing theoretical perspectives relevant to the broad research question from literature review that I observed that the concepts of 'images' and 'interface' were critical for the study. Otherwise at the start of the research process, I only focused on the theories of NGO interventions and project designing, which were based on my experience in the field and my earlier studies on social development. The research purpose and conceptual framework were necessary for the development of research questions, as shown in the figure and explained further later in this chapter. In dealing with interface images and meanings, however, it was important to keep important data validity considerations in focus.

Looking at the descriptive and interpretive validity of the information collected enables assessment of the quality of data that the researcher is going to generate during the study (Maxwell, 1992). I thought this was one of the critical issues to consider in the research design. This is because the orientation the researcher has towards data and its quality will affect any lessons, theories or knowledge that could be claimed from the study. According to Maxwell, descriptive validity has to do with the accuracy of transcriptions of what interviewees actually said and what was actually observed in people's interactions and their environments. Interpretive validity, on the other hand, has to do with the manner in which the research process allows for people's concepts and meanings to emerge. Otherwise research results could actually be based on the evaluative judgments that the researcher imposes on the situation being studied.

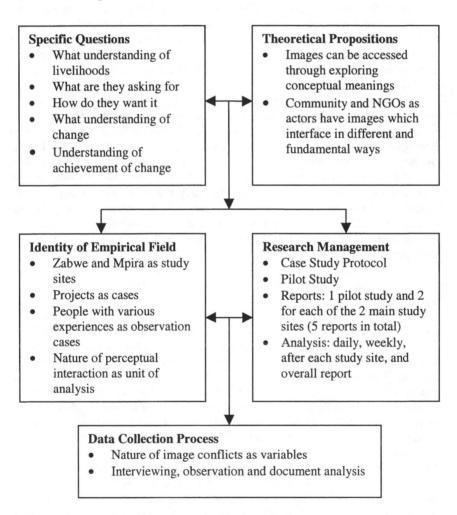

Figure 4.1(b) Research design process: the case study framework

In designing the case study, although the main areas where decisions were required were mapped out as indicated in Figure 4.1(b) above, only some of the components were filled with what was going to be done at the beginning. The other aspects of the case study design were included as they became clearer while conducting the study. For instance, I had a clearer mind on the conceptual assumptions and what the research was going to focus on (the identity of the empirical field) from the paradigmatic understanding discussed above. These components helped in defining the 'theoretical propositions' of the case study design (Yin, 1998). The conceptual design aspects of the study were enriched from presentations of a project proposal made at World Vision UK office and at the DSA NGO Study Group meeting. The input at World Vision UK strengthened my thinking about the possible relevance of the study outputs to the challenges that NGOs face, including accountability and working with governments. From the NGO study group meeting, the research focus shifted from emphasis on people's learning processes to an actor-oriented conceptual framework, on the NGO and community interface.

Even with such fine-tuning of the research proposal, however, the specific research questions, data collection process and the management of the case study process could not be fully developed away from the field context. They were being developed and adjusted as the research was going on. This was because, besides the fact that the field could not be predicted from the theoretical framework, I did not come across any research conducted in this way from my literature review. This is where I found conducting the pilot study before the main study played a critical role. In the rest of this chapter, I reflect on how I worked my way through the case study design, with a focus on the choice of the study areas, the pilot study, specific research questions, data collection process and the management of the case study process.

Getting to the Field

Having decided on the case study approach for the inquiry, a choice of the NGO projects for this study had to be made. Some of these choices were made before leaving for the field, based on the research design logic, discussed above, while the other choices were made in the field. These were choices that came as the experience of conducting the field research unfolded. For instance, before leaving for the field, I envisaged that the study required the 'Embedded, Multiple-Case design'[2] (Yin, 1994). This was because in the research questions, I used the concepts of 'NGO' and 'community'. Both of these concepts are problematic in that NGOs are of different types just as communities embrace diversities of different kinds within them. For a proper study, therefore, I needed to understand interactions at the more general level of community and NGO interface but from the understanding of cases at some specific levels that reflected the differences within them. Therefore, I chose to conduct the study in two community sites so that I could gain some insights that could come from understanding similar types of interactions in another setting. In this context, I also considered that some familiarity with the area of study would be helpful for negotiating access, as Morse argues,

It is foolish for the researcher to put too much work into a study that must be conducted in one particular setting unless he or she can be assured that access will not be denied (Morse, 1998, p.60).

As a result I chose to conduct the study in Malawi, where I come from, and one of the sites, Zabwe, was a project in which I worked before this study. Familiarity reduces problems of access that arise from role-playing in the community, in a researcher versus people's expectations (Cotterill and Letherby, 1994). The other site was left open for decisions to be made while in Malawi, after learning from the results of the first case study.[3] To avoid being blind to some presumptions, which I might overlook by studying a community in which I worked before, I planned to choose the second site from an area where I never worked before. This was to be another region of the country, with people of a completely different culture and language. When I actually went into the field, however, some changes were made to this plan based on the lessons from the first research site.

Firstly, I noticed that familiarity with a research site was more complex than I first thought because, as it occurred, there were a number of issues I had to contend with in that community. In the first place, having spent earlier years working with the community was not a guarantee that all the people would know me. It was mostly people who were either committee members or direct beneficiaries of NGO assistance during the years I worked in the community that remembered. The other people had to be reminded, which I chose not to do because I was equally interested in conducting the research as a new person in the area. To such people, I was as much a stranger as a researcher who has not been to the community before. Therefore, I did not assume that people in this community knew me, and therefore did not dwell on it as an advantage.

Instead, I reckoned that the most important familiarity for a researcher is with people's cultural expectations rather than personalities because personalities are very diverse and difficult to completely accommodate in a short period. I thought as a researcher, I needed to have the skill to enter different settings as long as I can gain a good understanding of their social-cultural life styles. In this case, I took advantage of my cultural awareness of the community in order to deal with communication barriers that could have arose because acting out of tune with the role expectations of a community (Cotterill and Letherby, 1994). For those who knew me, I had to carefully explain my change of role to that of a research student, without connections with NGOs that were working in the community. I actually introduced myself as a researcher from the University of Malawi, following the letter that was obtained from the University Research Coordinator. In this way, my past relations with the community were turned into strength, in that people were not afraid to give examples of what happened in my time in order to explain their images.

Secondly, from my analysis of data from Zabwe, I learnt that image-conflicts were in the areas of the quality of assistance and how this assistance was managed in the process of having the different people or groups of people in the community access it. On the side of NGOs, the areas of quality and management of assistance were seen to be associated with the NGOs' ideological and management orientations. As a result, I considered it more insightful to follow up on the nature of image-conflicts in another community where the same NGOs were assisting. The same combination of NGOs was only possible if I sampled within the same district. In this case I thought that, strategically, each NGO would be using much similar management and ideological approaches in the two sites. Therefore, I would maximise possibilities of deepening my understanding of the different or similar nature of image-conflicts from the two communities. This was the basis upon which the second site, Mpira, was selected. This meant that I could not go to the other regions of the country for the study as initially planned.

Learning from the Pilot Study

A pilot study was conducted for six weeks (from November to December 1998) in Mwenga community, away from the case study sites. The community had 4 villages, with 160 households and was undertaking project activities with assistance from NGOs. At the end of the pilot study, a report stipulating the study process and what I learnt from it, was produced and discussed with my local supervisor, some NGO and government staff operating in the area. I also discussed my findings with some of the community members and NGO fieldworkers in order to check on my interpretation of some of the main concepts that were generated in the study. The lessons learnt from the pilot study are incorporated in my discussion, on the conduct of the research in the main study in the two sites, in the following sections.

Sampling of Cases within Projects

Whereas the pilot study was conducted with wealth-rank categories as the main criterion for sampling the people to be interviewed, it was learnt that wealth ranking did not show anything about the nature of interaction between NGOs and the people. Instead, there were some identifiable patterns of images that people formed, following their experience of NGO assistance. Therefore, in the main study, the sampling logic was mainly based on the experience of NGO assistance. The socio-economic category of individuals was taken as one of the important population characteristics, together with age, education and gender, which I found important to consider in the analysis. I, however, still gave it a biased focus because of the interest of NGOs that design projects for social transformation to target the poor. This meant that if, for instance, the transformational focus was on gender the sampling process would be biased towards gender.

From my analysis of the data that was generated in the pilot study, I categorised the people's experience of assistance from NGOs in terms of leadership, which included being a village leader or committee member. The other aspect of experience was based upon the different levels of people's involvement in a particular project. In this case, it meant either a person was a direct recipient of

NGO assistance, receiving a loan for instance (direct participants), or an indirect recipient, for example, carrying bricks for a school (indirect-participants). There were also people who had just heard about the NGO assisted projects but had neither the knowledge of which NGO was involved nor the form of physical participation (remote participants). These people were considered also as participating in this remote sense because although they had a vague idea of NGO assistance, they still formed their images of assistance. They 'positioned' themselves in a particular way towards possible NGO assistance.

In the final analysis, I sought a compromise between experience and social-economic category of individuals (established through social analysis of the community), as a useful guiding principle for preparing the sampling frame in the main case study as shown in Table 4.1 below. The aim in this case, was not to obtain a representative sample from the population. Instead, it was to get a sample from the population that would strengthen my understanding of the nature of images that arise in the interaction between NGOs and the community (Mason, 1996). In other words, I was focusing on getting as wide a range of the kinds of image interactions with NGO assistance in the community as I was able to understand. Since the images that people formed in the course of these interactions could not be accessed prior to the interview, the sampling frame was only a logically constructed guide for locating observation units. For the first community, the sample size was 65 and was categorised as shown in Table 4.1 below.

Table 4.1 Sampling frame prepared for case studies in Zabwe

Well-being	Local leaders	Direct project participants	Indirect project participants	Remote-participants
Very poor	8	7	7	7
Middle- poor	6	4	4	4
Better-off	6	4	4	4
Totals	20	15	15	15

In Table 4.1 above, the leadership category had more people in the sampling frame because I learnt during the pilot study that the leaders made most decisions for projects and hence images they formed of NGO assistance were important, as gate-keeping orientations. Secondly, the frame was also deliberately biased on the poor in all the categories because of the NGO's social transformation focus on the poor. Other characteristics such as sex, education and ages of participants were also accommodated into the sample during the actual sampling process.

The immediate experience I had with this sampling frame in Zabwe community was that as I analysed the information on a daily basis, I was able to get the different images that people formed of assistance. However, I had to bear in mind that the comparison was focused on the nature and meanings of images rather than the population category from which they came *per se*. Therefore, I had to make sure that I understood these images clearly. In other words, if the inquiry had meant to find out the images that a particular category of people formed of assistance, I would have just gone on collecting information from these categories as indicated in the sampling frame. In this case, however, my interest was on the nature and meaning of images that existed in the community and then, as a secondary issue, who in the community formed these images.

Such an interest in the nature and meaning of images led to more sampling from a category or a number of categories, even where the target number, in the sampling frame, was already reached. This kind of sampling was meant to enrich my understanding of the images of NGO assistance in those aspects which I had not yet adequately understood, 'selective coding' (Strauss and Corbin, 1998). This was necessary because I observed that the image a social actor would form of assistance was not exactly the same as the experience they had of that kind of assistance. Therefore, I had to include more people of a known type of experience, but unknown images that they formed of a particular form of assistance, until I understood the nature of their images of that assistance. In Table 4.2 below, I have summarised the nature of this sampling logic.

Table 4.2 Summary of the logical progression of the sampling process

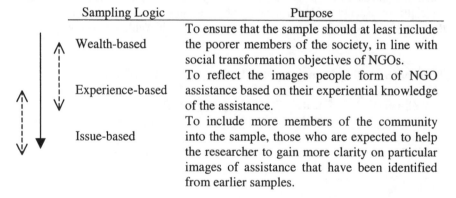

Sampling Logic	Purpose
Wealth-based	To ensure that the sample should at least include the poorer members of the society, in line with social transformation objectives of NGOs.
Experience-based	To reflect the images people form of NGO assistance based on their experiential knowledge of the assistance.
Issue-based	To include more members of the community into the sample, those who are expected to help the researcher to gain more clarity on particular images of assistance that have been identified from earlier samples.

In Table 4.2 above, the arrows show the direction of the sampling process for selecting observation units. The continuous arrow implies that the general direction was from wealth-based to issue-based sampling. The double-sided arrows imply that experience-based sampling was the main criterion but always with reference to both issue-based and wealth-based criteria.

Specific Research Questions

Although I had already set my main research questions, as part of the research design (see Figure 4.1 above) I needed a set of questions, which would be more 'topical' or 'specific' so as to enable generation of information at the field level (Stake, 1995; Punch, 1998). I would then link back to the main research questions, in the form of 'theoretical abstraction', when interpreting and evaluating the findings against theories I set in the conceptual framework. With the paradigmatic position of this inquiry, it was not possible to develop such specific research questions outside a social setting because I needed to be context-specific. The paradigmatic understanding only gave me a picture of what the data might be, in order to develop some strategic questions at the field level. A pilot study was hence conducted from 'sensitising questions' (Strauss and Corbin, 1998, p.77) in order for necessary questions to be constructed.

Upon analysis of data generated from the pilot study, I observed five categories[4] of areas in which images people and NGOs formed could be put and compared. These included the type of assistance, the form they wanted it to provide, an understanding of change that was expected and an indication of whether they saw this change achieved or not. I then turned these categories into specific research questions that formed the basis for the choice of research methods in the main study. The framework below shows the analytical picture that I formed of these questions.

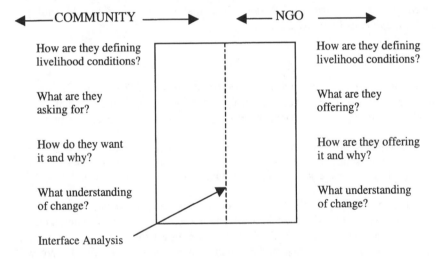

Figure 4.2 A framework of specific research questions

The framework in Figure 4.2 above shows 'topical' questions for both sides of the interface, the community and NGOs. Methodologically, I concentrated on finding ways of understanding images people formed of assistance and I made similar questions apply to the NGOs. This enabled me to compare images that both the community and the NGOs formed regarding the same experience of assistance and the negotiation process involved. It was based on these specific questions that the relevant research methods were selected and used to generate data. The first question relates to the first main research question. The other two pairs that follow relate to the main research questions on the role of assistance, the second main research question (focusing on change), respectively.

Working with Methods

> Data of whatever form do not just appear or lie around waiting to be casually picked up by some passing social researcher but have to be given form and shape in order to qualify as data; made relevant, in a word, to a research problem (Ackroyd and Hughes, 1992, p.3).

Operating from constructivism with an actor-oriented approach to data sources, meant that for whatever method I saw fitting for generating this data, I needed to think in terms of people as meaning makers of their experience. In this case, although they individually make meaning of their encounters with projects, these meanings are still shared from a social or cultural point of view (Walker, 1996; Arce and Long, 2000). This is because people's actions are partly influenced by assumptions they make on each other's meanings as members of the same social system. In this case, where NGOs were involved, a social relationship was created in the context of a project. From this understanding, I used individual interviews, focused groups, observations and document analysis, for providing the multiple sources of evidence in the case study.

Interviewing

All interviews were approached from a Personal Construct Theory (PCT) thinking in an attempt to deal with language problems in accessing meanings that people and NGOs made of their experiences with projects. With PCT it is understood that,

> Our discriminations of the world inextricably involve contrast; when we characterise something in some particular fashion (applying a construct to an element, to use technical terms), we are also indicating what it is not (Walker, 1996, p.17).

We cannot, therefore, rely on what people say without exploring what they are not directly saying, but which we know exists in their framework of understanding. We have to actively seek for both sides of the contrast through our conversation with them, for us to get to their understanding, as it exists in their minds. We will otherwise jump to conclusions of what we think people mean, especially where something sounds familiar to us. It is this active seeking for meanings as they exist in people's frameworks without impeding the flow of the conversation, that makes this kind of interviewing different from the other types of open-ended interviews. From such an approach, PCT becomes an effective tool for managing both the people's articulation of their images and the researcher's own predispositions and judgements.

The use of the PCT approach in these interviews, however, was in the 'informal sense' (Dalton and Dunnett, 1992, p.123), which uses ordinary conversation with people. In this case, I did not manage conversations with interviewees using a Repertory Grid technique.[5] This was because the people I mostly interviewed had literacy problems since the sample was biased towards the poor (see Table 4.2 above). With such a group I feared that the written Repertory Grid would provoke expectations of an intellectual exercise, which would make people provide constructs of how they think things should be, rather than what things are at that moment (Becker, 1998). Furthermore, as Seur (1992) observed in a study conducted in rural Zambia, the technique requires a lot of explanation to the interviewees before they can supply information necessary to use in the grid. In the process, Seur observed that he ended up defining categories, which interviewees emulated as theirs. You then wonder whether what people are saying reflects their true constructs or not.

Although operating with a PCT approach in the informal sense was effective, I had to keep thinking actively throughout the conversation, in order to understand the interviewee or otherwise put forward an appropriate probe. This was a challenging exercise because with constructs supplied in this way, their implicit meanings often emerged out of several sentences, rather than one word or phrase as happens with a written Repertory Grid. This meant that I had to carefully refer the interviewee back to some point made earlier in the conversation, if that is where a construct seemed to have emerged. With such an intellectually demanding exercise, I could only afford a maximum of two interviews a day. There were also times where I came back to the same interviewee on another day for clarity, after having analysed the conversation further. This technique was used in both individual and focus group discussions but was easier in the former than the latter.

Overall, I found the approach useful, except that if one is thinking in PCT terms, they need to be aware that there is a danger of getting too deep into people's personal lives and provoking other negative feelings against other people. In my case, I had to be aware of the fact that if not careful with my depth of probing, I could provoke negative feelings of the people against NGOs or their leaders. This would become an ethical issue. Because of these sensitivities, I found it difficult to employ research assistants in this fieldwork. There is need for finding a way of recruiting and offering appropriate training if this approach to interviewing has to be used with such help. I did not develop this aspect of the research process. In the following sections, I briefly discuss my experience with individual and focus group discussions from this understanding.

Individual interviews A total of 117 individual interviews were conducted in this study (67 in Zabwe and 50 in Mpira). More interviews were conducted in Zabwe than Mpira because Zabwe was the first site and I was still learning to use interviewing skills and generate good data. From the analysis of the pilot study data, I noticed that people's constructs were in forms of both the ways the general community looked at things and their own images. For their own images, people required space in which they could communicate effectively. Where this space was not provided, they tended to quickly provide the general community images. It appeared that they felt safe communicating what everybody was generally saying in the community and I had to carefully work with them towards their personally held images. In the quote below is an example of such a process where the interviewee uses that space to share her image of the structure of the village through which information about her needs has to go before the NGO can get it. In this case, it was linked to the political power of the traditional leaders versus women.

> *FT*: Is there no other way whereby you can get what you want to be known by the village headman?
> *Tafwa*: There is no way that is available, all of us think about different things.
> *FT*: So we stay with our different problems and ideas?
> *Tafwa*: Yes, besides this we are also different in our level of lack; some are better than others are, and once those who are not in problems decide for something, it goes that way. Those of us who are in problems should have to decide on what we can do on our own.
> *FT*: Do you say that to the village headmen?
> *Tafwa*: No, we do not say it instead we look for our own individual ways of alleviating our poverty.
> *FT*: What makes it difficult for us to say it?
> *Tafwa*: May be we are afraid.

Such pauses as 'may be we are afraid', which were not fully opened in order for the interviewer to understand 'why' they were afraid when talking about certain people or issues that were deeply felt to the interviewees. This is where I found that creating of space for interviewees does not always mean interviewing them just by themselves. The interviewee quoted above, for instance, is a woman and was interviewed in presence of her close friend because I noted that women were freer in presence of their friends than on their own. Husbands were generally not good partners in this process because they tended to take over the interview. Some of them could intervene with what they thought was the right answer, despite explaining to them that the objective of the interview was not about right or wrong answers. This however, does not mean that any grouping of women made good partners for this space of communication. Otherwise, the best partnership that I observed was where the woman being interviewed was interviewed in presence of a friend in whom she normally confided. Women would easily invite their friends to the interview where necessary. Men on the other hand were mostly free to enter into a dialogue on their own. It was this difficulty in getting to deeper level constructs that also influenced the manner in which I used focus group interviews.

Focus group interviews Thinking in terms of sociality and culture, meant that, as argued above, although people as individuals formed their own images of NGO assistance, there was an extent to which they understood and shared these images of their relationship to NGO assistance. As such they could be in a focus group discussion and validate each other's accounts based on what they know of the community's interaction with NGOs (Krueger, 1994; Morgan, 1998). As a result, I linked focus group interviews to the individual interviews. There were eight focus group interviews conducted in both Zabwe and Mpira (five and three respectively).

The first step was to interview people in the sample individually. Upon analysis of that data a number of perceptual issues were noted as common to most people in the village. These were mostly those that had to do with assistance meant for the whole village, such as water and schools. In this case I gained more clarity on their images in a focus group discussion, as people would be asking each other questions and encouraging each other. I always included a few of the people from the village, whom I had interviewed individually in the previous days, without disclosing their names to the group. The purpose for including the few who I interviewed before was to make them act as a check on my ability to understand their images. In most cases they would, after the group meeting, give me some feed back on how they thought I understood what they meant when I met them on their own. From my observation, focus group discussions were very useful for these general issues, as people would remind each other of real examples of NGO assistance alongside their explanation of images they formed of it. With the examples, I could easily get the meaning of what they were talking about.

However, focus group discussions were not easy to use for probing on more political images such as where committee members were seen as not managing NGO assistance well. Part of the problem that I observed was preparing a discussion of a homogenous group. This was difficult because there were a lot of factors, which characterised peoples' relationships. In this study, for instance, community people feared each other more on suspicions of witchcraft than on economic status of a household. Such a factor as witchcraft would cause lack of openness in the group. This was especially the case when I tended to follow through issues to get to deeper meanings and how they were mediated in the community. Categorising people on the basis of witchcraft was not possible because it was practiced in secret but from the way people talked, it was powerful in influencing people's relationships in the village.

Observations

I was able to enrich my understanding of most of the concepts that people were using in their verbal accounts during the interviews when I observed them engage into some interactions with NGOs. Dingwall (1997) argues that observers, as opposed to interviewers, 'find' data as people act out their lived experience (p.60). However, in this kind of inquiry, where it was meanings of those actions that were important, these observations required careful exploration to get to the meanings of concepts that were implied in them. There were several ways of doing this. For instance, I observed the interactions during meetings and project activities, which was a more direct type of observation, the 'participant as observer' approach (Adler and Adler, 1994). In this case, I observed what the NGO was emphasising and what people from the village were commenting on. I took note of points where I thought people were happy or not happy, as seen from their body reactions. I also took note of areas where they asked more questions or agreed without problems, including looking at who was doing the 'agreeing'. The same was the case on the fieldworkers' side. I then followed up with an interview with some members of the community members and the fieldworkers so as to validate these observations and their meanings.

Another way of observing was during interviews, where I observed the interviewee's conduct in both individual and focus groups. This was an important aspect for contextualizing the images that people and NGOs formed of assistance because, as Collins rightly argues,

> ... interviews are social interactions in which meaning is necessarily negotiated between a number of selves (and in which power may be *more* or *less* shared) (Collins, 1998, section 1.6).

Since, as an interviewer I was also a social actor, shaping the reactions of the interviewees during those interviews, I needed to take the interactions themselves as forming a context of the interview. More importantly, the changes in tone of voice when I asked about certain things, such as assistance in connection with village leadership or NGO fieldworkers, would show me something on which to seek further understanding. In this case, they were related to people's social relationships, which were mostly related to power. In focus group discussions there were changing group dynamics as people questioned each other, agreed and disagreed, some by whispering, some by motioning with their hands. I would probe more into these forms of communication in some ways during the interviews or after the interview but also documented them as part of the context of data. Ultimately, these observations assisted me to generate the 'moving picture' aspect of data, reflecting the changing behaviour of the interviewees during the interview (Catteral and Maclaran, 1997).

These observations were not always planned. I came across some of them as I moved in the village or when I suddenly met an NGO fieldworker. Many times I learnt more from such encounters than planned ones, such as the encounter I had with Melu documented below,

Melu: Where are you going?
FT (myself): To *Ndengule* village, I have to meet a few people for my research. Where are you coming from?
Melu: I am coming from the *Muta Hall* where we were supposed to have a training session. People from *Ndengule* village do not really want to be assisted; they are not serious.
FT: What has happened?
Melu: You can't believe it Mr. Tembo. Last week we told them that since they have been complaining about hunger and money, we now have a programme where we can give them small ruminants such as goats for them to rear and eat or sell. They were very happy to hear this and we even formed the first group with ten members. Since they have not kept goats before, we liased with Veterinary Assistants on a training plan, where they can teach them on good animal husbandry practices. The training was supposed to start to day at *Muta* but you can't believe it! [Shaking his head] They say they want training allowances rather than us giving them food. All they want is money and yet when they get the goats they will just give back the first two goats from the offspring to their colleagues in another group in the village. Is that not already a great benefit? Can you understand this Mr. Tembo?

The first thing I observed as a researcher in the midst of interactions such as the one quoted in the above was that both the people and the fieldworkers often put me in the role of a mediator or sympathiser with their images of the other. I made sure

I appreciated their concerns, while at the same time did not want to get caught up in such a role, because it could have compromised my role as researcher. I, however, did not close off people who wanted to express themselves in this confrontational manner because they often appeared to communicate from their deeper feelings. These were also moments when I could get access to the dilemmas they faced in engaging into NGO assisted projects. Similarly for fieldworkers they would communicate their personal struggles with a defined group of people, their organisation or even their role as fieldworkers, in terms of the pressures and frustrations associated with it. They would communicate as if they found a sympathetic ear in me, which they had been looking for all the time.

As such, these were the best sources of data on image interactions that I could get. The fact that people reflected on an incident that had just occurred provoked even stories and examples of other similar instances in the past on which I built more inquiry and got more understanding. I, therefore, was following up on such issues on both the community and the NGO side and got better insights on the image interface. In the example quoted above, for instance, I went to the village concerned and stayed there until late in the night. I was then able to meet some of the people who were part of that meeting in order to get to their live reflections. My interest was not on settling the conflict but understanding where in that kind of assistance they had conflicting images with NGOs.

The problem with such observations, however, was that they needed to be naturally occurring and as a researcher with a fixed time schedule, I could not just wait for them to happen. I, therefore, continued with interviews while keeping 'all my senses' wide open to any observation opportunity (Adler and Adler, 1994). Furthermore, observations are a case of a situation where it is difficult to keep to your initial sampling frame because the units you might have put in the sampling frame might not be the ones involved in this observation opportunity. This was not difficult in this case because I kept the sampling frame flexible in order to focus more on understanding interactions rather than being limited to categories in the sampling frame.

Documentary Analysis

> Textual communicative practices are a vital way in which organisations constitute 'reality' and forms of knowledge appropriate to it (Atkinson and Coffey 1997, p.47).

NGO fieldworkers in this study appeared to share particular persuasions of the images that they formed of their interventions; even in cases where people in the community initiated these interventions. These persuasions were discernible from the language they used in project documents, which were partly reflected in their verbal articulations. I found that NGO documents contained more concepts than their conversational language, perhaps because with documents they could write and review before putting them to public use. They were, therefore, a vital source of data. However, I could not understand the meanings of these concepts just from reading them in a document. Even where I had some kind of understanding I did not want to assume my interpretations were the same as NGO interpretations.

Instead, I sought explanations from NGO fieldworkers. In this case, therefore, I read through each document and summarised it, while taking note of concepts being used, for instance,

> The strategy stipulates that the key components of Credit and Education are MOTIVATION and TRAINING and argues that without these two, POTENTIAL credit association members might never take the first steps to increase their incomes through loans and improve health and nutrition in their families. Field Agents embody these elements. These are to ensure EMPOWERMENT of the members to manage their own Credit Associations (CAs) and hence improve their own lives. Field Agent's primary responsibility is to MOTIVATE potential members to belong to CAs where they are to access loans and have information on their family health and nutrition.

Such concepts as those shown in uppercase in the notes above were then part of the guide for interviewing staff of the organisation. The key personnel in this inquiry were those who worked in direct contact with people in the field. As established in the last chapter, NGO fieldworkers are the mediators of images that NGOs form of their interventions at the interface with the people. Fieldworkers do not carry documents to refer to in their interaction with people in the community. Fieldworkers included in the study comprised of development workers at field level and their immediate supervisors. At the end of the fieldwork, I debriefed the NGO officers at the regional, and in some cases national level, as part of my exit procedures. I used the opportunity for clarification on the understanding of certain policies within the organisations.

During the study I consulted documents such as project reports, project proposals, evaluation reports and project baseline information. The community hardly kept any document on these projects, except for minutes of meetings with the NGO, which were also analysed where available. Whereas documents were vital in helping me to formulate better interview guides in the context of my research questions, they were very selectively provided by the organisations, with some organisations more open than others. Fieldworker's were not sure which documents were improper for external consumption, and which ones were not. In some cases, I was refused access to some of them, especially in the case of policy documents.

Data Management: Ensuring Trustworthiness

The fact that the sampling logic was evolving as data was generated, so that issues could be adequately followed up, meant that data had to be transcribed and analysed frequently. Given that I could not develop any theoretical themes at this stage, my main concern was with the quality of data as it was being generated. This was with regard to ensuring adequate descriptions of actual data and contexts from which it was generated and ensuring that interpretations of the people were understood and recorded properly. This has been indicated in the framework as 'descriptive' and 'interpretive' validity questions, taken after (Maxwell, 1992) (see

Figure 4.1). With this approach, as noted earlier, I managed to conduct only two interviews a day, so that I could transcribe and partially analyse the data I collected on the same day. An hour-long interview would take an average of three hours to complete because, although I recorded most interviews on tape, they were in local language. I translated them into English, making sure that the conceptual content of the local language was preserved. I checked most of my earlier translations with some of the local people, in order to check that the conceptual content had been preserved.

The translated version then was imported into the Non-numerical Unstructured Data Indexing Searching and Theorising (NUD*IST) computer software package, where I consolidated my analysis. As the name suggests, the package is meant for working with textual data by way of grouping into key thematic areas, searching these areas in terms of their interrelationships. It thereby assists the analyst to develop theories from the data. In any case, computer programs cannot be a substitute for the 'analyst core role' of searching for meanings behind any given data set (Kelly, 1995, quoted in Catterall and Maclaran, 1997). I chose this package after an initial exposure to *ATLAS/ti* and *WinMax97* during a CAQDAS software training session conducted at the University of Surrey.

The NUD*IST software package was chosen because I noticed that the indexing system related very well with a PCT approach to data generation, where different levels of the meanings that people form of NGO assistance can be charted. For example, where the image of assistance was *'It is free'*, I found that, for fieldworkers, this image found its application when the assistance was for construction work and not for loans. For the people, on the other hand, the same image would also be linked to loans in other ways. Therefore, in coding such an image I needed to put relevant contextual images under it, which was easily done in the index system provided in NUD*IST. This was related to the 'laddering' and 'pyramiding' process in PCT, where the former implies getting towards a person's deepest images of life, following the 'why' question. The latter concept means getting the person to show concrete examples in their everyday life, following the 'what' and 'how' questions (Dalton and Dunnett, 1992). I was able to map out these processes properly an index tree in NUD*IST, so that at each point, I had always to ask myself whether I needed to get more data to understand a specific issue or not to. This was the process that mainly informed my issue-based or 'theoretical' sampling (see Table 4.2).

It was through this logic that, using NUD*IST functions, I organised my data into what Buston (1997) calls 'descriptive', 'conceptual' and 'base data'. The descriptive category was for putting together data that reflected the interviewee's descriptions terms and interpretations that, in different ways, depicted the images they formed of NGO assistance. For such descriptions I used literal translations of the local into the English language so that I could retain the conceptual originality of accounts of the interviewees. Hence, I was made to use concepts in the form of phrases such as 'As they wish', which was a literal translation of *'mwenemumo'* or *'momumo'*, as concepts which people used in connection with certain decision making aspects of the project design process. If I had interpreted these concepts without using the people's descriptions, I should have missed the contextual expressions and emotions with which people used them. These were important for my understanding of the power dynamics in their relationship with NGOs and among themselves, for instance. Interpretations based on my analysis of the descriptions and interpretations of interviewee's accounts using my own evaluative and theoretical mindset were instead put in 'conceptual categories'. For instance, if from my analysis of an interviewee account I thought power relations within the household, or between the fieldworker and her/his supervisor was significant, I could use the concept 'locus of power', even though interviewees never mentioned power.

These conceptual categories were developed alongside 'document memos', which NUDI*ST also provides for. These memos were what I wrote as my 'floating' thoughts about an interviewee account or the observation I made about their reactions during the interview or the nature of their locality, and my surprises or confusions. I could revisit these preliminary thoughts on a later date and develop an understanding from them while analysing the transcribed accounts and my field notes. This process often encouraged me to find out more in order to strengthen some areas of data. Since these memos were dated, they served the purpose of a written research diary that shows my different ideas at the different phases of the research. The advantage of using NUDI*ST memos was that they were easily retrievable and could easily be related to other aspects of data. Finally, 'base data' was for the basic information that had to be collected from all interviewees, including age, sex, education, experience of the project and wealth rank. These data were useful in the later process of developing broad themes from data and then exploring how they appeared to occur in the population. In other words, gaining a picture of where in the population a certain image of NGO assistance or conflicting image of assistance with NGO fieldworkers was occurring. The idea, however, was not in order to generalise to the whole population but to make some theoretical observations in order to answer research questions with more rigour.

The different interrelations among the conceptual, descriptive and base data categories were also developed using some searching functions in NUDI*ST. It was from such a process that the research results and discussions in the following chapters were developed. This, however, had to take a data management process that entailed production of reports to myself at several points during the data generation process. The package allows print outs of simple documents or a combination of results from a certain inquiry one wants to make on data so that I could explore and interact with data as I went on with the research. This was done in order to see if I was generating the data that I was looking for, and how this data was helping in movement towards answering research questions. From these reports I compiled other reports, two after each study site, which were shared with my supervisors. The two reports for each site included one on community perceptions of the role and purpose of NGO assistance and the other on NGO perceptions of the same. I did not combine them because, at this point of data generation, I was not able to start developing theoretical themes. Therefore, including the pilot study report, there were five reports compiled, which later on after using them to discuss, as feedback, with some community members and NGO staff, became the summarised data source for further analysis.

Ethical Considerations

Ethical issues arise when the researcher deliberately conceals his or her position, while living among people, who are being studied, in order to get into their personal lives without their consent (Bulmer, 1982). In conducting this research, I clearly stated the purpose of the research in all the documents where permission of access to study areas was sought and where verbal negotiation was being made, especially at the individual level. This, however, does not imply that I achieved a clear understanding of the conceptual purpose of the research with all participants. To achieve this understanding would also imply influencing the results of the research, where participants know the answers with which the researcher will be happy (Hammersley and Atkinson, 1995). In the case of the conduct of the interviews, I controlled the depth of probing into people's lives, so as not to leave them with guilt because of the role and purpose conflicts with NGOs or other members of the society. This can occur because, during the elicitation process people form new constructs, which if not well supported, can leave them with feelings of self-defeat (Dunnett and Dalton, 1992).

Conclusion

In this chapter, I concentrated on tracing the logical path that characterised the movement of the research process from the conceptual framework and research questions to an empirical study in the field. A case study design was the main centre for the development of this logic, as informed from an actor-oriented approach. Through a multiplicity of methods, in interviewing, observations and document analysis (mostly developed through the use of NUDI*ST), I emerged with theoretical themes of interactions between NGOs and the people as conflicting in terms of images of the role and purpose of assistance. In essence, these themes were the containers of answers to my research questions. In the following chapters, I dwell on the results, exploring the nature of these image-conflicts.

Notes

[1] Punch (1998) refers to situations where principles of ethnography are just applied rather than followed in detail, because of time and resource limitations, as an 'Ethnographic Approach' while Fetterman (1998) calls the same 'Applied Ethnography'.

[2] According to Yin (1994), an embedded multiple-case design is where more than one study site and unit of analysis are chosen for purposes of 'literal replication', which entails understanding the same issues in different sites and levels of analysis, and where the results are assumed to be similar.

[3] I sought for permission from the NGO in which I previously worked before I left for Malawi. I also wrote to the University Research Coordinator in Malawi, with my research proposal, for permission to conduct the study in Malawi. I managed to get the

written approval, which was used for seeking further permission to conduct the study
from the District Commissioner in the district where the site was located.

[4] Strauss and Corbin define categories as 'concepts, derived from data, that stand for
phenomena' (1998, p.114). In this case they stand for the phenomenon of perceptions as
characterised from peoples' images of NGO assistance.

[5] A Repertory Grid is a matrix that is used for eliciting constructs based on defined
elements of the object in view. The constructs are elicited in their bipolar forms, one
opposite the other and then an overall construct of the individual defined from the
matrix (Dalton and Dunnett, 1992).

Chapter 5

Constructing Livelihoods

Introduction

In this chapter, I present and briefly discuss the results of comparing and contrasting images that NGOs and the people had of the condition of people's livelihoods in Zabwe and Mpira. The focus of the data generated in this connection was on the construction (or meaning making) process rather than defining the state of livelihoods *per se*. In other words, it was about comparing what NGOs and the people were considering in defining the condition of livelihoods in these communities. This was an important background for understanding how NGO assistance was placed in people's livelihoods, becoming part of meanings they formed of different aspects of their life. Understanding the NGO's construction of these people's livelihoods also formed the basis for my interpretation of meanings that NGOs formed of the role and purpose of different forms of assistance that they rendered to these same people.

Since it is important in an actor-oriented approach to recognize your own framework of analysis as a researcher (Long, 2000), in the first part of the chapter I explain the general definitional issues, of what I understand about livelihoods, based on literature. This forms the basis on which livelihood issues, as from accounts of the people in the two communities and as NGOs described them, are interpreted and discussed. The chapter concludes by highlighting the critical interface issues that emerge from this process. This forms the foundation for discussions on images that NGOs and the people formed of the specific interventions in the chapters that follow.

Theoretical Standpoints

The Reader's Digest Universal Dictionary defines livelihood as the 'means of support; subsistence' (DIGEST, 1987, p.899), which implies that the focus is on things from which people find support for their day to day life. This definition has been qualified in literature in two main strands: a more socio-psychological view on what livelihood entails and an applied definition, providing entry points for external interventions.

A Socio-psychological Orientation

This theoretical position includes a definition, which looks at livelihood as,

> ...individually and jointly constructed and represent patterns of inter-dependencies between the needs, interests and values of particular sets of individuals (Long, 1997, p. 12).

What is central in such a conceptual position is the attempt to understand people's livelihoods in the context of their personal lives connected to the material, social and spiritual worlds. Life is seen in its holistic and not disjointed context. Long qualifies this understanding of livelihoods further by defining people as 'striving to make a living' (ibid., 11). This denotes the making of a living in an environment, which in some way demands people's effort to draw from it what is necessary for living to be possible. It also relates to the notion of human agency as 'knowledgeable and capable' even under constraining circumstances, discussed in chapter two. In essence, this construction of livelihood is more basic and theoretical, rooted in the socio-psychology of human life. In a more applied sense, however, definitions of livelihood are more inclined to provide entry points for external interventions, working towards sustainable livelihoods.

Towards Sustainable Livelihoods

In this position, authors tend to construct the notion of livelihoods as a foundation for developing approaches to achievement of sustainable livelihoods (Chambers and Conway, 1992; Carney, 1998; Scoones, 1998; Bebbington, 1999; Rakodi, 1999). In developing an understanding of people's livelihoods, therefore, they emphasize issues of capabilities, assets and access. These qualities of livelihood are further linked to the concept of sustainability, which brings with it issues of people's abilities to cope with shocks and stresses on their livelihood over a period of time. On the whole, the approach is one of looking at livelihoods in a broader context, seen in terms of 'capital'[1] which people draw upon in order to make a living. The purpose of external interventions, therefore, becomes that of expanding 'capital' in order to build people's capacity to handle life situations along with its shocks and uncertainties.

These approaches appear adequate for informing practice towards sustainable livelihoods. Bebbington's (1999) theoretical framework, for instance, provides a clear point of entry for NGO interventions in people's livelihood. The framework logically links the process of access to resources to how these resources are utilized and transformed. This process, he argues, takes place within relationships that people have within the spheres of the state, market and civil society for purposes of claiming, defending, transforming, receiving and challenging of rules governing access to assets. With NGOs seen as playing a critical development role in civil society, they have a positional advantage to ensure that access and capability issues are advanced in favor of the poor.

This was the kind of orientation that NGOs working in the two case study areas had in understanding people's livelihoods conceptually. For instance, the underlining ethos of their interventions was said to be 'capacity building' and 'empowerment', with the ultimate objective of enabling people to achieve improved well-being. Well-being in this case was characterized, for instance, as reduced malnutrition, increased incomes and improved accessibility to markets. NGOs referred to their involvement in people's livelihoods as 'enhancement' of objectives which individuals or groups own and pursue for improving their livelihoods, as shown in the interview account below.

FT: What are you implying when you talk about enhancing the capacity of the community in this case?
Sara: This means, for instance, in food security, we will enhance the capacity of people to cope with problems of food insecurity. It will be folly for us to say 'we will provide you with food, or we will help you to do the actual gardening in the field'. No, what we shall do is to help farmers so that when we have gone they should be able to address their life situations. That is why we aim at sharpening their skills through some training, we are supporting them with resources and we help them to get organized so that they act on their own. What we are trying to do is to build the capacity whereby we ourselves are declared redundant.
FT: Where they don't need you any more?
Sara: No, they don't need us any more, instead of us doing it on their behalf; they should be doing it on behalf of themselves.

Interview accounts such as the one with Sara above, show that the general framework of livelihood approaches that NGOs in the two communities deployed fit in very well with the 'capital' approach discussed earlier. The emphasis is on building on strengths and objectives of people themselves, with the implicit assumption that there is a shared understanding of livelihoods between the NGOs and the people involved. In this position, the NGO agenda becomes that of designing projects meant to expand the deficient capital through various strategies together with the people and to improve people's well-being, as an end product. The agenda is focused on 'what to do' and 'how to do it', assuming that the 'why to do' has been settled already. In the following sections, however, I will show that this assumption is simplistic because there are often fundamental differences in the understanding of livelihoods between people and NGOs.

Firstly, I will present the general description of the livelihood conditions in the study sites, Zabwe and Mpira, from people's accounts. I will then compare this general understanding that I formed of the two communities with what I got from NGOs, also as their general understanding of livelihoods. In essence, this builds on the description of the people and NGOs working in Zabwe and Mpira that has been presented in chapter one. The difference is that, whereas chapter one presents the picture of who was there in these areas, the focus in this chapter is how those people and the NGOs found in these areas construed livelihood conditions. This is done through an in-depth exploration of meanings from their own accounts.

Describing Livelihoods in Zabwe and Mpira

As explained in the research design chapter, it was part of my case study protocol to establish a general understanding of each village in which I studied before getting into deeper aspects of the research. During this preparation stage, I talked to some key informants in these communities, especially local chiefs and community members in general who were willing to brief me about their village. Since I was staying in the village, even the house owners where I lived were very useful in this regard. I also read some documents from the District Commissioner's office on past research work that had been conducted in the area and talked to government extension workers in the area. As the research was going on, however, my key informants were also the guides, whom I recruited in both Zabwe and Mpira. I used to ask them on anything that I was anxious to know or was just not sure about, as we walked through the villages. This enriched my field notes on general livelihood issues in the communities.

Through this process, I generated information that included issues such as how leadership was organized in the community, where people were grazing their animals, traditional dances for both men and women, the relationship between youths and elders, religious and general beliefs and so forth. I also generated more statistical information about the area including agriculture, health, education, population, roads and markets, mainly from documents from government offices. This information was then enriched when I started interacting with fieldworkers and selected individuals in the villages, for interviews. I then used this information in order to set an agenda for mediating focus group discussions in both Zabwe and Mpira. This resulted in conceptual maps of their descriptive understanding of the livelihood conditions shown in Figure 5.1(a) and (b) below. They have been translated them into English for purposes of presentation in the book.

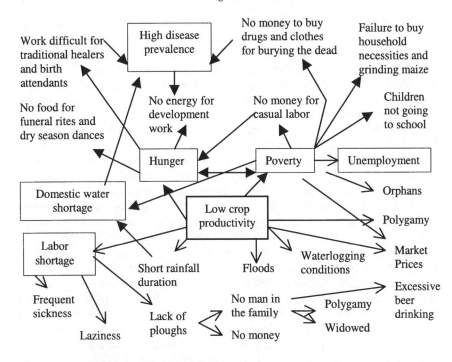

Figure 5.1(a) Livelihood descriptions in Zabwe: transcribed version

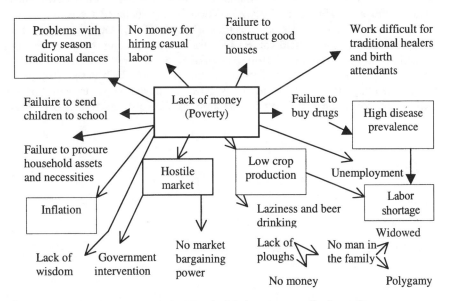

Figure 5.1(b) Livelihood descriptions in Mpira: transcribed version

In the conceptual framework above, textboxes in thick boarder lines reflect issues people considered the most critical in their livelihoods, as they were experiencing it at that time. Those on the lower side of the figure (in open arrows) reflect the 'why' of the critical issues while those in upper side (thick headed arrows) reflect the 'what' of the same critical issues. This was constructed from the 'laddering' and 'pyramiding' processes, discussed in the methodology chapter rather than forming direct connections as the arrows suggest. In each case, I started facilitating an open discussion before the conceptual maps were drawn and then I transcribed them to the form they have been presented.

As shown in the conceptual maps, whereas the most critical issue in Zabwe was seen as the low crop productivity, resulting in poverty and hunger; in Mpira it was seen as poverty, characterized as lack of money. In Mpira's case, it was critically related to hostility on the input, product and commodity market. Whereas unemployment for the secondary school leavers was critical in Zabwe, it was not reflected in Mpira community as critical. Community members in Mpira put the effect of lack of money on their traditional dances as critical, which was not the case in Zabwe. Issues of labor shortage, disease prevalence and water shortage were common to both Zabwe and Mpira. I discuss how these aspects of livelihoods were interrelated and understood in the following sections. This is where I also discuss the other aspects of livelihoods shown in mapping above. Firstly, however, it is important to compare this broad conceptual picture to the NGOs' broad framework for understanding livelihoods in both of these communities.

The broad conceptual framework of poverty in the case of NGOs was informed from the government of Malawi's situational analysis of poverty. The difference was in the adoption of this framework to particular NGO development philosophies and values. For instance, World Vision included Christian witness and advocacy in their strategic directions (WVM, 1995). Otherwise the broad understanding that NGO fieldworkers had was one of assisting the government or 'complementing government efforts ... so that we are not accused of getting beyond the boundary', fieldworkers often remarked. In which case, NGOs were 'complementing' the government in its poverty alleviation strategy for health, agriculture, education and income generation, as shown in the framework below.

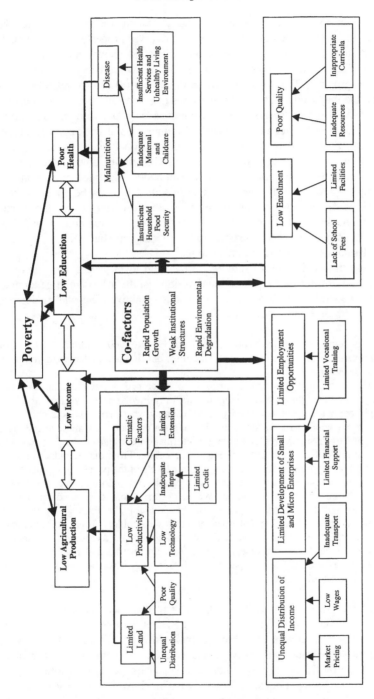

Figure 5.2 Conceptual framework of poverty alleviation in Malawi (adapted from GOM, 1995: 7)

Looking at the poverty framework above, which was the basis for NGO operations, the first impression I formed was that it was properly compartmentalized into poverty areas. That of the people, on the other hand, shown in Figure 5.1 (a) and (b) above, had so many interrelationships that it was difficult to delineate the connections properly. The arrows shown in Figure 5.1 (a) and (b) reflect what were seen to be the major relationships, for purposes of presentation to others. Otherwise, arrows needed to be crisscrossing into a complex web and in many directions. In terms of differences between the two general frameworks, it was apparent that of the people included other social life issues such as traditional dances, funerals, laziness and beer drinking. The guiding framework for NGOs on the other hand, was with a technical focus, meant to improve people's livelihoods in defined poverty areas and with stipulated strategies. The immediate argument that could be posed is that this framework was a national one and therefore, there must have been a more specific focus at the grassroots. This was also noted during the research and I found that the actual NGO strategies were flexible in these projects but within the general framework relating to the one presented above.

This was the case because, although at the field level people were involved in the generation of information about their livelihoods, the information generated fell in the same general livelihoods categories discussed above. This was evident in my interaction with Seji, the fieldworker.

FT: Concerning *Zabwe*, you have said that you started with general development and then went into small enterprise development; what were you doing in general development?

Seji: This is a broad area and as far as I am concerned, I was the first person to be employed and everything was coming out with my involvement. We first of all had to do rapid appraisal in the community so as to know what people were doing so that it could be our benchmark for our activities. We learnt a lot from that exercise because people had to say their problems. We got information and ranked the problems so that we could know the degree of the problems, in Zabwe. From that exercise we came up with four major problems including low-income levels of the people, low productivity of crops, poor access to education and poor health and nutrition. We developed the program based on this information. We also carried out a detailed survey in the community so as to know the depth of the problem, the findings of which were presented at general meeting that involved other stakeholders. These stakeholders then knew the extent of the problems in Zabwe and committed themselves to support our efforts. Local leaders, government experts from the district and regional offices and representatives from the church patronized the meeting. It was at that meeting that the programme was fully launched.

As reflected in this interaction, projects were designed based on the people's 'productive' life conditions. The data were collected in a context of direct contact with people as individuals and through their different representative groups or committees. These data were, however, facts about the condition of life of these people as seen by fieldworkers, without perceptual images that people attached to these aspects of living. Focusing on the 'what' and 'why' for these meanings to emerge (see Figure 5.1), the differences in images of livelihoods between NGOs and the people become apparent. The first one to be discussed is the understanding of poverty, which was the central issue in the NGO livelihood framework, in accordance with the aim of alleviating it, as discussed in chapter three.

Defining Poverty

The literal translation of poverty in the local language is '*ulondo*' in Zabwe and '*ukavu*' in Mpira. When translated in this way, people were inclined to interpret it as lack of anything of value in their lives, in absolute terms. In this case everyone, in these communities, perceived themselves as poor. When these terms were put aside and poverty explored in terms of the 'what' and 'why', in relative terms, however, several forms of poverty emerged. The project approach demands that this information be related in terms of means and ends, which then clearly provides for entry points for interventions (Kabeer, 1996). This was the framework from which I approached the focus group discussions in Zabwe and Mpira, in order to produce linkages shown in Figure 5.1 above. However, as noted above, there were a lot of problems in defining the relationships among the various aspects of livelihoods because they formed a complex network of interrelated issues. I then learnt that this was the problem with my facilitation approach, which was that of wanting to put people's livelihoods into a 'means' and 'ends' mould.

A Means and Ends Image of Poverty

There are perceptions of poverty that are to do with inadequacies of people's essential needs, including food, health, education for children, housing, clothing and household commodities. These are constructions of poverty from what Kabeer (1996) terms 'ends perspective' (p.3). The focus is on the result of failure to meet the need, for example, disease prevalence because of lack of drugs. There are also those meanings of poverty, which people construct from looking at what is lacking on their resource base. They are seen as affecting their livelihood because they make them fail to produce what is required in a particular aspect of life. In Figure 5.1 above, these include labor shortage and lack of ploughs. This is looking at poverty from a 'means perspective' (ibid. 1996, p.3). According to Kabeer, this categorization tends to provide entry points for interventions, meant to address poverty. The 'means' perspective provides for interventions that focus on expanding the resource-base under the command of the poor. The 'ends' perspective, on the other hand, provides for interventions that deal with the inadequacies in basic essentials of life.

From the data I generated, NGOs used information about the stocks of assets that households possessed and information on specific qualities of life in order to gain understanding into the extent of poverty. Researchers consulted people in the community in order to develop a list of assets that households possessed in the area and how they were valued. This provided them with a checklist against which household surveys proceeded and an overall community picture on wealth was built up. These assets, in Zabwe and Mpira, included dwelling houses, radios, beds, chairs, oxcarts, ploughs, land, cattle, chickens and goats. On the specific qualities of life, NGOs looked at the levels of education for children, adult literacy, average crop yields per family, distance to water sources, nutrition status of mothers and children and prevalence of diseases. The household assets and the social indicators together brought out a picture of the socio-economic status of the community, based upon which specific interventions were designed. This approach, therefore, also drew on the means and ends approach to poverty alleviation.

In this means and ends categorization, however, fieldworkers could not accommodate the issues of people's social behavior in the community. These included, for instance, lack of wisdom, laziness and excessive beer drinking, which related to so many directions of poverty by the people, as shown in Figure 5.1(a) above. These behavioral issues, however, were a significant part of living to the people. Excessive beer drinking by men as soon as they have money from their crop sales, for example, made the family suddenly vulnerable to poverty again. Women in families with this type man perceived this behavior as very detrimental to the quality of life in their families. In such cases, as Wright (1999) rightly argues, the definition of well-being cannot be equated to a rise in income-levels because poverty is not reduced. Similarly, issues of lack of wisdom and laziness, in Figure 5.1, also came out clearly as affecting people's quality of livelihood. This was the case because they affected the quality of labor and general family welfare, as evident in some extracts from my field notes.

I tried to probe into what poverty in terms of wisdom and laziness might mean in these societies and noted that when people talked about natural wisdom they referred to several behavioral aspects of livelihood. Some of them included the ability of a community member to provide good guidance, if he/she is a leader, respecting older people, if he/she is a youth and being able to provide for his family, if he/she is of middle age (20–50 years old). A person who continually begs was not always seen as just poor materially but also in terms of wisdom. This was closely related to laziness '*ukata*' in that people knew very well those community members who were lazy in doing manual work were also lazy in their own fields. They, therefore, could not expect much from them in any other work. Wisdom on the other hand is essential in the community, as *Gotha* the village leader explained.

FT: What is that wisdom about?

Gotha: We look at how a person talks with people and we see that he/she is able to stay well with people. But sometimes some people can be clever and can bribe some village elders so that they take them when it comes to leadership. They may give them beers or money, such behavior is not wisdom. True wisdom is where people are left to support you based on what they know of you freely, without being coerced through a bribe. True wisdom is where you stay with people peacefully and are able to handle gently even the difficult ones. As a leader you have to get all people involved, especially in development work where you have to call everybody, men and women, to a meeting and table the issues there. You have to allow both the ones who are fools and the ones you consider wise to say something and you let them guide others properly. It is not good to say such and such are not people they are people and not animals. You have to respect people as they are and let them respect you by what you say.

In this context, however, field workers found it difficult to see how behavioral issues could be part of the project design; they were either a problem or not, and were part of what the community needed to be dealing with as they participated in a project. As a result, in a project design, they were treated as part of the assumptions of the project. In this case, it was the inadequacies in livelihoods or lack of resources, as seen from the means and ends perspective were the issues that formed the center of action for the project. Goals of the project were stated in terms of increasing incomes, reducing illiteracy and decreasing disease incidences, for example. They made no reference to the social behavioral aspects of livelihood in any way. The same was the case with the understanding of assets in relation to poverty.

Assets and Poverty

As pointed out above, NGOs drew out the household asset picture of the community from surveys conducted in the community, where people participated. The definition of what constitutes poverty, in terms of assets in these communities, therefore, can be representative of the state of poverty in these communities. At this point we assume that methodologically, there was no interference with validity of data, which could occur through faulty instrument design, for instance. Judging validity of that data is not the subject of this study. What can be observed, however, is that this data did not accommodate perceptions people had of their assets. Fieldworkers met these realities in their interaction with people in the community. However, they were surprised at the behavior of people being different from what they expected.

> Over 60% of households in Zabwe and Mpira community keep livestock, especially, cattle. Small animals like pigs, goats and poultry are overlooked. Ownership of cattle is prestigious symbol of wealth. It is also kept for dowry, security and funeral rites. Since livestock is kept for social reasons, it is not managed with prudence as business entities.
> The problem in Mpira is that they have herds of cattle but they rarely sell some to solve the problems. They would rather keep it and use it in times of bereavement than sell it. I have the incident of somewhere where I saw a child naked and I asked the parent why not sell one of the cattle he has so as to solve the problem. What he said was, 'I cannot do it because if I do, may be my son-in-law will pass away, how am I going to appear before my relatives at the funeral.' It appears that in the past there was more value in the herds of cattle than in the person; and death was more respected than the wealth of a person (Sara, fieldworker).

As in the example above, the people's uses of their assets were seen as prestige, based on the image in the field worker of these assets. In this case, it was that cattle were assets that needed to be sold and become the means for meeting people's needs. For the farmer, however, the cattle he had were for fulfilling a funeral obligation on the death of his son in-law. This was the image attached to cattle as an asset under his command. In other words, these funeral rites, securities, dowry and keeping cattle were part of their livelihoods, with their own priority ordering. Otherwise, the fieldworker's labeling of the people's keeping of assets, as prestige, was an explanation for the invalidation of their own meanings (Leitner et al. 1996). In essence, therefore, the NGO had a list of assets as an indicator of the wealth or poverty of the people but not of the meanings that people formed of these assets in relation to their livelihoods.

This points to the fact that projects were designed based mainly on NGO perceptions of poverty, or at least with assumptions on what people's perceptions were. NGO perceptions themselves were shaped by a means and ends rationality imbedded in data collected from emergent facts of people's livelihoods. How people managed their assets in relation to their poverty was interpreted from this rationality and not from the meanings attached to these assets. Social behavioral issues, that were a significant part of community life in relation to these assets, were not accommodated in this rationality and therefore external to what the project was about. In the project design, they were part of the assumptions that project management made about the people, as explained above. A very similar scenario, though with a different nature of images, emerges when the problem of hunger was understood from this analysis.

The Question of 'Seasonal Hunger'

In the areas studied, people use the local language '*njala*' for a wide range of intensities of food shortages. This '*njala*', however, should not be translated as famine nor hunger but 'seasonal hunger' or 'starvation' (Devereux, 1993). This is because the food shortage in Zabwe and Mpira was not a situation of total crop failure leading to mass death, which, according to Devereux (1993), is famine. This was reflected in the communities in various ways as I observed and interacted with people, as some of my field notes below show.

> I gathered historical accounts from some people in the villages from which I generated data and from their experience, facing seasonal hunger or food shortage in each year for some people is a common phenomenon in the community. Some of the reasons included sicknesses, poor soils, lack of seeds and fertilizer for their maize to yield adequately. These people survived through '*ganyu*' (casual labor) where they are paid either food or money, which they use to buy food from those who produce better yields. In Zabwe, however, there were unfavorable climatic conditions for three years, which drastically reduced food production in the area. These climatic conditions included short rainfall period, which was followed by heavy rains in the following year that caused floods and gullies and then too late rains in the third year. This meant most families lost their seed and general production capacity in their fields but none of the cases resulted in total crop failure for the whole community. Short rainfall period and late rains also affected Mpira community but not heavy rains resulting in gullies and floods.
> (*Source*: Personal field notes)

It was in this context that NGOs collected facts about the extent of food shortage in the community as a basis for designing interventions. The approach to the appraisal was that of a food-gap analysis. Most of the survey questionnaires had information gaps indicated as follows,

16. In the last 12 months, was there a time when it was more difficult to feed your household so it was necessary to eat less or eat poorly?
    1. Yes GO TO QUESTION 17
    2. No. GO TO QUESTION 21
17. How long did this period last? _____ (Months)

(*Source*: sample survey questionnaire from Mpira).

From this information, the household was pictured as not having adequate food to cover the whole year. This information was then related to other livelihood indicators related to food use in terms of the nutrition status in the community. The nutritional status indicators, for example, showed that 75% of the mothers in both Zabwe and Mpira community were anemic. According to the report, these mothers were anemic despite 70.2% of them knowing that anaemia were caused by lack of food and by the high incidences of diseases. They even knew, mainly from exposure to such information at antenatal clinics, that eating vegetables, eggs and meat or fish could prevent anaemia. Looking on the food production statistics, at least 63.3% of the households kept chickens, 56.2% owned cattle (ranging from 1 to 100 per household), 40.1% raised pigs and many people grew various types of local vegetables. Since there was no other variable, which could explain this disparity, the consultant researcher concluded that there must be other factors playing a crucial role in causing anaemia in mothers. NGO field workers, however, attributed these problems to the problem of improper food use in the community.

It is very funny if we talk about *Zabwe* because it is a rich area in terms of production but the way food is being used is a problem (Lameck, fieldworker in Zabwe area).

This understanding was formed in relation to maize and tomato production in the rich alluvial soils of the river in a good year, as explained in chapter one (p.10). However, when we examine the 'what' of hunger, shown in lowercase in Figure 5.1, there were more aspects of people's livelihood calling on food use, where food for individual family intake was just one of them. Food use was associated with significant social engagements in which the households were involved. Some of the important practices that were observed in these communities as I generated data are quoted from my field notes below. They were part of the conceptual framework of poverty in Zabwe and Mpira, shown in Figure 5.1 above.

In the case of bereavement in Zabwe community, relatives spend two to three weeks at the home of the deceased during lean periods (crop growing seasons) and up to a month in dry season (after harvest). They sometimes spend longer periods depending on the status of the person who has died. They all contribute food and eat together during such occasions, where contributions themselves vary with the nature of relationship with the deceased. A son in-law, for instance, is expected to contribute a cow, a white cloth, and baskets of flour to the deceased family. If a son-in law has failed to contribute these materials, they are not allowed at the funeral and the wife is not allowed to join him until he meets his obligation. Some families never allow cash as a substitute for actual materials. These funeral rights however, are not just about eating and condolences.

Instead, this is where elders and relatives discuss matters of significance, such as settling land disputes and other social misdemeanors that just occurred in the village. They need food to keep them going for some days before they disperse. In Mpira community, they only meet for a day or two and disperse but they have other important social-cultural beliefs and practices. At Mpira, they have an organized traditional dance, called *Malipenga* during the dry season. This dance involves inviting their friends from other areas for a whole week at most. There can be up to twenty invited groups from other areas into one village and these people require proper feeding. This dance is for men and is organized in close association with the traditional leadership structure. In order to ensure seriousness of this organization, leadership positions and responsibilities that bear titles of the military ranks such as regiment commanders, sergeants, sergeant major, soldiers in general and team doctor. There are elders assigned to look after each dance group with stipulated codes of conduct such that any breach of conduct has specific punishments. It brings a strong social identity and unity in the community and is used for reinforcing discipline and obedience among the youths as part of their upbringing. It also brings to the community some pride as they compete and exchange gifts with other villages, some from far off places. (*Source*: Personal field notes).

This reflection shows how different and important cultural processes were taking place in these communities, to which food use was connected. The same was the case for Traditional Healers and Birth Attendants who were basically volunteers in the community but who required that people should contribute food. Such purposeful organizations and cultural norms, therefore, were as much part of the legitimate demands or 'calls' on their food stocks as was feeding their families (Maxwell and Wiebe, 1999). There were certainly some priorities, which these households set, in their competing wants, but they were situated in a context of their cultural values. These cultural values made it difficult for outsiders to quickly understand and predict people's behavior, even in times when it appeared logical for families to keep food use to the individual household. However, it should also be noted that from people's recollections of the past and present situation, there were significant transformations to these practices in these societies. For example, the duration of stay at a bereaved family's home in Zabwe was said to be getting shorter over the years. We could also be wrong, however, to quickly attribute these transformations to the shortage of food in the community.

Therefore, whereas it is true, based on statistics, that food was a problem; food use was attached to so many practices and beliefs in a society. The meaning of food was part of these practices, rather than intake *per se*. Food use was situated in people's 'social capital'; it was part of it and not a different undertaking. Incidentally, this reality was not hidden from fieldworkers but was seen as a hindrance to development. This meant that it was not an issue for negotiation but to be addressed alongside food security goals. However, by taking the social behavior of the people as 'problems', the design process did not accommodate the important basis for people's engagement with the project as regards food security. These issues will be followed and presented in the next chapters. A much similar situation, but different nature of images, arises when labor shortage, as one of the critical livelihood assets in Zabwe and Mpira communities is analyzed.

Labor Shortage

As shown in Figure 5.1, labor shortage was one of the critical livelihood limitations on crop production and hence also related to hunger discussed above. In terms of meaning, people saw labor as the manpower available to accomplish a piece of work in a given time, especially in agriculture. Labor shortage was, therefore, with respect to what members within the household can do, given their physical, social and cultural limitations, at a particular time. In this connection, when an 'active member' (in social-physical terms) of the household left the family in order to work for *ganyu* (casual labor) in search for food or was sick while at the same time there was work in the field, there was labor shortage. It therefore, took different forms and intensities in different households and with different tasks at hand. In the two communities, labor supply was perceived as a problem especially in association with farm practices during the season for growing crops (from December to April).

In Zabwe, the soils were said to be very dry and hard for them to do any preparation, in terms of ploughing or ridging, before the rainy season. They could only do so when the rain started coming and the soil was sufficiently wet. This, however, meant that there was so much work to do within a short period of time, because the rainy seasons were short. Many households also had several fields scattered in many parts and different soil types, in order to diversify and minimize risk of crop loss. In this context, the more active members available in the household, the more capable they were in completing the tasks within the prime time that was available. The quality of labor available was critical for each household. In this context, however, people saw the use of ox-drawn implements, including ploughs and oxen, as making a big improvement to the quality of household labor supply. My interview with Lide is a good example of this image.

Lide: The soil in this area requires ridges for the crop to do well or otherwise you will not get a good crop yield.
FT: What makes making of ridges a problem?
Lide: The problem comes because in this area we have three or four plots per individual, which are scattered in different parts of the area. Once you start making ridges in one, by the time you get to the second one the first one has weeds grown up requiring weeding. If you come back to the first one you will delay on the others. If you have ploughing oxen on the other hand, you are able to plough all the fields within a short time and plant the crop and be ready for weeding.

The alternative to having better farm implements, for people like Lide above, was to hire more people to work in the field on particular tasks in exchange for food or cash. Given that these activities took place during lean periods, in terms of food stocks and cash, not many people could afford hired labor.

In this situation, NGOs documented information on the extent of these problems and their statistics showed that only 6% of the households, in Zabwe and Mpira had ploughs by the time of the baseline survey. This was related to production figures; for instance, the fact that farmers were producing only an average of 2,000Kg per hectare of maize compared to the crop potential of

5,000Kg per hectare. This was attributed to poor technology and other factors also identified in the survey. For example, only 15% of households were using chemical fertilizer, according to the NGO survey. As argued above, it is a factual representation of the condition of livelihoods from a means perspective and provides for perceptions of interventions that focus at labor supply as a factor of production. This reflected their broader framework of low productivity in agriculture, taking after the government, as shown in Figure 5.2 above. This thinking provided a way for making available assistance to the community in the form of loans. However, when we examine the 'why' of labor, it was socially constructed with respect to gender and other forms of social behavior in both communities (see Figure 5.1). I understood the social construction of labor as follows:

> The society perceives working with cattle as a man's job such that it is also men who own ploughs. In this case, therefore, households where there are men are at an advantage, in terms of labor, to those where there are no men. This however, does not always apply because women in polygamous families are given their own fields, although they all assist the man in his fields. Men usually concentrate on cotton (in Zabwe) and rice (in Mpira) as cash crops. In terms of ploughing women's fields, the woman who is the eldest gets the first opportunity to get her field ploughed and then the others follow. In years of late and short rainfall, a difference of a day can mean a lot on yield of crops. Most women in polygamous marriages, therefore, perceive themselves as suffering from as much labor shortage as those from female-headed households. There is another difference, however, to this gender-analyzed labor shortage. Women with male children who can manage to work with oxen are in a better position than are those that have girls only. In this case, therefore, the sex of ones children makes a difference between female-headed or polygamous family households. The same is the case when the man is an excessive beer drinker such that he is only part of the productive household by name (*Source*: Personal field notes).

The situation sited above, as also shown in Figure 5.1, meant that labor was the most complicated and variable asset in the households. The fact that use of technology was socially constructed around gender perceptions of the society put the men at a comparative advantage over women. This situation, as Quisumbing (1996) argues, is not a factor of women's human or physical capital, in terms of capabilities. It is, instead, a socially constructed privilege of men over women. In the case of the two communities, the use of ox-drawn implements was seen as a man's job. When I asked them why, the reason they gave was that it requires toughness, because oxen can be aggressive and get out of control, making it difficult for a woman to control. The ploughing itself was also seen to require more energy than women can afford. These images were accepted as part of life in the society, for both men and women, and hence any difference between them, created role conflicts. This means that these images were part of their shortage of technology, or otherwise shaped the nature of the technology itself.

Therefore, whereas labor is regarded as the only commodity that most people use to expand assets under their command (Sen, 1997), employment of this labor is perceptually mediated. Ownership and use of technology is constructed in a particular way, and hence determines returns on labor. However, when labor shortage, general poverty, food security and other forms of livelihoods are understood from the market side, different images emerge. In this arena, people in the two communities saw the market conditions, where their assets were traded, as not just a problem but as being hostile to their livelihoods.

Hostile Market

Almost everybody I interacted with during the study, attributed part of the deteriorating livelihoods to the operations of the market. In attempting to best express the nature of these perceptions, Bates's (1981) analysis of the markets is more helpful. He argues that farmers' real value of profits is dependent on conditions at the intersection point among three markets. These include the market of their agricultural commodities, market of factors of production and the market for consumer goods. In these case studies, people perceived the market from this intersection point as hostile, because it reduced their real incomes. Furthermore, their productive asset base, which they accumulated in the past, was also seen as having been drastically eroded, as Riche explains.

> *Riche*: Things were better before than these years because now money is difficult to get while in the past if you had MK10 it would be so much money but now MK10 is like MK1 that is why there is a lot of poverty now than before. In the past we would buy clothes with MK20 and now MK100 is not enough for a cloth. That is why we feel things were better that time.
> *FT*: What about food?
> *Riche*: In the past there was no hunger because we were not selling much of our crops. As of these years, we are selling a lot of it in order to get money. One needs to sell a lot of cassava in order to raise enough money for a piece of cloth and hence a lot of food is being sold. In the past the same amount of money could buy three cows. As of now, we are able to grow crops and get something but it is as if we are getting nothing because there is no money. This year even ADMARC is failing to buy our crops because they have no money and this threatens our food security because we are selling our crops to the Tanzanians instead of ADMARC who would store it and we would buy from them again. People are selling their maize because they are looking for money.

This market hostility, which Riche refers to in the quote above, was seen to have the effect of reducing household incomes and eroding the asset base of the people and hence living difficult.

Reducing Real Incomes

Debates about incomes in the rural areas show actual calculations are difficult because people's incomes are largely non-monetary and hence not easy to value in terms of money (Smiller, 1994; Hulme and Mosley, 1996). However, taking income, as mostly coming from people's agricultural produce, as is the case in the two case studies, real incomes constantly become lower. This is because the cost of production is higher than the price at which crop products are being sold at the market. This is worsened also, because whatever is raised from the market meets higher prices at the consumer market (as in Riche's account above). People perceived themselves as not having any bargaining power on these markets, especially that markets operated under the influence of government policy. Commentators on Malawi's agrarian economy have attributed this situation to the effects of market liberalization, a component of structural adjustment programs (Peters, 1996; Chilowa and Chirwa, 1997; Devereux, 1997).

This situation presents a picture of the economy where people's incomes are low and getting lower. NGOs working in these communities also collected information on income levels and related it to other indicators; levels of protein energy malnutrition among children, for instance. From this analysis emerged an image of community with low incomes, and that was affecting their health status, particularly that of children. This was supported with information, as argued earlier on, where women demonstrated knowledge of the needed practices to improve nutrition but were not putting them into practice. Women indicated that they did not have money to do what they were taught. Therefore, in the NGOs' understanding, these women needed economic empowerment, as Sinera the field worker explained,

> The issue is that when people, for instance, go to the hospital they are told to take three food groups but yet they do not give them those foods and people are poor. They cannot on their own manage to get that food and therefore, we should first of all give them loans. Once we give them loans then we will be saying 'when a child is sick give him such and such foods', and because they are running a business from the loan, they will be able to buy those foods from the profits they are making (Sinera, field worker).

The conceptual image that the two communities formed of this need for money, however, had two interpretations. The first interpretation was that of cash meant for buying a good or service as an end in itself because a particular aspect of livelihood is threatened. This, for example, would be the need for money to buy drugs in order to get healed and other social needs shown in Figure 5.1 above. The second aspect was where cash was needed as a mechanism for converting one form of assets to another of more value than the first one. For example, in both Zabwe and Mpira there were people who saw their livelihood conditions in terms of lack of money to hire casual laborers who could work in their plots (also shown in Figure 5.1 above). In which case, it was a problem of converting labor to crop yield production. This is a form of expanding assets through investment, where direct exchange of the two forms of assets is not possible. Hulme and Mosley (1996) refer to the two aspects as 'protectional' and 'promotional' needs for credit, respectively.

Given the desperation arising out of difficulties in liquidating their assets on the market of their agricultural produce, the two images were mixed. In other words, people who would have sold their produce and bought their drugs and hence come to the NGO for money for business were the same as those who would still have come even if crops were being sold because they did not have any crops to sell. In such a situation, focusing on these needs with an interpretation of a promotional requirement for money was conflicting with those that were there for 'protection needs'. How it affected the nature of engagement of the people in the projects will be shown in the next chapter.

Erosion of the Asset-Base

As shown discussed above, the need for money forced people to sell their produce in markets, even when they knew that they would make a loss. The distortion between the produce and consumer market forced them to sell more produce per unit than before. In the case of the two communities, alternative markets were difficult to find because the road infrastructure to the township, especially for Mpira, was poor. In such a situation, the perception of the NGO of women as requiring economic empowerment interfaced with their image of a hostile market, where they had no alternatives. As will be shown in the next chapter, it only created a 'labor trap' for the women involved (Razavi, 1999). They, however, still got involved because of other images they formed of NGO assistance, also discussed in the following chapters.

Conclusion

This chapter has demonstrated that despite the factual evidences of what NGOs perceived of people's livelihood deprivations and assets, people had their own images of what these goods could do for them. In other words, it shows that the 'why to do' indicated in the second section of this chapter, was negotiable and not to be assumed as already settled through people's problems. NGO perceptions of these aspects of people's livelihoods, therefore, needed to work through images that people had of their livelihood reality, even when seen from 'facts and figures'. From this understanding, it will be shown in the following chapters that it is right to support Hutson and Liddiard (1993) in asserting that 'definitions can act as gatekeepers'. Definitions of livelihoods in these two communities, as provided by NGOs, influenced their choice of assistance to provide to each community. Could we similarly argue that definitions that people had of their livelihoods influenced the assistance they asked for from NGOs? The next two chapters demonstrate that this was an area of bargain based on the NGOs and some of community member's 'gate keeping' behavior. In this case, there were conflicts in the interfacing images of the role and purpose of NGO assistance.

Note

[1] Capital is defined as, 'the basic material and social, tangible and intangible assets that people have in their possession. ..., based from which different productive streams are derived from which livelihoods are constructed' (Scoones, 1998, p.7).

Chapter 6

Conflicting Images on the Role of NGO Assistance

Introduction

This chapter brings out image-conflicts that were observed with regard to the images that people and NGOs formed of the role of specific forms of assistance, which NGOs were providing in the two research sites, towards improving people's livelihoods. These were image-conflicts that occurred in the process of NGOs and the people placing assistance within their construction of livelihoods, as discussed in the last chapter. This process marks the first step towards understanding the nature of agency that both NGOs and the people had at the interface. This is where both NGOs and the people placed assistance, in people's livelihoods, within their constructs of the 'expected role performance' of each other. As explained in chapter three, these 'role performances' are created in the images they form of each other, as part of their relationship, mediated through project assistance. Any image-conflict observed from such an understanding, therefore, relates to the nature of engagement that the actors involved have with the project in question.

The chapter starts with a presentation of the dynamics of interactions between NGOs and the people during the initial phases of their relationship, where the different forms of NGO assistance were decided. Apparently, this formed a stage for much of what Goffman (1969) calls, the 'front' performance, implying a kind of performance that the actor projects on the stage, for the purpose of creating a good initial impression to the observers. In which case, most of the image-conflicts at this stage were disguised rather than openly expressed. This is then followed by a presentation of the image-conflicts that were unearthed through probing into the images of the role of assistance. The chapter ends with a summary of the nature of image-conflicts that characterized the interaction between NGOs and the people, with regard to the role of NGO assistance. People in these study sites were diverse in terms of their socio-cultural characteristics and also the experiences they had with NGO assistance. Therefore, I have attempted to explain the interaction with NGOs in the form of some distinct categories. These categories are still broad but they give some understanding of what was happening in the community.

Setting the Stage

As Kelly (1995) indicates 'ROLE relationships involve understanding the other's process of construing more than the content of constructs' (cited in Epting, et al. 1996, p.311). This means that the role-governed relationship between NGOs and the people should be seen in the context of how they construed processes or each other's behavior, as mediated through the various project activities. In this case, either people or NGOs could have what the other would have seen as wrong interpretations of their actions and meanings. Nevertheless, the issues of interest here were image-conflicts and not the accuracy of meanings people and NGOs formed of each other. Even the wrong interpretations inform the nature of agency or potential and actual actions at the interface between actors. From this position, I sought firstly to gain some understanding of the processes that characterized the movement from defining people's livelihoods to deciding on the appropriate assistance.

When I questioned NGO fieldworkers about this topical area, they immediately said that projects were based on people's 'priorities'. One field officer put it clearly, 'We do not impose projects on people, we are community-driven!' However, while moving from one village to another, I was amazed with the similarities in the forms of assistance that NGOs provided in each case. In every village people pointed at wells, schools, clinic shelters, loans, cassava and sweet potato cuttings and others. It was difficult to imagine, in this case, how priorities in all these villages would follow such a similar pattern and also be associated with particular NGOs. If it were people's priorities, could it not be the case that if in village A, the priority problem was hunger, an NGO could be faced with that problem and not water, which was the most critical problem in village B? Is it that people presented all the problems and NGOs selected what problems to tackle? If that was the case, what was the basis for selection, given that these NGOs came to these communities at different times? The answer to these issues from NGO fieldworkers was, 'we cannot do all things' and 'we have to prepare good projects'. I, therefore, sought to understand what these concepts meant, from which I learnt that these concepts represented a discourse that was useful for the negotiation of 'priorities' in a project.

NGO Priorities

It was apparent from fieldworker's accounts that NGOs constructed their priorities as within priorities of the people but within the type of assistance that the NGO was already poised to provide. Take Manfred's explanation for instance,

> In our organization we fund diverse types of projects. We can fund secondary schools, primary schools, dispensaries or health centers, under-five clinics, piped water schemes and bore hole projects. We can fund even forestry and land reclamation projects, dam projects, roads and bridges. All these things can be funded but for them to be funded the main thing is that we are community driven. We do not impose projects on the communities. Out of all these things, the community should have a need, which they can

tell us. The community must therefore sit down and look at the problems they face in their community then prioritize their needs. The one they have chosen is the one they indicate and ask for assistance. We respond to what they have actually demanded, otherwise if they have asked for an under-five clinic we will not go there with a school and say, no, your school is dilapidated and hence we should start with the school. That is not what we do; when they have asked for an under five clinic we fund them on that and upon completion they can ask us to fund something else like the school in accordance with their priority list. They will be moving with their priority list. They might have five things on their list, which can be funded; we move according to their priorities, so we are community driven that is the main thing.

When we are funding a project we do not just fund a project as one entity but we consider several things. For instance when we are funding a school block we will make sure that we provide pit-latrines, which they might not have included when asking for assistance. We provide them because we consider sanitation as an important factor in these constructions. Also even if they don't include desks we will provide them. Also knowing that it is at school, sanitation cannot go well without water. We, therefore, also provide a borehole at the school and then the money that comes can also be used to buy some seedlings for any type of tree that can do well in their area at least to improve the environment. So at the school you would have trees planted at least to contribute to the environment and pit-latrines, which once full can be repaired. In this way, instead of polluting the environment by digging latrines all over, they can use the improved ones permanently. These VIP latrines can be mopped with water, which we provide through boreholes. Children coming to school should be sitting on desks and not on the floor. So we fund a complete set considering the different areas of development.

We do a desk appraisal where we remove projects, which are not within our mandate of support, such as a providing a grinding mill. Income generating activities are left to other organizations like Malawi Rural Finance and SEDOM. Those that have passed desk appraisal are the ones for which we do field appraisal with the people, in order to verify if that is what they want (Manfred, NGO fieldworker).

In this case, therefore, 'we cannot do all things', reflected the image of assisting communities within the NGO's philosophical and operational boundaries and not providing assistance responsively *per se*. In essence, it was also closing off on some forms of assistance, as reflected in Manfred's accounts above. This kind of selectivity was also observed within the same form of assistance. One NGO, for example, indicated that although they provided loans to women, they would not assist women who wanted to open an enterprise in beer brewing as a business.

Focusing on 'priorities of the people', therefore, referred to addressing people's problems and not necessarily the most critical problems at that time. With this image of 'priorities', other forms of assistance, which people never mentioned, were also provided. In this case, they were provided because they were seen as necessary for 'good projects' to be prepared. For example, I observed that certain forms of assistance were 'a donor requirement', and that was adequate to warrant their inclusion in the project design. This was the case with, for example, assistance that had to be gender sensitive and environmentally friendly. Most of these gaps were, besides the desk appraisal, noted during preparation of proposals as they developed the objective hierarchies. They needed to ensure that the hierarchy was tight and linking well to objectives. For example, if the objective was to reduce incidences of water-borne diseases they needed to provide clean water and also include digging pit latrines, even if people did not mention or articulate that assistance.

The process of placing assistance in people's livelihoods was therefore, not just about isolating some problems from the complex livelihoods of the people according to the means and ends rationality, as discussed in the last chapter. Instead, the project system, NGO missions and pressures from the funding chain, conceptualized in chapter three, also shaped the decision making process as to what was necessary for the project to focus on. In other words, this was the source of influence for shaping the interventions (see Figure 3.1). However, this was manifested at the interface with people, where regardless of the influence from NGOs, people also shaped the nature of interventions in unpredictable ways. Therefore, we need to see what was happening with people, from their images of this process of placing assistance in their livelihoods. In this case, there were three main image categories, based on the concepts people were using to communicate their images. In coding of these concepts I directly translated from the local language to English and the phrases were, 'As they wish', 'Construction' and 'For the Community'. These concepts characterized the expressions of the people with regard to explaining their approach to communicating their priorities to development agencies. Interestingly, these images emerged following certain experiential characteristics of the people, which could also be traced to other characteristics such as gender and well-being.

People's Priorities

'As they Wish' was a concept in people's mention of assistance as whatever the NGO or the community leaders wanted to do. This perception was most prevalent among the very poor people in the community, especially women and also among traditional leaders. As for the very poor women, who were also mere community members, they had little knowledge about specific NGOs and their assistance. Most of these people found the articulation of the NGOs that were assisting them, and with what assistance, difficult. They referred me to their traditional leaders as the ones who know what should be happening, which they then had to follow. They, however, often remarked that they provided information to NGO fieldworkers during surveys and PRAs conducted prior to the start of project activities in the community.

As for traditional leaders, this concept was associated with their desire to have a funded project in their community, just like their neighboring villages. In essence, they were open to have any NGO activity in their communities. For the middle-poor and better-off community members in this general sense, it was the concept of 'Construction NGO' that was prevalent. The image of 'Construction NGO' was where the mention of an NGO's name would cause people to say, 'that is a Construction NGO' implying all the NGO was known for was construction of infrastructures. The same would go for water, loans and so on. In this case, people's preoccupation was to align their requests with what an NGO was providing, in a sense of defending their position for assistance even when the critical problem was something else. Consider, for example, an interview I had with Menala, a community member.

> *FT*: You said these children are yours [I saw them playing at home during school time]. Do they go to school?
> *Menala*: No, most children fail to go to school this time because they are hungry. They go to school but stop during the season of hunger when we have no food.
> *FT*: What makes it difficult for us to properly discuss our hunger issues with the two NGOs working in this community?
> *Menala*: Because it cannot happen that they assist us in three things at the same time, building schools, intervening on hunger it cannot be possible and that is what makes us afraid to ask them.
> *FT*: What makes you think that way?
> *Menala*: We have never seen it.
> *FT*: You said one of the NGOs has been here for eight years and the other for three years?
> *Menala*: What we know is that the organizations you are talking about construct schools. We do not know that they could also assist in other things.
> *FT*: Who asks for school?
> *Menala*: We asked for school.
> *FT*: Do you mention those other things to them?
> *Menala*: No, they do not explain to us properly what they are about.

This image of 'construction NGO' was also easily connected to community assistance. 'Community Assistance' was an image of NGO assistance where the explanation was that assistance was for the benefit of the whole community. There was a 'community assistance' image of the role of NGO assistance that was prevalent mostly among traditional leaders and men. Most of the poor were enrolled into such projects, for the good of the community, yet at the neglect of their individual poverty situations and hence it created role conflicts in most of them.

> When you want to mention a problem that affects your home you are told by the village leaders not to disturb but to just go to the office of these NGO officials and complain there. When you try to go to the office they say that they require MK2,000 as deposit for their assistance. As a poor person, where can I get that money? We just get discouraged (*Helebu*, community member).
> Even if I want to say something, my friends may say they do not want it mentioned. I if I say I do not have a blanket, will they assist me (*Tafwa*, community member).

Helebu was a middle-poor man while Tafwa was a very poor category woman who lived in the same village. There seems to have been a gendered manner of reflection on how prepared they were to explore for their individual needs in a project, having aspects of 'power from within' (Townsend, 1999). In both cases, however, it shows that there were power dynamics both within the village and with NGOs that affected the people's agency for them to support the 'community assistance' role of NGOs.

Looking at the people's articulation of their priorities, therefore, shows that they were framed in the role they formed of NGOs and the various social actors of influence within their society. At the NGO interface, most face-to-face negotiations for assistance were through traditional leaders, men and middle and better off members of the community. These leaders' presentation of the people's priorities was framed in the context of what NGOs wanted, showing traces of role conflicts in their statements, as reflected in one village headman's explanation.

> We never asked if they could assist us on our hunger situation. We just fear by ourselves because we were saying, 'these people are for construction work, if we ask them to assist us on our hunger, will we understand each other? (Village headman).

Furthermore, government extension workers working in the area were playing a critical role in this perceptual build-up in the community, prior to face-to-face negotiations with NGOs. People in the community often told me that extension workers said, 'This is your only chance'. They could then realize after the project starts that the assistance was not as was publicized by the extension workers. In Table 6.1(a), (b) and (c), below are summarized occurrences of these images as they were presented, reflecting people's priorities at the interface with NGOs. They were calculated from the coding of mentions in NUD*IST. I then used 'matrix searches' to trace them to the various community characteristics. 'Number of mentions' stands for the number of times that the interviewees used the concept in each transcribed interview. For example, every account where interviewees mentioned 'As They Wish', were coded under 'As They Wish'. Since the sampling was purposive, I had to calculate the average number of mentions per individual from the total number of mentions in a category and the number of people interviewed in that category. The figures just assisted me to get an impression of the inclinations of the various categories of the people that were interviewed, towards NGO assistance. They are not representative of the population from which the sample was taken.

Tables 6.1(a), (b) and (c) below, clearly illustrate that the people's images of their choice of assistance in their interactions with NGOs was that of leaving it to NGOs to provide what was necessary assistance in their livelihoods. For the very poor category and women, it was their leaders who knew the necessary assistance. They also perceived NGO assistance as for the whole community needs rather than for their individual household needs (see also page 95). The tables below show that average number of mentions among traditional leaders was much higher than other categories on 'as they wish' and 'construction NGO' and yet these were the people who represented the people in most decision-making meetings with NGOs. This means that traditional leaders primarily wanted the NGOs themselves to take the lead and provide the type of assistance, which they had in store, in the NGOs' images of appropriate assistance to that community.

Table 6.1(a) Images on choice of assistance analyzed by gender

Perceptions	Gender/No. interviewed		No. of mentions	No. of mentions per individual
As they wish	Male	64	210	3.3
	Female	53	192	3.6
Construction	Male	64	127	2.0
NGO	Female	53	57	1.1
Community	Male	64	106	1.7
	Female	53	67	1.3

Table 6.1(b) Images on choice of assistance analyzed by position

Perceptions	Position/No. interviewed		No. of mentions	No. of mentions per individual
As they wish	Traditional leaders	22	99	4.5
	Committee members	23	60	2.6
	Community members	72	243	3.4
Construction	Traditional leaders	22	56	2.6
NGO	Committee members	23	28	1.2
	Community members	72	100	1.4
Community	Traditional leaders	22	26	1.2
	Committee members	23	30	1.3
	Community members	72	117	1.6

Table 6.1(c) Images on choice of assistance analyzed by well-being status

Perceptions	Well-being/No. interviewed		No. of mentions	No. of mentions per individual
As they wish	Better-off	20	46	2.3
	Middle-poor	43	80	1.8
	Very-poor	54	276	5.1
Construction	Better-off	20	24	1.2
NGO	Middle-poor	43	55	1.3
	Very-poor	54	105	1.9
Community	Better-off	20	3	0.2
	Middle-poor	43	50	1.2
	Very-poor	54	120	2.2

Ultimately, from my interpretation of information in the tables above, people were using their perceptions of NGOs to construct their own approach to successfully negotiate for assistance. In essence, they did not actually represent their livelihoods as understood from their social-cultural constructions, discussed in chapter five (see Figure 5.1), but from the means and ends picture of NGOs (Figure 5.2). There were, therefore, image bargains at work in the negotiation process for particular forms of assistance to be provided (Mosse, 1995). The focal point of influence for this bargain was the manner in which NGOs sought to address the priorities of the people. In terms of role conflicts, however, they were not apparent to me at this point. The fact that there was this image bargain suggested that image-conflicts were implicit in the interactions between NGOs and the people. This required probing into meanings that the people and NGOs formed of assistance.

The question I had at this point was, 'If people asked or accepted these forms of assistance based on images they formed from the influence of NGOs and other members of the community, what are their 'real' images of assistance? In other words, what assistance could they have asked for if they were to exercise their agency in line with what they wanted? This is where the second specific research question on the role of assistance (Figure 4.2) was useful. It was also a critical part of the research because; how people and NGOs 'placed' assistance in livelihoods was dependent upon this image of role of assistance. My interest here was not necessarily in getting to the exact role of assistance. Instead it was that, in the process of searching for this role I would get to know the nature of image-conflicts that people faced and how they were negotiating them, as a form of their agency at the interface with NGOs.

Such a question, however, gave me a methodological challenge, because it suggested that I needed to elicit people's 'real interests'. Eliciting 'real interests' of people is epistemologically contestable and not easy because the justification that one has arrived at the real interests of someone else is difficult to ascertain (Clegg, 1989). For example, if I asked people directly as to what assistance they would ask for and why, they would probably intellectually think of what is socially expected. In this case, this would include what was socially acceptable to me as an interviewer; and seen as another social actor by the interviewee. An interview is a context of 'negotiating selves' and not socially neutral (Collins, 1998). The best approach I thought of in this situation was to use Personal Construct Theory techniques in an informal sense (see p.61). In this case, I elicited constructs on the role of assistance descriptively and then probed in order to elicit deeper constructs.

Descriptive Role Conflicts of NGO Assistance

People and NGO fieldworkers, in each interview, were asked to describe the various activities and forms of NGO assistance involved in their projects. In essence, I asked people to educate me on the kind of assistance that NGOs and other development agencies were offering in the community. From their narratives and descriptions, I formed the understanding that NGO assistance was provided in four broad categories, including assistance as consumables, infrastructures, loans and training. Of these four, NGOs, but not the people, mentioned training as a form of assistance. Otherwise, people saw training as a facilitating activity attached to the process of receiving some kind of NGO assistance. For instance, leadership training was perceived as an activity prior to receiving assistance on infrastructures, mainly as a way of ensuring effective community organization. In this thesis, therefore, I have not discussed training as a form of assistance in the way it featured in the NGO project documents.

Assistance in the form of consumables[1] was described as assistance, which was freely provided to people to address their sufferings or vulnerabilities. This was where, for instance, 60 per cent of the under-five children were identified as malnourished and 'free' soybean flour was distributed to mothers with such children. This assistance was seen as different from assistance towards the construction of infrastructures, where NGOs also offered 'free' materials. This assistance, towards activities such as building of roads, bridges, school buildings and clinic shelters, assisted the community with essential services as a basis for future well-being improvement. This was the 'physical capital' for the community (Ostrom, 1995). The difference, therefore, was in purpose of assistance and not in the conditions of provision. The difference in the conditions of provision was noted instead of the provision of loans. In this case, the critical differentiating feature was the requirement for individuals to repay assistance that they received from NGOs.

From my analysis of these descriptions, I noted that the similarities and differences that people could see among the different forms of assistance were constructed around concepts such as 'free', 'repayments', 'individuals' and 'community'. In broad terms, we could say that these perceptual constructions centered on the conditions with which assistance was offered and to whom. However, as shown in Table 6.2 below, there were also descriptive ambiguities in the understanding of assistance on infrastructures between NGOs and the people on both of these construct categories. Most people said, 'we are provided with free materials for constructing infrastructures but we contribute our own materials as well.' A similar ambiguity was apparent on targeting of benefits, where some of the people indicated access to benefits from infrastructures, but not in a definite manner as they did with loans and consumables.

This lack of clarity in the understanding of assistance through infrastructures showed obscurity in the role people perceived of this form of assistance. The pronoun 'but' suggested probable existence of role conflicts between what they had as assistance and what they perceived as assistance. This is where the 'laddering' and 'pyramiding' processes, explained in the methodology chapter were used. The latter meant asking people to give life examples and compare them with experiences they had with other forms of assistance, from NGOs or other external agencies. The former meant asking people what makes them to think in that direction amongst the many alternatives that could be available. Apparently in doing so, perceptual differences were observed even in the case of consumables and loans where there were 'emergent' similarities, as indicated in Table 6.2 below.

Table 6.2(a) NGOs' descriptive images of assistance

Emergent pole	Consumables	Infrastructures	Loan	Contrast pole
Free	β	ß	✔	Repayments
Individual benefit	✗	Ý	✗	Community benefit

Table 6.2(b) People's descriptive images of assistance

Emergent pole	Consumables	Infrastructures	Loan	Contrast
Free	β	ß✔	✔	Repayments
Individual benefit	✗	✗ ý	✗	Community benefit

Free = β, Repayments = ✔, Individual benefit =✗ , Community benefit = ý

Essentially, image-conflicts illustrated in the Tables 6.2(a) and 6.2(b) above, occurred in the conditions that NGOs (as informed from their ideologies and project systems discussed in the last chapter) set for provision of assistance and targeting of people in the community. In the following sections, I present the nature of image-conflicts that were observed upon probing into meanings that people and NGOs formed of the role of these specific forms of assistance.

Role Conflicts: Meanings of Assistance

As shown in Table 6.2, assistance in the form of consumables was seen as similar to assistance through infrastructures, in that both were provided freely. In their provision, however, they were different, in that consumables were provided to address sufferings and vulnerabilities in the community. Infrastructures, on the other hand, were for physical capital, meant to generate future development. In other words, people had to be seen as poor and desperate in order to receive consumables. Otherwise, they could only access 'free' assistance through infrastructures, which were for the reduction of the poverty of the whole community, and not of isolated individuals. The reason that fieldworkers gave was that the desperately poor could not find the required support from their weak resource base, at a point when their lives were threatened. They required, therefore, instant and 'free' support. The overall NGO role in this case was described as 'filling the gap' so that people would then continue with their own development. It was, this role of 'filling the gap', however, that was a center for role conflicts for both fieldworkers and the people.

Filling the Gap

From the accounts of the fieldworkers that I interviewed, the NGO image of 'free assistance' was that of 'filling the gap' with money-based resources. To build a school-block, for instance, would cost an estimated 2,000 pounds. Such amounts of money were seen as not affordable for people in the two communities because people were poor, they did not have the money. This situation, therefore, also required provision of free assistance in order to procure materials with high money-value; those bought from shops, and skilled labor. Accordingly, resources that required unskilled labor were seen as already available or 'locally available resources'. These would include, for example, bricks, sand and water. On the other hand, assistance towards food security, in the form of material provisions such as cassava and sweet potatoes, were provided freely without looking for any labor contribution. This was because of the image of the desperation of the recipients, as explained above.

Given that in both cases people were seen as poor, this boundary was left to the judgment of fieldworkers of the different NGOs. In essence, some people would be seen from one perspective as desperate and then from another as not desperate and being expected to contribute through their labor. The same would happen with different NGOs, where one NGO describes a group of people as desperately poor while another NGO sees them as a resource for labor-intensive projects. This created role conflicts in fieldworkers in the event that communities or some members of the community behaved differently, as one of them explained,

We give them freely because they cannot buy. The protocol is that we are the hope for the poor and if we make everybody to buy then he is not the poor then. We take everybody as a poor man despite some are rich but because the area is taken as poor everybody is poor. It is difficult to say buy because we will be contradicting ourselves. We give them free school blocks; everything is free. Only the fruit tree breeders will be given money so that we can thank them for doing something good for the community. Where I have seen problems with these people in *Zabwe* is with construction work and I really do not know what the problem really is. The way they have accepted our organization seems to be saying that they want the organization to do all things for them, they do not see their role as to participate, like in carrying of bricks to the site. In *Nkhandwe* village, for example, they molded a lot of bricks but for them to carry them to the construction site it is very difficult, they struggle to contribute money for hiring some means of transport. Sometimes when you are handing over a structure to the government and community they will demand for being taken care of. When we were handing over the health center for example, they were very furious in that we did not slaughter a cow for them to eat at the function. At *Mwela* village we are constructing a TBA shelter so that we improve services she renders to the community. They started very well after convincing them that it was for their benefit but then they suddenly stopped working on it and it has taken us a very long time than expected. Very few people are coming to carry materials. We are about to start drilling of boreholes in the area and people are expected to mould bricks for the boreholes but very few people are doing it. At the community level, the village headmen are not even influencing people to work. When you chat with some people we are told that they are saying that we are eating their money as facilitators. They are saying that the whites sent the money for construction of these things but these people are saying we should be doing it. It appears there is a misconception somewhere, which I don't know. This is surprising because things at *Mpira* are different in that they actually scramble for work. They have bricks ready for any assistance that might come their way. In this community we are even afraid to propose anything for an area when our bosses suggest some developments. We are often worried and afraid of committing ourselves to something that will not work. I often use my effort and sometimes I have to give my money to the village headman say MK100.00 and then he is very happy and calls for people to work, their own thing. This community is very much behind on development; it needs a lot of education (Lernard, NGO fieldworker).

As further shown in Lernard's accounts above, he explained his conflict by comparing Zabwe to Mpira communities, with people in Zabwe as in a worrisome situation requiring education. This was because they were not 'participating' as expected in that condition of assistance as those in Mpira. This was from the framework of enhancing people's strengths or capacity, as a livelihood framework, as discussed earlier. As argued, the major assumption for this framework, where assistance is perceived, as filling the gap, is that there is shared understanding of the existing assets and capacities. With such an assumption the focus is just on what and how to do the project. My study experience in both of these communities showed that Lernard's kind of role conflicts were also noted from all the fieldworkers that I interviewed.

When it came to the people, in Mpira community I noted that women, general community members and the very poor people had conflicts with the role of NGO assistance. In this case, they perceived the work of contributing materials as 'too much', in terms of the demands put on them in the context of other calls on their labor. This included household chores and casual labor, for instance, as discussed in the last chapter. The 'filling the gap' image, on the other hand, was strongly expressed among the traditional leaders and better-off members of the community, often with animated statements.

As for us we work in such a way that they do what they are supposed to do but on our side they ask us to mould bricks and make them ready, also with sand and identifying and paying contractors. They will provide cement, planks, iron sheets and the like but that we should be the first to do something for ourselves so as to show that we really need the things we are asking for. They just help us to go forward just as a person who asks for assistance on his work, which he has already started himself. Those people who are assisting do not do all the work, they help him to a point and he has to continue and complete it himself (Traditional leader, Mpira community).

Even with these statements of support for NGOs 'filling the gap', however, looking at the images that women formed of assistance and the power dynamics in the culture of Mpira community, brings a different picture. In this case, I formed the impression that the good co-operation that fieldworkers were talking about in Mpira community (for example, Lernard above) should be because of the supportive images that men, traditional leaders and better-off people formed of NGO assistance. These categories of people were in a position of power and were making decisions on behalf of the community, including sanctions on labor-based contributions. As explained in the introductory chapter, although Mpira had more cross-cultural interactions than Zabwe, both communities had strong traditional leadership from those tribes than were owners of land. Men were also more influential than women were, under the patriarchal marriage system. From this position of influence they were possible 'validation agents' (or mirrors) for the images that women and the very poor had of assistance (Leitner, Begley et al. 1996; Willutzki and Duda, 1996). As a result, these images cannot give a proper picture of the nature of interaction that women and the very poor had in Mpira. This suggests that getting a proper understanding of the power dynamics involved in negotiating external assistance is an important issue to consider in designing a project. They significantly affect the nature of agency of some of the actors within the same 'community' or group of people.

In Table 6.3 below, I have summarized the occurrence of these images of role of assistance in Mpira community across position in society, gender and well-being status of the people that were interviewed. In the tabulation, 'some materials' was the concept used to reflect the fact that NGO assistance was only part of what people were contributing to a given project, in order to 'fill the gap'. 'All materials' was the concept used to signify that NGOs had to provide or financially support the acquisition of all the resources (mainly material) that were required in specified project. This was seen as the NGO's necessary role in the context of assistance. The total picture shows that Mpira community was properly aligned with the NGOs' understanding of their 'filling the gap' role in people's livelihoods. This was the kind of self-help spirit that the government of Malawi underlined in its policies. The Mpira case would make most NGOs working with communities in Malawi, argue that they are people's own choices and priorities and not a reflection of NGOs' 'interests and ideologies' as Malawian commentators, such as Kishindo (2001, p.303), contend. In which case, the results from Zabwe, presented after Table 6.3 below, provide an interesting contrast and a proper basis for conceptualizing role conflicts regarding 'assistance'.

Table 6.3(a) Images of assistance on infrastructures in Mpira: gender-based analysis

Perception	Gender/No. interviewed		No. of mentions	No. of mentions per individual
Some	Male	22	111	5.0
Materials	Female	10	4	0.4
All Materials	Male	22	19	0.9
	Female	10	11	1.1

Table 6.3(b) Images of assistance on infrastructures in Mpira: position-based analysis

Perception	Position/No. interviewed		No. of mentions	No. of mentions per individual
Some	Traditional leaders	9	42	4.6
Materials	Committee members	5	29	5.8
	Community members	18	44	2.4
All Materials	Traditional leaders	9	n/a	n/a
	Committee members	5	n/a	n/a
	Community members	18	30	1.7

Table 6.3(c) Images of assistance on infrastructures in Mpira: well-being analysis

Perception	Well-being/No. interviewed		No. of mentions	No. of mentions per individual
Some	Better-off	6	35	5.8
Materials	Middle-poor	12	32	2.7
	Very-poor	14	48	3.4*
All	Better-off	6	n/a	n/a
Materials	Middle-poor	12	n/a	n/a
	Very-poor	14	30	2.1*

In Table 6.3 above, the average number of mentions for traditional leaders and men is much higher than in the other categories. However, all categories, except women, had a higher number of mentions on 'some materials' than on 'all materials'. This shows that the people in Mpira were more for NGO assistance 'filling the gap', just as was the case with the NGOs, as noted above. The starred figures (*), however, are surprising because they suggest that the very poor also were in line with 'filling the gap' as their traditional leaders and the NGOs, although on a much smaller scale. This could mean that their interaction with their leaders framed their images of the role of NGO assistance in their livelihoods. This is because when we take women on their own, who were mostly in this very poor category, the image of filling the gap with 'some materials' is lower than 'all materials'. In this case, it was the very poor men who aligned themselves with their leaders. This interpretation makes sense when we consider the fact that most of these very poor people were not part of those who had direct experience with NGO assistance, they were not part of project committees. However, my study experience at Zabwe community was a clear contrast to that at Mpira and provides interesting illumination on image conflicts regarding role of assistance.

Zabwe community is where fieldworker's (such as Lernard, above) experienced a lot of role conflicts. Despite experiencing these role conflicts, however, fieldworkers explained most reactions and statements from the community members as based on rumors and not as representing fundamental image-conflicts. The case of Lernard, where he notes that people say 'whites sent the money for everything' and then he takes it as just one of the community 'misconceptions' of NGOs, is a good illustration of this observation. With these reactions regarded as misconceptions, rather than emanating from image-conflicts, they had to be explained properly as projects were being implemented. Alternatively, they were included in the project design under interventions in the form of awareness creation through community meetings and training. In project reports, explanations for slow progress of work were stated with blames on the people such as, 'clinic construction was not completed because people did not carry bricks to the construction site'. In some cases, some villages were even punished by shifting assistance to other villages that were said to be ready with materials. It never appeared in fieldworker reports and project designs that these community reactions could reflect role-conflicts.

When I explored images of the role of assistance in Zabwe community such concepts as, 'NGOs have the money' and 'it is not our responsibility' and 'too much work', characterized their accounts. Mostly women and people in the very poor category, as in the case of Mpira community explained above, used the concept of 'too much work'. Given the importance of the other concepts in explaining the nature of NGO interaction in such conditions of assistance, I briefly reflect on two of these concepts in the following subsections.

NGO has the Money

In this case, people associated NGOs with having money enough to cover even what people were being asked to contribute. The image was that of the existence of donors outside the country providing money for assisting communities for all the work involved in construction. Where this was not happening, it created role conflicts. In this case, NGO fieldworkers, as people entrusted with disbursement of these financial resources, were seen as appropriating the money for their advantage. In many cases people were angrily reflecting their interaction with NGOs, as reflected in the interaction quoted below.

Henry: The issue is that they cheat us. What happens is that they say that it is our development to work ourselves but what really happens is that when money is coming there is money for sand, bricks and for everything required to construct a school for instance. When the money comes to these NGOs they change the language and tell us that we should be contributing these materials. The money comes but they misuse it, they use the money on our heads.

Chimutu: I have not been to school myself but I know what happens in the village. We are three villages adjacent to each other and we should have been working together to form one force and make things happen.

FT: That does not happen?

Chimutu: No it does not happen, what we hear is that the NGO is conducting a meeting in Chasu village and not our village. You can even look at their list of attendance and you will not see anyone from my village.

FT: How come we are not able to ask the organization or the Group Village Headman about this?

Chimutu: So many times we tell them but nothing is happening that is why we are saying we are ready for anyone who can assist us quickly. We told the project manager about this but nothing is changing. Do you know a lion?

FT: Yes.

Chimutu: When it has caught a cow where does it eat it?

FT: I don't know.

Chimutu: It goes to the forest and this is the forest.

FT: What does this mean?

Chimutu: What we perceive is that these organizations are using our villages to eat their money because when a lion catches a cow it goes hiding far away in the forest. This is what happens with these organization officials. When money comes to assist us in the village they just use it themselves and report to donors that they have assisted such and such areas. They say everything is all right and yet things are not all right. We just look at them because we are not educated ourselves.

If we compare these accounts with those in the example for Mpira above (see page 103), we find that the leadership category had role conflicts with NGO assistance when in Zabwe. This could explain the difficulties that fieldworkers had with project implementation in this community because the leaders were the link between NGOs and the people. This role conflict was exacerbated with the people's image of NGOs as responsible for providing resources for infrastructures. These resources included those that NGOs regarded as 'locally available resources'.

Not our Responsibility

This concerned mainly construction work that involved a whole village or more than one village such as roads, schools and water, seen in this case as 'public services'. The understanding in this case was that the government has to serve the people through provision of, for instance, good roads, good schools, and water along with many other services. NGOs were in this context seen as taking government responsibility. In essence, many people regarded NGOs as sent or called by the government to serve the people. In such a situation, NGO demands on people's participation, through contributing labor-based materials, was seen as a deliberate substitution of people's labor for what NGOs were meant to provide.

As a general observation, the same categories of people, men, better off people and people in leadership positions that had supportive images in Mpira, perceived assistance as where NGOs provide 'all materials' in Zabwe. If we take the analysis based on gender and position in society, as an illustration, men and traditional leaders mentioned assistance as 'all materials' almost twice as much as women and general community members. Table 6.4 below, shows the picture in Zabwe community, reflecting on gender and leadership for illustration purposes.

Table 6.4(a) Images of assistance on infrastructures in Zabwe: gender-based analysis

Perception	Gender/ No. interviewed		No. of mentions	No. of mentions per individual
Some	Male	39	12	0.3
materials	Female	28	16	0.6
All	Male	39	249	6.4
materials	Female	28	103	3.7

Table 6.4(b) Images of assistance on infrastructures in Zabwe: position-based analysis

Perception	Position/ No. interviewed		No. of mentions	No. of mentions per individual
Some	Traditional leaders	12	12	1.0
materials	Committee members	15	6	0.4
	Community members	40	10	0.3
All	Traditional leaders	12	96	8.0
materials	Committee members	15	65	4.3
	Community members	40	191	4.7

Given that the traditional leaders in Zabwe were in the fore with regard to expecting NGOs to provide all materials in their projects, it is not surprising that projects could not progress well. This was because they had the role of mobilizing the community, as people and NGOs agreed when designing the projects. The same argument about the direction of community leadership in shaping the participation of the people can be made here. In this case, Zabwe leadership formed images that were conflicting with the 'filling the gap' image of NGOs and hence because of their strength, the rest of the community could not move forward on such projects.

From this analysis it is possible to see that the struggle that people, particularly in Zabwe community, had in attributing 'free assistance' to assistance on infrastructures was located in the image they formed of the role of NGOs. In this case, the conflict was that, whereas NGOs provided assistance as 'free' in order to fill the gap, people were looking at who NGOs were in relation to their broader picture of livelihoods. In the case of Zabwe, it was evident that they saw NGOs as 'providers' (Curtis, 1991, p.101) who rescued the poor from their poverty. In this case, it became a role conflict to make people suffer with labor contribution as a condition for access to the assistance. This reflects the 'situatedness' of labor in communities rather than the image of abundant rural labor, as discussed in chapter five. Ultimately, this analysis shows that it was not only NGOs that framed the conditions for what was proper assistance to communities. In other words, people were not simply being 'coopted at the implementation stage' into NGO projects (Kishindo, 2001, p.303). Instead, these people had a frame of understanding of the proper role of NGO assistance in their livelihoods right from project initiation phases of interaction with NGOs. They had their own conditions that shaped their understanding of role of NGO assistance in their livelihoods. These conditions were based on differences in understanding of livelihoods but also in relation to the presence of NGOs. This framework of understanding was, apparently, not brought to the open during the initial negotiations for assistance, as discussed above.

However, the conditions that people set, in which they framed the proper role performance of NGOs cannot be adequately understood from this analysis on its own. We need to explore the contrast in the images that people formed of assistance to NGOs providing 'free assistance'. This is possible because the conditions that NGOs set for assistance have been revealed as 'free' assistance and 'repayments', which are already contrasts. We also know that from the general descriptions that people and NGOs gave of assistance, having their emergent contrasts. As discussed above (see Table 6.2), there was already a difference between NGOs and the people. This meant that the NGOs were already offering different conditions for their assistance. Therefore, we need to compare the nature of role conflicts, under the conditions of 'free' assistance to the role conflicts, under the conditions of 'repayments'.

Role Conflicts: Situation Analysis

The argument in this situation analysis of role conflicts is that if role conflicts are of similar nature under both 'free' and 'repayment' situations then there was more to the role conflicts than the conditions that were set by the NGO. If on the other hand, they are different, it means that it was the conditions that NGOs set for their assistance that were a problem. In this context, the differences between Zabwe and Mpira in the images formed of assistance as 'free' was an opportunity for deepening the insight into the nature of image interaction between NGOs and the people. This was because the same NGOs were assisting Zabwe and Mpira communities, where the former had role conflicts while the later had minimal role conflicts. Therefore, it is possible to look at role conflicts in the two communities when conditions of assistance changed to 'repayments'. In this section, therefore, I focus on loans and the nature of role conflicts that occurred in the two communities. I also look at the activities and how they were carried out in those situations of role conflicts because they constitute the way NGO conditions were executed on the ground.

In the case of loans, with the image of NGOs providing assistance, people in the two communities accessed loans for various enterprises. Apparently, loans were not new in both communities, because the government had been providing agricultural loans for some years. During the negotiation process when provision of these loans was being decided, there were no conflicts (at least in the open) and people from all wealth categories were involved. This is likely because of the image bargains between people and NGOs, discussed above. However, conflicts emerged after NGOs started demanding repayments from people including use of coercive means, such as confiscation of defaulters' property. [2] This meant, to the people involved, that loans were not 'assistance', as it occurred in their images. In fact what was important to them, before this repayment campaign, was that the NGO took down their names as the poor who needed assistance to have their incomes improved. The common phrase in this case was, 'I or we registered'.

> *Situ*: When they were coming they told us that they have come to assist people who are poor and hence village headmen and all of us were very happy to have such assistance. However, when we were given loans we later discovered that there were cases where we could be convicted in court. We were surprised because we thought we heard them say that donors want to assist the helpless in these communities so that they get better in their lives. When you have been told that this thing we are giving you is assistance then it has to be assistance.
>
> *Chibwe*: They asked us village headmen to call all people to a community meeting to hear about the goat project. I called all people in my village saying that anyone who wants free goats should go for a meeting at the school. Those who wanted went to the meeting and those who did not want did not come. However, it is just the same because even those who registered have not received goats.
>
> *FT*: What did people who attended do for you to say they registered?
>
> *Chibwe*: The organization staff wrote down our names.
>
> *FT*: Did they say that means you are going to receive goats?
>
> *Chibwe*: Yes, that is what we people in the village think it means, why should I register my name if I am not going to receive?
>
> *FT*: If you already have goats, how is it that you want to go into a loan?
>
> *Chibwe*: I am doing it for my wife. I have four wives and I have seen that one of them is hard working and takes care of my goats hence I am wanting to give her a chance to keep goats on her own.
>
> *FT*: Is it not possible to just give her from your stock?
>
> *Chibwe*: No, those are for my children, they are not hers and also those other wives will cause problems.

As can be seen in the quotes above, people closely linked the process of receiving a loan to the process of 'needs' analysis that NGOs conducted in the area. The role conflict resulted in formation of other images of NGOs and their assistance. Chibwe, the village headman, for instance, was calling people for 'free goats' and yet goats were on loan. He then explains it in connection to the process of registration. The poor are said to be helpless and that is what made them get loans. Since these people already knew about loans even before NGOs came to the area, it meant that they formed an image of assistance where it was to be humanitarian. Role conflicts in this case raised other images, including that NGOs were generating their own profits, loans would just make them go into prison and were not good for business enterprise in their areas. In Table 6.5 below, is a summarized presentation of the picture of images people formed of NGO loans in Zabwe.

Table 6.5 Images formed of 'repayments' in Zabwe

Perception	Gender		Position		Well-being	
NGO	Male	1	Traditional leaders	2	Better-off	4
profit	Female	n/a	Committee members	1	Middle-poor	n/a
generation			Community members	n/a	Very-poor	1
Threat of	Male	1	Traditional leaders	1	Better-off	n/a
imprison-	Female	6	Committee members	2	Middle-poor	3
ment			Community members	5	Very-poor	3
Business	Male	2	Traditional leaders	n/a	Better-off	4
not good	Female	n/a	Committee members	2	Middle-poor	2
			Community members	1	Very-poor	5

As reflected in Table 6.5, 'NGOs making their profits' was an image that most men, traditional leaders, committee members and better-off people formed of loans. This was explained with reference to NGO fieldworkers insisting on loan repayments even when, according to people, they saw that crops had failed in the field due to drought. This meant that NGOs were not caring about people's livelihoods, but getting what they planned to profit from the loan provision. Related to this was the image of loans as 'threats for imprisonment', which women, community members, middle and the very poor category formed of loans. In this case, they saw themselves as liable for imprisonment because, unlike the better-off people, they had no assets, which NGOs could confiscate and sell upon their failure to repay the loan. Getting imprisoned was to them a likely result, especially looking at the pitiless stand of fieldworkers in collecting loan repayments, as stated above.

The 'business not good' image, on the other hand, was associated with problems of marketing in relation to these loan repayment periods and interest rates. Although this image was reflected among men in Zabwe, it was the prevalent image of loans in Mpira community. Since most of the people engaged in trading of agricultural commodities, they had difficulties in selling these commodities as they put all their hopes on ADMARC markets. These markets, as explained in the last chapter, were not open in these areas, as was the case in the past years. Despite this reality, however, NGO fieldworkers continued to press for loan repayments within agreed dates, even if it meant people selling other assets to repay the loan. This was because projects had to be sustainable. Many women, however, indicated that they were repaying loans from the same money they received as capital, as shown in my field notes below.

Most women are spending several days going to the lake to procure fish to exchange for maize or beans within the community. They are hoping to sell maize on the ADMARC markets but these markets are not open and they have nowhere to go with their maize and rice. Some women are saying that this failure to open the market also means that people in the community have no money to buy the fish that they (women in business) are selling directly. Instead they are selling these products to primary school teachers and workers at a small hydroelectric plant on credit. They are waiting for some credits to be settled at the end of the month, when debtors receive their salaries. However, the NGO requires loan repayments weekly. According to fieldworkers, these loan conditions were agreed upon with another organization, which was contracted to oversee the implementation of the project. All women are doing in this situation is to take part of the same principal they received in order to repay the loan. This, however, means that they are having less and less capital with which to continue with the business. They are also worried with raising enough money to repay the interest when the amount they received runs out, a psychological captivity of NGO expected actions. (Personal field notes).

The role conflict, in this case, was not so much about the loan itself as a form of assistance, but the way NGOs managed it, with respect to the business environment within which they were assisting people. This suggests that if the business environment was good or NGOs were flexible to the prevailing business environment, loans were going to be seen as 'filling the gap', as construed by the NGOs. In other words, assisting people with capital for generation of income for meeting their livelihood needs. This is different from the case of Zabwe, where image conflicts started from the definition of assistance itself and how loans were located in it. NGO rigidity in administration of loan repayments, because it was part of their policies, exacerbated the role conflicts leading to negative images.

Emerging out of this analysis, therefore, is the understanding that the interaction between NGOs and the people was based on the conditions they both set to frame the role of the other in negotiating assistance in people's livelihoods. The fact that there were role conflicts indicates that these conditions were different. The first difference was in the understanding of NGO management of assistance in a technical sense, as in the Mpira case. The second was the difference in the definition of NGO assistance itself. Therefore, the two positions also suggest differences in the nature of agency of the people as the actors at the NGO community interface in the formulation of project objectives and implementing projects. Apparently, the nature of people's agency during choice of assistance, as participants through PRAs and community meetings, was in the form of satisfying the NGO conditions for provision of assistance. Their primary agenda was to get the assistance regardless of how it fits their purposes, which is further elaborated in the next chapter. In this next section I provide further evidence of people setting conditions, in their images of the role of NGO assistance in their livelihoods, which were different from those of NGOs and resulted in conflicts. These role conditions had to emerge in relation to the expected distribution of benefits from specific forms of assistance and affected the implementation of projects.

Role Conflicts: Targeting of Assistance

As shown in Table 6.2, the descriptions people gave in comparing the various forms of NGO assistance, had emergent discrepancies in terms of either individual or community benefits. In this case, NGOs favored provision of assistance to groups or the whole community rather than directly to individuals. This construction was based on an image of benefits that are common to all, such that an individual benefiting from that good or service cannot deprive others from benefiting at the same time. These benefits included, for instance, children learning in a school block, a village drawing water from a protected water source and the community growing their rice or vegetables using an irrigation system. This assistance was, therefore, provided to a village or a group of villages in the mind of a community working together for the good of all. In the case of groups, used especially for the provision of loans, they were seen as strengthening the people's solidarity and reducing transaction costs. The issue of transaction costs also relates to the demand on them from their donors to reduce administrative costs and increase value for money, discussed in chapter three.

As for the people, however, whereas they asked for assistance in the image of the good of all, 'for the community' or group, in terms of meanings, there were three categories. There were those projects where individuals could hardly monopolize benefits derived from success of a project. The second case included projects that were for the community but with inherent possibilities of certain individuals benefiting more. The third and last case comprised of projects, which focused at a community or group, where individuals were to directly derive benefits through working together. Therefore, people had different role expectations as to how they could benefit from NGO assistance, according to these categories, which resulted into image-conflicts in cases where there were differences with these expectations.

Individual Working for His/Her Community

This category concerned projects like schools and water, where members of a defined community were working together in molding bricks, carrying sand and water to a construction site. In most of the villages in Zabwe and Mpira, working together on a project for common good was not a new practice. In the past they had worked on projects like school shelters, mostly made of poles and thatched with grass. There were also cases where brick-walled and iron-roofed buildings were constructed with funding from the local church, especially the Roman Catholic Church, in both Zabwe and Mpira. There were also some clinic shelters and school blocks with iron-sheets and brick walls, which were funded by the government. All this occurred in the 1970s under the National Youth Week Project (most of these buildings had the label 'Youth Week Project, 1978'). Apart from schools, people also worked together on sinking shallow wells and repairing or opening up new roads.

However, in the context of NGO assistance, leaders in Zabwe perceived their work as worth some rewards from the project, named as *ilopa*, which stands for blood. There is a proverb in their culture, which they cited and translated as 'no butcher can slaughter a cow without blood being spilt on him or her'. This proverb meant that just as a butcher gets a piece of meat by working on meat, they needed to get monetary rewards for working with NGO money on a project activity. The lack of provision for such rewards or 'fringe benefits' (Curtis 1991) created role conflicts. The case of a project chairman in Zabwe is a good illustration of these conflicts.

> What I see is that we have a problem of transport as Committee members. We have been asking them to assist us by giving us bicycles but they are not doing it. The other thing is that as we are leaving our jobs in our homes and doing this work but we are not given anything. Although fieldworkers are saying that it is our own development, we leave our jobs in order to work for this development, especially myself as chairman. I travel in the area a lot almost everyday because I have to see that work is progressing in every area and I use my own transport and food and yet I have no assistance coming to me. I am just doing it because there is nothing I can do and yet those NGDO employees come here by car and then go back and claim allowances from the office. They don't do that with us as if we do not want to have good things also.
>
> The other thing, which people are complaining about is the practice of giving us food during meetings; people are saying that we don't want food but money so that I can buy something for my family. I can buy soap because as I am traveling in this project I get dirty but have no soap to wash my clothes. I spend most of my time at this work, how do I buy clothes? They should have been sparing some money for us to be assisted (Project Chairman).

NGO assisted projects were said to be different from their past projects, where they worked on their own. This was because in their projects of the past (before NGO assistance), people were devising systems of ensuring contribution of an equal amount of labor or time to a project. This was necessary because they were prone to 'free-riding'[3] (Ostrom, 1990). This equality of labor input was socially constructed for community members of different social status and not necessarily based upon equal man-hours per person. For example, daughters-in-law who were just joining the society were drawing more water for the project activity than could be done by elderly women. Such a case would still be seen as equality as long as all women of that category are apportioned the same size of work. Any deviation from this rationality, however, was handled using socially accepted forms of punishments or otherwise it created conflicts within the society. Persistent conflicts would result in work delays or stopping the project activity all together. It was this socially constructed equality that kept individuals working for their community and made the difference between the different sections or villages within the same community. This was in terms of the number and pace of project activities.

In the context of an NGO funded project, however, people perceived the project as a special and different programme from their own self-conceived community project. This was because of the extra resources (financial) and the faster pace of activities that NGOs demanded from the people, in order to continue funding the different projects. As a result, these new ways of doing things and resources destabilized the socially constructed 'equality' principles in the communities. The faster pace of the projects implied developing a management structure that could handle the work at the pace demanded. In this case, for instance, people were asked to elect committee members that had the ability to handle the complexity of funded projects, in terms of amount of funds and the time required to attend to the details. For example, for one NGO, committee members said that they were expected to meet on every 15th day of the month and then at least twice in every three months, with NGO fieldworkers.[4]

In the case of Mpira community, on the other hand, traditional leaders referred to the extra time and labor that they provided to attend meetings as a sacrifice for the development of their community. Committee members, however, pointed at the high NGO expenditures in organizing training sessions and when feeding them during committee meetings. They considered this as an indication of the NGO's financial capacity, which could easily and rightly be extended to provision of some direct rewards to committee members in recognition of their extra effort. They also found a contradiction in the claims of NGOs that the financial resources were for the community, when the community did not have control over the use of the resources. To this extent, committee members in Mpira could be said to have had similar understanding of their role in the context of NGO assistance. Although there were these role conflicts, since most traditional leaders in Mpira were in favor of the 'sacrificial spirit' of leadership, image-conflicts could not come to the open interface with NGOs. In Zabwe, where traditional leaders also formed image-conflicts with community-wide project benefits, most conflicts came to the open.

Community Working Together: for Individuals Serving the Community

This was the case mainly where the community was involved in construction of infrastructures for some individuals in the community, who were serving the community with special functions or skills. This concerned mainly Traditional Birth Attendants (TBAs), who were helping expectant mothers in the society in all maternity requirements. There were also traditional medicine specialists, who also were assisting with cure of certain diseases in the community, which in many cases were seen as not curable at the government hospitals. Lastly, they constructed infrastructures for witchdoctors, who often combined their practice with traditional medicine. The common thing for all these traditional practitioners was that they never accepted payment from their community members because they said it was their special call, often coming from spirits of their forefathers. Accordingly, communities constructed special houses where these local practitioners could do their work without charging them for community labor, a form of reciprocity. However, when NGOs came in with assistance on these infrastructures, role conflicts emerged. I will cite the case of TBAs, for example.

I observed that communities were constructing TBA shelters adjacent to the TBA's dwelling house, out of poles and thatched with grass. NGOs, however, noted in the data they collected on community health services that these shelters were unhygienic. This created a risk for mothers and babies who were born in these shelters. They, therefore, decided to promote the construction of improved and permanent shelters for TBAs in these communities. In this case, people were also asked to mobilize 'locally available resources' of bricks and sand. People became excited with this offer, as they usually would do, through their traditional leaders. When it came to implement the project, however, instead of choosing the TBAs' premises as sites for constructing these structures, people chose sites away from the TBA's homes. They argued that these structures were now for the community and not for TBAs. If they constructed them at the TBA's home, they would use them for a time and upon their death their families will inherit the property. This would mean that their families would be made wealthier than other families in the community. As for TBAs themselves, there were mixed images and choices were difficult to make. On the one hand they were excited to have an improved structure but having it away from their home dwelling meant spending a lot of time away from their families. This is because the work of assisting mothers would involve long hours of waiting because delivery times are not predictable. When they assist mothers closer to their homes they would wait while also attending to their household chores. This was especially important because the work does not attract any payment from the community, NGOs and government. On the other hand, to accept to have the structures constructed at their dwelling homes would make them vulnerable to jealousies from community members, some of these would even bewitch them. These jealousies would arise from the fact that community members contributed their labor in constructing the improved structure. The NGOs provided free iron sheets, cement and other money-based materials. In this case, people saw the possibility of the TBA using the structure for her personal household purposes and therefore, in a better position than others. (*Source*: Personal field notes).

A closer look at these perceptions, however, shows that it is also the difference in the ability to access NGO assistance that was at stake and not labor *per se*. If these same communities were able to provide labor and construct a shelter at the home dwelling of the TBA, we can explain their refusal to construct the same structure with NGO assistance as the perceived advantage of an individual TBA in accessing free NGO assistance. This is especially the case because the quality of the structure would be much better than any other owned house in Zabwe. The same was the case in Mpira, where they agreed with fieldworkers and work was said to be proceeding well. In Zabwe community, on the other hand, there was still a struggle in most villages even after agreeing to shift the sites from the premises of a TBA to a community owned land. As Lernard (quoted on page 100 above) explains, they could not mould the bricks required for these structures.

Community Working Together: for Direct Individual Benefits

This category was for images people formed of assistance when working together, in groups, such as loans and irrigation projects, storm drains and so forth, where benefits were directly accruing to individual participants. For NGOs, this was meant to enhance community solidarity and gain from mutual sharing of experiences and knowledge. These groups would also reduce transaction costs when it came to seeking external advice on their enterprises. In this case, I will use the case of an irrigation project in Mpira community to illustrate the nature of role conflicts that arose when NGO assistance was involved. The project was called *Kasanga Self-help Scheme*, which started before NGOs came into the community.

In this case, people were working together to divert water from Mpira River and were able to grow rice twice a year on the same piece of land. The project was conceived out of the desire of a few people in the village who organized to work together and produce rice in dry season. When the NGO looked at the project in the light of the low crop productivity figures that they collected from their survey, they decided to expand the programme and allow most people, especially the poor in the community, to join. A wider and more permanent main water channel was constructed using cement bought by the NGO. After construction of the main channel, using paid skilled labor, people were required to divert small channels into their fields on their own and then organize for maintenance of the main channel. However, people did not do it. Instead, the original group of people continued to irrigate their crops using their old channel. When I found out why, I was told that the new channel was going to include people who are lazy in the village to join and would cause maintenance of the channel to be difficult. These people will eat on other peoples' sweat. It was difficult to reject anybody on the new channel because it was seen as for everybody because NGOs provided the resources to construct it. Anyone who dares to stop somebody from benefiting from such projects can even be bewitched. In this case they found it better to work on an old channel but with people who were already committed to work together (*Source*: Personal field notes).

This role conflict in the irrigation project was due to the circumstances of the incoming NGO resources that destabilized the equality principles, which were used when the people had organized themselves. This destabilization can be said to have occurred because the bargaining power, which sustains togetherness, could not operate properly (Curtis, 1995; Ostrom, 1995). We could also add, however, that bargaining power was eroded because of the image of 'free assistance', explained above. This image must have given power to the poor but 'lazy' people (see discussion on livelihoods in chapter 5) to lay equal claims on the possible benefits of the project. Free assistance put all people at the same level because, as discussed earlier, none of the community members labored for this assistance.

When we look at the targeting of assistance, from the conditions that people set rather than those that NGOs set, therefore, we find that it affected the nature of participation significantly. These conditions reflect the social relationships, which were apparently left to assumptions, in the project design because they could not fit into the goal formulation processes, as discussed in chapter five. This section has shown that role conflicts were based on the nature of negotiation activities between NGOs and the people around these social relationships, rather than the forms of assistance *per se*. In essence, the changes in participation in relation to targeting of NGO assistance have shown that there were differences in the forms of agency of the people. In other words, the people's nature of agency was affected in different ways, with respect to both the choice and management of assistance.

Conclusion

This chapter has shown that the role conflicts that characterized the interaction between NGOs and the people in the two study communities were of two types or forms. On the one hand were role conflicts that were based on the differences in the expectations of the management of 'assistance for the poor', pointing to technical aspects such as time and amount of assistance. On the other hand, however, role conflicts were based on the definition of NGO assistance itself, pointing to the core understanding not just of assistance, but also of NGOs as organizations for the poor. The discussion has also shown that people set their own conditions in which they shaped the nature of their participation. These conditions were based on images that they formed of the distribution of benefits from NGO assistance, which were linked to their social relationships. In which case, as discussed in chapter two, these people were still active agents in these interactions, despite the set NGO conditions. The question that remains, however, is the nature of the exercise of this agency in relation to empowerment objectives. This ultimately, shows that the analysis needs to go to a much deeper level; that of the understanding of change expected from experiencing NGO assistance. This will be the subject of the next chapter.

Notes

[1] Geoff Reiss defines a consumable resource as a resource that 'is consumed as it goes into task' and a non-consumable resource as one, which, 'can be used and used again' (1992, p.85).

[2] According to fieldworkers, this action was already put in the loan agreements, which all people who got the loan signed before getting the loan. Therefore, it was legally appropriate to do it.

[3] As Ostrom explains, 'Whenever one person cannot be excluded from the benefits that others provide, each person is motivated not to contribute to the joint effort but to free-ride on the efforts of others' (1990, p.6).

[4] In actual sense, they were only meeting when NGO fieldworkers invited them to meet because of what they called 'logistical problems' of food and transport. When NGO fieldworkers called them to a meeting, they provided both food and transport to committee members (where transport meant having the NGO vehicle take committee members to and from meetings).

Chapter 7

Conflicting Images on Change Resulting from NGO Assistance

Introduction

This chapter focuses on conflicts in the images that NGOs and the people in the cases studied formed of the purpose or expected change from NGO assistance. This is necessary because, as noted in the last chapter, the image-conflicts that were identified with regard to the role of assistance were associated with the meaning of assistance and the way that assistance was managed (operationally). The former could not be understood properly with an analysis focused on 'role' of assistance on its own. In other words, there was need for a deeper analysis that delves into the core aspects of the images that both NGOs and the people formed of assistance. It is at this level of analysis that the nature of agency of the people and NGOs, in relation to the achievement of empowerment objectives via projects, was conceptualized. Whereas 'role conflicts' arise due to differences between the expected and actual performance of social actors, image-conflicts with regard to expected livelihood change emerge from differences in the outcome-values of this performance.[1] A contemporary life example of someone from a different life-world assisting another person with a coat might illustrate this conceptual landscape.

Let us assume that person A from a life context X negotiates with person B, living in a significantly different context Y, over B's livelihood situation and identify a number of problems of which one is lack of protection from cold weather. Let us further assume that A decides (based on A's understanding and agreement with B) to provide a coat to B in order to reduce B's lack of protection from the cold. In which case, a coat has the role of 'warm clothing' in both A's and B's images of coats (influenced by their ideologies, philosophies, social backgrounds etc.). Surprisingly for A, however, B is still seen on the road without a coat. A is disappointed because, in his or her image, change has not taken place in B's life. For B, however, the coat is a vital material for warmth in the bed (as a blanket) and hence does not want to risk it getting wet while walking outside. The warmth of the night is better, because he/she can have some sleep, than the warmth of the day where walking itself is a warming exercise. This according to B, is the purpose or change that has significantly taken place in life as a result of A's intervention. This, however, represents image-conflicts as regards change expected or resulting from A's assistance despite their agreement over the 'coat' having the role of providing 'warmth' to B.

In this illustration, the relevant question might be, why did A and B not sort out their misunderstandings as they negotiated B's livelihood in the first place? From the last two chapters, both livelihood and role of assistance negotiations involve image bargains that are imbedded in preoccupation with achieving successful projects, for NGO fieldworkers, and access to NGO resources on the side of rural people. In the illustration above, B might consider that A will only assist when change expected from the coat is abstractly presented as 'warmth' while in specific sense the need is warmth in the bed and not outside the house. For A, providing warm coats for outdoor use is better because the change will be visible to B's neighbors as well as A's supporters. A can easily receive credit for providing good assistance, from people other than B, from these outdoor performances. In project design terms we could say that there are image-conflicts with regard to project purposes that could be achieved from project outputs. These image-conflicts are not easily noted because not all changes that are important to people are considered good livelihood changes by NGOs. The data that provided this understanding, discussed in this chapter, were generated following the set of 'topical' questions that focused on the understanding of change (see Figure 4.2).

The chapter starts with a presentation of the general setting in which image-conflicts regarding the purpose of assistance were analyzed. The setting is based on the discussions in the last two chapters and the methodological issues that I encountered in the generation of data on images of change. This setting then forms the framework within which the images of change formed by people in the two communities and NGOs were compared, and conflicts identified. It becomes apparent in this analysis that whereas NGOs focused on the achievement of material and non-material results by following specific activities, the people perceived changes in their livelihoods in different ways. There were image-conflicts on both material and non-material aspects of change. The chapter concludes with a summary of the areas of conflict regarding change.

Setting the Stage

Concomitant with situations where role conflicts were identified, the differences in the characterization and definition of people's livelihoods between NGOs and the people, forms the major premise for analysis of the nature of purpose conflicts. In chapter five, it was noted that the NGO's articulation of people's livelihoods was centered on 'means and ends' rationality. As for the people, the understanding of their livelihoods was a complex web of interrelated social, political and economic aspects of living. NGOs interpreted some of these aspects of living and relationships as problems, which to people themselves were part of their capital. With regard to the placement of NGO assistance in such a context of differences in the construction of livelihoods, were role conflicts, as discussed in the last chapter. These role conflicts were identified in both the conceptual and operational aspects of NGO assistance provision. Similarly, conceptual and operational aspects of assistance formed the premise for identifying purpose conflicts in data.

The Conceptual Basis for Purpose Conflicts

Conceptually, the understanding of change was in the form the material and non-material aspects of life of individuals, groups or communities. The material types of change were those changes that were tangible or could be quantified, while non-material changes were qualitatively described or quantified only in terms of defined categories. In the case of NGOs, the images that they formed of these two types of change were mostly stipulated together in the project design documents, for example:

> Decrease the prevalence of micro nutrient deficiencies (Vitamin A and iron) for mothers and under-five children (M).
> Improve nutritional status of mothers and under-five children by reducing the prevalence of major diseases (M).
> Increase local capacity for health and agriculture (NM).
> *Source*: Health and Nutrition Project Document (Mpira)

In this case, (M) represents the material or measurable aspects of the goals while (NM) represents the non-material changes. Fieldworkers mostly used concepts such as 'participation', 'capacity building', 'empowerment', 'equity' and 'sustainability' in their communication of non-material change. Although these concepts form the center of social development theory in literature, I sought to explore how fieldworkers could describe such concepts using real life examples. These descriptions, focusing on project activities, were then compared to descriptions of change that the people involved were articulating, from the same project activities. For NGOs, for example, people needed to carry out project activities in a participatory manner in order to achieve not only material change, such as increase in crop yields, but to become a more participatory community as well. I methodologically, therefore, focused on the project activities (both of the past and current) and noted how fieldworkers used these non-material concepts either as a 'means' or an 'end'. I then would look at how people were describing the performance of these activities in their own concepts rather than the NGO concepts, as 'empowerment'. It was in this process that I noted that fieldworkers had specific operational ways, which they believed would result in the achievement of both the material and non-material changes. This was how the operational premise to the understanding of purpose conflicts came into the analysis.

The Operational Basis for Purpose Conflicts

As noted above, these were the project operations, which when conducted were believed to result into change. In this case the non-material changes, which fieldworkers would not physically point at, would be described with confidence based upon the evidence of the performance of these activities. Since people were involved in the performance of these activities, as the primary actors, they also formed their images of their performance. In my analysis, the people's images of their performance in these project activities, was an important interface area. I am particularly, referring to the understanding of non-material changes because for material changes, such as the increase in the number of women attending literacy classes, there were often shared images. The differences were in the actual figures, with some cases where NGOs were mentioning higher figures than the people to whom they were referring were, and vice versa. The non-material aspects in these cases were, for instance, what this increase in attendance at a literacy school meant to the people and the assisting NGOs. If the attendance of literacy classes by the women, as a performance of a project activity was seen as empowerment, how were the women involved describing their attendance to literacy classes? In this case, my analysis of performance was with the process rather than isolated actions.

In this regard, the involvement of people in identifying problems on which the project would focus was, according to fieldworkers, the enhancement of the decision-making capacity of a community, as an aspect of empowerment and participation. This process initially involved everybody, or at least everybody in a community or village, was called for involvement in surveys or PRAs. However, only those people whose category of needs was selected were further organized in readiness for NGO assistance. For example, some communities were identified as lacking good school infrastructures for their children and hence were considered as 'the concerned' when it came to assistance on schools. In short, the people who were participating in various project activities were said to be concerned because the information gathered on their state of life showed that they were suffering in particular aspects of their livelihood. This was the image orientation on the part of fieldworkers, as one of them explained:

> Particular attention is paid to the state of women who bear the greatest burden of ill health and poor nutrition. Women from the beneficiary communities will not only benefit from increased coverage of health services, but even more importantly, from participation in the planning and design process, implementation, in village-level committees, and in monitoring of project activities.

In this case, women were placed in various forms of participation including decision-making, in planning and in implementation. However, they were placed there, not because they were concerned in that manner themselves. Instead, in the NGO's understanding of livelihoods, they fell into the category of people that required that kind of attention. This was also a reflection of the NGO agenda and performance pressures, as explained in chapter three. In this case, participation was centered on 'mobilizing their will' to identify themselves with their categories and then participate further in project activities (Srinivasan, 1990). In essence, the project design shaped the nature of participation, because from that point onwards, people had to work in accordance with the project system demands and other specific NGO requirements.

For the people, on the other hand, being mobilized 'for their will' was not difficult because their own identification was with the assistance rather than with the problems into which they were categorized by the NGOs. The kind of concepts that people used to describe this kind of involvement included, for example, 'registration' and 'attending NGO meetings'. The registration exercises and meetings were, according to the people, part of the preparatory processes necessary for their access to NGO assistance. In other words, in as far as people were concerned, in their images of assistance, these activities, which for NGOs were for their empowerment, served the purpose of facilitating the inflow of external resources. Furthermore, selecting some people out of the community meant qualifying them for access to this assistance. They were known by the relevant NGO names, such as 'The Red Cross Committee'. When the external NGO phased out the assistance, the people also stopped their participation and left the name, as reflected in Mateyu's account below.

Mateyu: I am a member of the PHC committee; in fact I am the chairman, but the committee is no longer functioning because the government is not putting emphasis on PHC now as they used to do. As a result there is no communication with the government. In the past, the government had a separate department, which was overseeing these PHC activities and our committee was reporting directly to that section within Ministry of Health. They used to call us for meetings time and again, they would also train us and when we come back home we would hold committee meetings and send our minutes to the government who were also responding accordingly. In such a situation correspondence was there and here in the village; we could go and meet village headmen and even address people concerning PHC activities.

FT: Could you not operate just within the village without being linked to the government?

Mateyu: We could do that, but everything has to have a path through which it will go to some point and when people are talking to the committee they expect things to go somewhere and not end up at the committee. If there is no outlet for that information people lose interest in it. It is just the same as having a parent at home, and his/her children are discussing. They want the elder one to report to the parents. If he/she does not, they stop discussing altogether. Discussing just for the sake of it is seen not to be beneficial. Malawi Council for the Handicapped (MACOHA) was working with volunteers in this community, which were also being supervised by our committee. They of course have some committees in some parts of this community but they are also not functioning now.

FT: What makes MACOHA committees not functional and yet the office still operates at district level?

Mateyu: The office is indeed there and the District Officer is also there but since he stopped visiting and reminding us, we can see that there is also weakness with MACOHA. This is the same with the church, where if the pastor is not visiting you, even services start to go down. The pastor has to remind people all the time.

FT: What about water committees?

Mateyu: Those are functioning because the PHC committee facilitated election of the Water Health Committees who were trained so that even though there is a weakness, those people have already been trained and also people know the goodness of water. They have been told that that water is theirs and they have to take care of it. They have to maintain these boreholes when they break down, otherwise where do they get the water?

FT: How different is that from the PHC committee?

Mateyu: In the PHC committee if we were to discuss problems, where do we take them to if there is no one available to assist us?

Therefore, in the case of Mateyu, the people were not just singled out as the involved but they also isolated the NGO activities from their normal activities. The criterion for this demarcation was the association of project activities with money-based NGO assistance. Once this special characteristic that they used to identify the external agency was over, the identity also ceased. Furthermore, I observed that when a new NGO came to their communities, people did not provide an account of similar programmes in which they were assisted by other external agencies in the past. Instead, for instance, new committees were formed for the new NGO's projects. In such a context, the people's description of change was associated with the NGO, which was assisting them at that particular time. This was change as seen in project terms rather than in the context of their own construction of livelihoods, as demonstrated later in this chapter. Mateyu's further explanations below make a good illustration of such descriptive images of change.

> *FT*: So what made it difficult for you to inform the NGO about this PHC committee, which was doing active work before government pulled out?
> *Mateyu*: Because the NGO survey already brought out these things and therefore we thought we should just follow what they want. The NGO will be here for a short time and pull out their assistance and so we need to concentrate on something that will change people's lives.
> *FT*: How is this change like?
> *Mateyu*: We should see how people would change according to the survey the NGO conducted because they even put down percentages on every problem. They put such figures on those parameters in agriculture, health and education and their task is to reduce on those percentages.

As Mateyu explains, the targeted percentages of change were based upon the NGO's understanding and the assistance offered, based on the initial representations of needs in the community. In essence, people were saying, 'since the NGO identified us into this category and this intensity of need, they also know what change is best in our livelihoods'. This shows, therefore, that it was NGOs that shaped the indicators of change in people's livelihoods, within the project language, rather than the people who were experiencing this change. This was an operational premise for purpose conflicts with NGOs because committees were, for NGOs, the major mechanisms for achieving capacity building, sustainability and empowerment. The case of Lwesya's account below illustrates this NGO operational premise.

> The thing that we actually do is that as much as possible we do not just have to have the structure put in place, whether schools, boreholes or roads; no, we make sure we do the capacity building, we want to build the capacity in the community. One of the main things is capacity building and again community empowerment is in finances. We believe you cannot empower a person without giving them the finances, he must be taking charge of the finances and then we will say you are now empowered because the scarcest resource is finances. So when we have approved for a project like a school, the community must account for the funds themselves. We do direct financing and the community is responsible for the procurement of both materials and even procurement of the skilled labor, the contractors. They will do the interviews of the different people

that might apply e.g. bricklayers and carpenters. They will choose from the list of people they have. The community decides the payment for the contractor. So it can be a project of up two million (Malawi Kwacha) but the community itself, using the project committee, will manage the whole of it. They keep their own stores ledger to control the flow of stocks. They maintain the cashbook so that they know how much money they have at the bank and how much money is released into the procurement of materials. They also maintain the petty cash book, which shows what the petty cash has been used for. We have both internal and external auditors who visit the projects. They previously used to audit projects quarterly, but this time they are doing it biannually, because it is quite a job, which would put some of our activities at a halt because we have so many projects. We also check their books from our office.

In essence, NGOs were doing all they could to ensure capacity building and community empowerment, despite the differences among the different NGOs. Where these project committees were not active, fieldworkers were very worried about the sustainability of projects. In order to ensure the continuity of project activities and good performance, committees were being trained, which was called 'capacity building'. Ultimately, this demonstrates the fact that people who were regarded by the NGOs as 'the concerned', and therefore to be involved in projects, were themselves identifying with concerns that were not stipulated in the project design. In other words, the project identification did not reflect the nature of the people's struggle in their livelihoods. This is understandable when we look at the fact that their livelihoods were more complex than the problems, which were being selected for project designing (see Figure 5.1). However, within this complexity, they had their own critical problems for which they sought solutions through access to external assistance. It is in this context that we find Mateyu above, explain that committees could continue working in the case of ongoing technical activities, like maintaining boreholes. This was because there was a tangible commodity, water, which was a critical need for the people. It is in this context that both the conceptual and operational bases of purpose conflicts, discussed above, were a useful starting point for this analysis. They pointed to the fact that although people used the NGO framework of change in the project context, they did not resign to the NGO's frameworks of understanding. They strategically used it to access assistance. This is where I turn in the next section, moving to a deeper analysis of purpose conflicts.

Purpose Conflicts on Change

This refers to image-conflicts that occurred with regard to images that NGOs and the people formed of the actual change that was or could result from NGO assistance. In a general sense, people spoke about this change in terms of physical relief, social relief, and financial relief. Physical relief included such change as reduction in walking distances to water sources or schools while social relief had to do with the pleasure of having modern facilities in their community. These modern facilities could be the new school buildings, roads and other new facilities that were built using NGO assistance. Lastly, financial relief was where people described their life in the context of NGO assistance as 'resting' from contributions of money or assets such as chickens to the community fund, in order to carry out community projects. All these descriptive views of change reflected their affirmative images of NGO assistance. There were some people, however, who saw themselves as 'getting poorer' in the context of NGO assistance. These people were mostly women and people in the very poor category, as they related their poverty to the time they spent doing community projects and attending group meetings in order to access loans. These loans were not profitable but only made them lose their assets in repaying the loan. As for one woman in Mpira, these loan procedures and demands from NGOs were 'dehumanizing' on their state of poverty.

Looking at these emergent descriptions of change in people's livelihoods, in relation to the images that people formed of the role of assistance, I observed that they were based mainly on the 'community' image of assistance. I suspected, therefore, that even in cases where they mentioned the different forms of relief from NGO assistance, they could harbor purpose conflicts of NGO assistance. Additionally, the 'getting poorer' image, suggested that the people concerned had images of change, which they expected from NGO assistance, that they did not fully disclose to me in their general descriptions. I, therefore, expected more issues from these people as well. Apparently, on the NGO side, it was clear that they were looking for more change than the people were articulating at this level of analysis. For example, whereas they were seeking to reduce walking distances to water sources, they were also aiming at reducing incidences of water borne diseases in the community. This meant that they were concerned with water, not only in terms of availability, but also in terms of quality. There was hence some kind of functionality[2] that NGOs formed of assistance, which needed to also be articulated on the side of the people, in order to get to their conflicts.

It was in this context that I found the use of the second topical question on change (see Figure 4.2) able to cause people to say whether the change in their livelihoods, which they formed in their minds, was being achieved or could be achieved or not. In essence, I was motivating them to look into the way they saw NGO assistance make an impact on their complex livelihoods, as discussed in chapter five. In this process, I noted that the images of change that people formed of the various forms of NGO assistance were solutions to the critical problems that they faced in their livelihoods. These critical problems were in the different dimensions of the people's physical, financial, spiritual, political and social-psychological aspects of life. What mattered to them at this point was whether they could access assistance, which could easily provide solutions to their critical problems. It was this understanding of critical problems and 'solutions' that was often different and conflicting with NGOs' construction of the same. In this case, people looked at particular forms of assistance in terms of availability, employment creation, cure and relationship to their socio-cultural practices. NGOs, on the other hand, looked more on technical quality of change, empowerment and preventive or investment characteristics of assistance.

Assistance Availability

In the case of assistance availability, people construed change primarily in terms of access to any form of assistance. For example, with loans, the primary issue was whether loans were available or not; similarly, if it was food, whether it was available or not. Change, in this case, was in terms of the extent to which people could access the form of assistance, which they saw as enabling them to meet their own purposes. These purposes were variable and situational and most people were not free to disclose them even during the research. This explained the difficulties for people to disclose these uses to NGOs in the cases where they were not in line with the NGO's frame of understanding change, because this was related to actual assistance from NGOs. In other words, they preferred to hide the actual uses as long as they succeeded to access assistance, which they could then use for their own purposes. It was through use of probes, sensitivity to discrepancies in the people's explanations of change and observing people's uses of assistance that I understood some of their actual uses of NGO assistance. As explained above, these uses were conflicting with the purposes that NGOs had of the same forms of assistance. I will illustrate these image-conflicts with an example of the construction of schools in the community,[3] with assistance from NGOs.

In the case of school construction, people stated that the purpose or change associated with their children going to school was avoiding ignorance. It was presented as such a critical problem that every parent wanted their children to escape from this state of life, despite parents themselves having failed to go to school in certain instances. Apparently, people found it difficult to express ignorance in simple words or examples, although it appeared obvious to them. Descriptively, however, they related ignorance to failing to know things, such as 'an ignorant person is not capable of getting employed'. This showed me that they were not necessarily looking at education in terms of 'wisdom' as stated in their descriptions of livelihoods (see page 80). I then noticed that people were critical of the results of the final class (standard eight) at their schools, even if achieving 'success' required that the teachers and children cheat in examinations in order to get selected, as noted in my field notes:

> People talked about schools with a reputation of high selection rates to secondary schools as having teachers with good passing skills. To this effect, a story was told of a headmaster in Zabwe who was evicted from a house because he could not cheat successfully during examinations and no one passed. The school was constructed with assistance from an NGO and people were angry because they wanted their labor contributions, through molding of bricks to result in good education for children. They indicated that all other headmasters had good techniques of getting their children selected to secondary school.

Therefore, despite understanding that selection to secondary schools was important, these reactions showed a purpose conflict with NGOs. Education, for NGOs, was a mechanism for the people's capacity building and empowerment. These changes were about literacy, which could enable people, especially women, to get into more of the decision-making strata in their societies and in the wider contexts. This, they expected, would make the women more effective in their different enterprises and in their own households. People, however, could not see any capacity building or empowerment in children who dropped off at a level less than secondary school. Their involvement in constructing schools was meaningless when their children were not getting selected and hence, they accordingly withdrew their contribution of labor to school construction activities. In my view, this shows that the availability of a school in these communities had a role of education but the purpose was that of selection to secondary school. NGOs on the other hand saw capacity building and empowerment through education in general and not limited to secondary school selection. This observation does not dismiss the necessity of literacy for human development as argued in literature but that in that context, it did not relate to the critical problems of the people. It is interesting to observe that Mukherjee and Benson's (2003) results of a recent study conducted on poverty in Malawi also show that returns on education in Malawi are lower in rural than urban areas. My further exploration as to what lay behind people's strong desire for secondary school selection was that it was seen to increase chances of access to formal employment.

Employment Creation

Employment was featured as one of the livelihood constraints in both Zabwe and Mpira, especially in Zabwe (see Figure 5.1). In eliciting meanings of employment and its links with education I focused on understanding how people were comparing the educated but unemployed youths with the educated employed. Most people quickly remarked to the effect that, 'Farming is for us who have failed to make it in education'. However, most of the youths were still living in the village after completing their secondary school education, complaining that they were failures in life despite their education. Their parents were also complaining of having spent so much money on education but their children were not getting employed. Therefore, the fact that farming was described, as an enterprise for those living in the village did not imply that employment was readily available for the youths who were educated. Instead, employment was seen as the most effective way for youths to improve their livelihoods, not only for themselves but also for their community. Education without employment was useless. There was, however, a difference in the nature of purpose conflicts that existed between Mpira and Zabwe communities in this regard. In Mpira community, for instance,

Jaki: The school is like a toilet, which you will need at some point in time. Whatever we will find in future will come while our children are well accommodated. That is what makes us get busy begging for some things now while we are constructing the school so that when a chance comes in future it will come while we are in good structures. So when World Vision and GTZ are assisting us they are assisting us saying let us do these things for them and let them find their own way to improve their lives.

Miriam: There are many things, which improve when children get educated. They can in future be presidents, members of parliament or ministers. If they become president or minister it means that all households in the whole area they come from will get assisted because they will be arguing for their area on development projects.

Choto: We have no boreholes in this area. If there was somebody educated coming from this area, they would be able to tell her/his friends that there is a lot of good land at Salaha but there is no water. They would inform a company responsible for water and they would come and see the area and do something about it. These children who are educated will have drawn assistance to this area. So education is not just about reading and writing but about being exposed to the wider community where the government would know them and listen to their requests.

With accounts such as in the three above, which were from one village headman and two ordinary community members, I formed the understanding that their concern for employment was also for investment, as was also the case of NGOs. However, it was more outward looking and hence their image of use of education was linked to selection to secondary schools and to formal employment. In the case of the people interviewed in Zabwe, however, the linkage to selection to secondary schools and to employment was of a different nature. In this case, they wanted NGO assistance to reflect that type of change within the project context and not as an impact for the future. For example, there were contentions over the posts of NGO fieldworker, particularly in Zabwe community. People in these positions had secondary school qualifications and hence similar to those of most youths in the community but all of the fieldworkers were from either other areas or districts in the country. This resulted in purpose conflicts in the community, as exemplified in the explanation below,

People are saying NGOs are not helping us because all benefits go elsewhere instead of coming to Zabwe, where the money was meant for use. The money goes to develop other areas where people are already developed and yet in Zabwe people are where they were. If we imagine all those field staff coming from Zabwe, would they fail to construct better houses in Zabwe and assist their relatives? They would also have educated their children. The example is the watchman who is working for the NGO and has now managed to construct a house. That is where NGOs have not helped us, by employing staff from elsewhere.

The employment implied in the Zabwe case in my view was 'waged' employment (Wield, 1992). Mukherjee and Benson (2003) explain this situation as being the result of very few 'remunerative economic opportunities' for educated youths in rural areas, rather than the problem of education *per se*. This study, however, even though NGO fieldworkers and officers understood education in projects to be offering opportunities in terms of self-employment in agricultural and trading business enterprises, the people did not make such a direct link. This nature of conflicts was also observed in the context of the people participating in the NGO projects in different forms. For example, training sessions were a major strategy that NGOs used for capacity building. This was done in order to enhance people's technical and management capacities in handling various project activities. As for the people, however, despite identifying themselves with the training needs, they had 'employment' images attached to these activities. This resulted in open conflicts in certain cases.

As this research was being conducted, for instance, one NGO organized a training session for selected goat farmers. These people had to be trained in goat management skills in order to ensure that they would successfully manage goats. These goats would be provided to them for nutrition and income generation, by the same NGO. The NGO prepared to give them food at lunchtime so that they could concentrate on the training. However, before the training commenced people demanded that they be provided with training allowances in cash and not food. Fieldworkers could not resolve the tension and referred to their bosses for assistance. When the NGO turned to the 'take it or leave it' approach, the people agreed and the training session was conducted, but with a lot of grumbling on the part of the community members. Fieldworkers were surprised and angry with the people, arguing that they were already beneficiaries of long-lasting assistance and should not demand payment for their access to the assistance.

The behavior of the people in this case, meant to fieldworkers that people were not genuinely interested in the project. When I interviewed the people who participated in this training session, however, they argued that they had the simple logic of asking the NGO to spend the exact money they spent on food to give them cash. This would enable them to use the money on what they wanted in their households. For fieldworkers, however, this would compromise sustainability of the project, as people would be used to receiving money for participating in their own development. They also said that it was against the policy of their organization to offer allowances to people. They were, instead, only providing cash allowances to people for their accommodation and food when training sessions were conducted in the township. As a result, I observed that people preferred holding any form of meeting or training in town rather than in their community. Fieldworkers often agreed to this compromise, in order to get project activities accomplished, because they had to avoid under-expenditures on their training budgets.

This same kind of orientation among the people and NGOs was also observed in the adult literacy classes for women and the conduct of the various committee members. In the adult literacy classes, I observed that instead of having women who had not been to school, these classes included women who said they had been to school in the past. They said that they had forgotten how to read and write. Some of them had completed their session and graduated but were still continuing, repeating the same lessons. They said that they were afraid of forgetting to read and write. However, as I probed into whether the changes that they were looking for were being realized through NGO assistance, their images of change emerged. A group of women informed me that fieldworkers said that they would be provided with home craft training materials in cookery and sewing if they continued to attend classes. They, however, were getting disappointed because this programme was not forthcoming. They favored home craft classes because they would easily get dresses, which they would sew for their children and also the food they would cook during the classes. They would have something to take home with them rather than just learning. Since this was not taking place, their friends in the community and their husbands were mocking them, saying that they were wasting their time.

For the NGOs adult literacy was for capacity building, in order to enable women to perform effectively in their enterprises. Fieldworkers indicated that they could mention other activities such as home management classes and loans to women, as future prospects of joining classes in order to encourage women. Otherwise, fieldworkers further indicated, they were just 'fringe benefits' but not the main change that NGOs were looking for. This, however, shows that for the people literacy training was the 'fringe benefit', while those other potential activities were the main prospects for change; hence they created conflicts. In other words, literacy came second (Rogers, 2000), assuming that they would be able to continue with classes if they managed to access the assistance that they critically wanted. Primarily, there was some kind of desperation in the community for assistance that would quickly meet their critical needs. According to fieldworkers, these people were focusing on the 'curative' rather than the investment or 'preventive' type of changes in their livelihoods. Preventive measures were, to fieldworkers, more sustainable than curative measures. In other words, projects were designed to provide curative assistance through a preventive approach. The best expression of this image came from health projects, where 'prevention' and 'cure' are commonly used technical terms. As concepts, however, they are also applicable to other contexts.

Cure before Prevention

The case of image-conflicts regarding Outreach Centers (or Clinic Centers) and nutrition projects easily emerged as good illustrations. Outreach centers, according to NGOs, were constructed in order to become central areas for immunization, growth monitoring, child health education and treatment of simple illnesses. For the people, however, it was the 'treatment of simple illnesses' aspect that caught their attention. According to their definition of their livelihood conditions, they saw themselves in a situation of many diseases, which could be cured if only they had access to drugs (see Figure 5.1). Since they did not have money, with problems of low crop production and low market prices, they expected assistance in the form of drugs. The local word being used for clinics was 'chipatala', which means hospital, although most people also knew that these were smaller in size, compared to the hospital at the district headquarters. Therefore, where there was a lack of drugs in the locality and at the district hospital, except where some types were being sold in the shops, the mention of clinics was easily associated with the opportunity to access some essential drugs, as one woman explained,

> They must have seen that we are in problems because our hospital is across the river, which is difficult to cross once it is full with water. With this clinic now, we will be getting our treatment from here. They have really assisted us. They are already assisting underweight children as of now.

The surprise, however, came when upon completion of construction of the center, all people could see were child immunizations and training of women in child-care for only one day per month. This happened because, for NGOs, curative assistance in the form of provision of drugs had to be done through a Drug-Revolving Loan (DRL) scheme. This was part of capacity building and would achieve sustainability, through organizing and cost recovery. Under this scheme Village Health Committees (VHCs) had to be instituted in the villages first and then trained in treatment of simple diseases. They would then be given start-up supplies of drugs, which people were expected to buy and the VHC to use the money to procure more drugs. The same was the case in villages where mosquito nets were provided, or to be provided to some villages, in order to reduce incidences of malaria.[4] In cases where people were not able to elect VHCs and get them trained, they were not allowed access to drugs or mosquito nets, which resulted into purpose conflicts.

For example, people, especially in Zabwe, saw entrusting of these drugs and funds to VHCs as problematic because, from their experience with projects in the past, such committees easily misused the money. As a result, they were very reluctant to elect these committees. Secondly, buying drugs would selectively favor those with money, and yet all of the people participated in constructing the Outreach Centers. This strategy, therefore, was seen as distracting their access to what they wanted in constructing these centers. In essence, they felt cheated and saw it as lack of commitment of NGO fieldworkers to address their problems as promised at the start of these projects. During the research process, I observed that most of these buildings were not cared for and left to termite attack. Most of them were actually only used once a month for the mobile under five clinic services that the government was rendering. This left most of the people in the community frustrated. Similar purpose conflicts existed in the case of nutrition projects, although they were manifested in different forms.

In this case, NGOs' understanding of the role of assistance was nutritional improvement especially among mothers and children, as discussed in the last chapter. The purpose in terms of change was reduction in the deficiency, for instance, of Vitamin A and iron, which would reduce protein-energy malnutrition and anaemia. With this understanding, community groups were provided with 'nutritionally rich foods' including different varieties of fruits, vegetables, soya beans and animals like guinea fowl. They were meant to grow these crops and include them in their food rations for the household. This was also a capacity building and sustainability strategy, because the NGOs were looking at long-term impacts of this assistance. Attached to this were IEC programs meant to bring changes in the traditional feeding and eating practices, which the NGOs saw as detrimental to the proper health of mothers and children. Among other activities, fieldworkers provided drama groups with information on nutrition and health problems of the community in relation to these traditional practices. The objective was to use the plays to tactfully stigmatize certain practices, using the safe 'speaking spaces' that theatre provides, so that people could change their traditional practices. This would, in turn, lead to improvement in the nutritional status of mothers and children.

However, from the images that people had of these types of project activities, it was income generation that was their central focus. In this case, income generation was to result from several routes, such as exchanging fruits or vegetables for maize (scientifically very low in Vitamin A and iron) or selling them for cash and buying household necessities. In essence, the people's consumption patterns were different from those that the NGOs formed of their assistance, and hence also not fitting into the NGOs' purposes of the projects. In the case of the IEC drama plays, most elders in Zabwe openly asked me as to where I was born. At the mention of my village they would say, 'Go and ask your parents about these things to see what they mean, every people have a culture'. A similar challenge was echoed at a project planning meeting, where government and NGO fieldworkers told the traditional leaders who were in attendance that the shortage of rainfall was because of the cutting down of trees. They said that instead of stopping the cutting down of trees, people were worshiping their ancestors in order to plead for rains. These resulted into an open conflict as traditional leaders defended the relevance of their traditional practices. In both cases, when I followed up with more probes, people argued that NGO fieldworkers have a job to do in order to be paid at the end of the month. Otherwise, where they come from, they also have their traditions.

This demonstrates the fact that in most cases, people were co-operative, in terms of giving appropriate answers to fieldworkers, in order to please them and have their access to NGO assistance. This assistance was in order to fulfill other purposes they already formed on their minds. They were negotiating with fieldworkers from a broad background of their experience in which they had critical problems to be addressed or cured. They were careful in their manoeuvring of negotiations with fieldworkers in order to find solutions to these problems. From this broad background of social and cultural experience, I also noted that even the nature of these critical problems was socially defined and so were the images that people formed of the purpose of NGO assistance.

Socially-defined Purposes

These socially defined purposes took different forms, depending on the nature of critical social problems that people were facing at a particular time. For instance, the youths and middle-aged men produced their crops and also grew vegetables as income generating activities for their household use. This, however, included participating in the *malipenga* dance during the dry season. When the time for this dance came, they would buy uniforms and other necessities and also invite their colleagues from other villages whom they would feed (see chapter five). This explains why traditional dances were seen as critical in Mpira. In Zabwe, on the other hand, the critical livelihood issue was taking care of relatives during funerals (see Figure 5.1). In such cases, people used proceeds from a food security programme, a loan and any other form of increase in assets, in order to meet their social necessities.

These social practices created purpose conflicts with NGO fieldworkers, because without sustained increases in food production or income, expectations of sustainability were not achieved. Such a community, as discussed, was said to require 'education'. Education in this case was seen as a way of getting a community to change their behavior, to become more supportive of project objectives. It was non-formal education for social change (Eade, 1997), but framed within project objectives. This would lead people to transform their social capital to forms that reflected economic viability of projects, as an indicator of sustainability. The transformation of 'capital' from one form to another is central in the pursuit for sustainable livelihoods. However, this analysis shows that such expectations of transformation are not based on the agency of the people concerned.

In the final analysis, therefore, the purpose conflicts that existed between the people and NGOs were based on the quality of assistance, in relation to the people's critical needs. These needs were not clearly articulated, as people negotiated with NGOs for assistance, hence were not reflected in the project design. NGOs on the other hand focused on merging material and non-material changes in people's livelihoods and hence focused upon forms of assistance utilization that reflected this frame of understanding. This, therefore, also explains why the actual purposes of the people could not be reflected in the project design because the people's primary orientation was to successfully access assistance. If they had based their negotiations on their genuine uses of assistance, they might not have been able to access NGO assistance.

Conclusion

This chapter has shown the areas in which there were image-conflicts between people and NGOs regarding change resulting from project interventions. In these areas, people saw changes in terms of solutions to their most critical needs, which were not articulated in the project design. In the context of these conflicting images of the purpose of assistance, any form of assistance was highly liable to misuse, in project objectives terms. This is because people saw assistance in terms of uses, which were different from the NGO purposes. The difference in the nature of image-conflicts between NGO and community interactions in Zabwe and Mpira reflected the differences observed in their definition of their condition of livelihoods. I do not explore these differences between Zabwe and Mpira further in this book because I was interested to see if the nature of image-conflicts could lead to understanding the nature of agency at the interface. The images of non-material change that NGOs had of assistance were in the form of the 'required' processes, which could bring about such change. In this case, the emphasis was on the managerial and technical aspects of these processes.

However, this chapter has shown that these processes were also conflicting with images people formed of them. This, ultimately, means that there were role conflicts regarding the quality of NGO assistance as it related to images of the expected or experienced change in people's livelihoods in both material and non-material terms. In the next chapter I reflect on how both NGOs and the people negotiated or dealt with image-conflicts, as observed in terms of the role and purpose of assistance. This is necessary in order to understand the nature of agency of NGOs and the people, in areas of assistance where these conflicts occurred so that we can discuss the practice of empowerment-based transformational development through projects. As discussed in chapter three, if we stop at establishing that there were role and purpose conflicts regarding NGO assistance, they suggest different agency but the nature of agency will not be understood.

Notes

1   As conceptualized in chapter three, both role performance and purpose or output values should be understood as socially constructed rather than in objective terms.

2   Sen (1997a) uses the idea of 'functionings' to conceptualize what people are able to do with goods or services.

3   There were other relevant experiences, such as men using loan capital obtained from NGOs to pay dowry for their wives immediately after accessing loans. In this case, loans were provided for increasing the levels of income, according to the goals of the programme. Interestingly, people in the community told me that they never disclosed these issues to NGOs because they were not acceptable.

4   There were examples of this cost recovery practice, which fieldworkers showed me but they were struggling with it in practice. On the one hand, this assistance was meant for the poor and yet cost recovery meant to them that they had to spend the money and recover it from the same activities so that they could use it again with other groups of people. They often settled for charging less than the actual cost of products and the transaction costs, which was mathematically not recovering all the costs. As a way of satisfying the demands of both sustainability and reaching the poor, they decided to link groups to government ministries so that the government could meet extra costs, after project phase-out. With cash budget problems, the government would find difficult to take such projects.

Chapter 8

Negotiation: the Politics of Managing Image-conflicts

Introduction

The analytical reflection on the research results in the last three chapters has shown that image-conflicts, which characterized the interactions between NGOs and the people, were in the main areas of choice, management and quality of NGO assistance. In this chapter, I will reflect on what was happening in these identified areas of image-conflicts. In other words, I will focus on what NGOs were doing in order to succeed in implementing projects, despite the underlying image-conflicts with the people. Similarly, how were people managing to work with NGOs in the context of these conflicts, where they had their own understanding of the purpose of assistance, often different from those that were stated in the project design documents? Both of these explicate the nature of engagement that NGOs and the people had at the interface, as conceptualized in chapter three. I am also interested in discussing the situation within the community because, as analyzed in the last two chapters, there were conflicting images among people of different characteristics from the same community. This suggests that there were differences in the nature of agency among the different people, within a particular community.

The discussion starts with a reflection on the conceptual and methodological understanding with which I approach the results from empirical data that have been presented and partially discussed in chapters five, six and seven. This is important because the various concepts that are used in this process, which include negotiation, power and politics have different meanings in different fields of application. It is from this premise that I elucidate on the nature of negotiations that characterized the choice, management and quality of NGO assistance. At the end of this chapter, I come out with a conceptual understanding of the design and implementation of social transformation projects, from a negotiation and agency position.

Conceptual and Methodological Premise

Images, Power and Politics: a Conceptual Relationship

It was conceptualized in chapter three that conflicting images of the role and purpose of assistance, occurring between NGOs and the people, provide an opportunity for an empirical understanding of the nature of the agency of the people in the specific NGO-assisted projects. At this point, looking at the nature of conflicts that were presented in the last three chapters, we can rightly conceptualize an interface of power dynamics as having characterized the interaction between NGOs and the people and within the communities themselves. In this case, the powerful exercised their power through their ability to validate and legitimize their images of assistance to the powerless. In other words, the interaction with the powerless produced a reshaped reality in which images of the powerless were subordinated (Epting et al. 1996; Leitner et al. 1996; Willutzki and Duda, 1996). Such an interpretation, however, also urges us to understand these interactions in the context of conflicts for their political characteristics (Lukes, 1974; Dowding, 1991).

In this connection, Dowding (1991) makes an interesting argument to the effect that, although not all conflicts are political, 'but all politics is conflictual and therefore any potentially conflictual act is potentially political (if other conditions obtain)' (p.50). In other words, conflicts are most likely to result into political action. This shows that it is possible for one actor to act in the genuine sense of achieving the benefit of the other. However, as long as the other interprets actions of the helper (interpretations over which the helper has no absolute control) as affecting his or her preferences or interests, he/she will tend to act politically. Since NGOs had no control over the people's interpretations, even with non-strategic actions, people were likely to take NGO actions as political and then act politically themselves. This should especially be the case in the context of the differences in priorities discussed in chapter six. It is necessary, therefore, to take political analysis of image conflicts between NGOs and the people, as central to our understanding of the nature of their negotiations. This also necessitates understanding interface interactions as negotiations.

Negotiation

The understanding that development projects are arenas of struggle and negotiation among the various actors involved is well known, in literature (Long and van der Ploeg, 1989, 2000; Scoones and Thompson, 1994; Elwert and Bierschenk, 1988). More recently, however, Leeuwis (2000) has made a compelling conceptual challenge against the theoretical and practical bases of participatory approaches to development, in favor of negotiation. He argues that, based on planning, decision-making and social learning models, participatory approaches fail to adequately deal with social conflicts and struggle over resources, despite acknowledging them. The contention here is that these approaches are based on 'communicative action' and yet the different stakeholders that are involved are not willing or able to communicate genuinely, as is being assumed. Furthermore, it is not possible to de-link power from participation in these contexts. Finally, he argues that participatory approaches are based on cognition as a motor for social change, ignoring other equally viable avenues of change, where cognitive change is the 'end' and not the 'means'. Looking at the nature of conflicts between NGOs and the people, in this study, I fail to conceive possibilities of smooth interactions in their negotiations. I, therefore, concur with Leeuwis's position.

However, several questions arise on the methodological approach that Leeuwis proposes for an alternative to participation based on communicative action. For example, how does one explore conflicts, select participants and secure their participation (which, according to Leeuwis are tasks at the preparation stage) without understanding what lies behind their conflicts? If we do so, we would be limited to managing observable conflicts, neglecting the subtle ones that are unobservable. They are disguised conflicts because of the power and political dynamics within the social context involved. On the other hand, from this research I have learnt that understanding what participant's images are and how they are used in the light of NGO assistance, appears to help the researcher to delve into these 'back stage' conflicts (Goffman, 1969). In a social context, the concept of interface is not limited in meaning to 'face to face encounters' but also includes the remote encounters, which have a bearing on the interface in which we are interested (Long, 2000). Therefore, similarly, we cannot limit the concept of negotiations, based on these interfaces, to observable and face-to-face dialogue. Instead, we have also to remain sensitive to the distant (observable and unobservable) negotiation strategies[1] with a bearing on the image conflicts identified.

Methodological Approach

Given that this research was focused on the images that people and NGOs formed of assistance, it was not designed to generate information specific to the nature of power and its role in negotiation of assistance in the cases studied. As a result, there was no question among the stated research questions that referred directly to the notion of power. However, the role of power was found to be critical as I continued to generate and analyze information on images on a daily basis. For both the people and NGO fieldworkers, I observed that there were discrepancies in their accounts that pointed to existence of power relations in their images and hence in their social environments. Phrases such as, 'we feared just by ourselves'[2] (see page 95) in relation to an interaction were pointers to such power-related actions. This meant that the actors were responding to the image they formed of each other, in the context of the other being more powerful. This, therefore, affected the nature of engagement they had with the particular actions in which they both were involved.

Approaching the study of power through 'discrepancies' was an approach that Gaventa (1980) used, with a focus on all three of Lukes's (1974) analytical dimensions of power. Shorthall (1992) also used the approach successfully in her study of power and powerlessness among Irish women farmers. Clegg (1989) strongly recommends this approach arguing that although based on Lukes's radical view of power, it avoids looking for 'real' interests as a measure of power. However, I consider this approach as prone to problems of creating a proper interpretive standpoint for the researcher and can lead to interpretive validity problems (Maxwell, 1992; Kabeer, 1998). For example, in Shorthall's (1992) study, the Irish widows were observed to be in direct control of their farms, playing roles that were played by their husbands beforehand. This was interpreted as an indication of a move to being more powerful; but we are not told whether these widows saw their situation as better than before in this context. Is it not a possibility that there were no other alternatives for these widows than taking control of the farm, which in a sense is just another 'fixed choice set' of the powerless (Dowding, 1996)?

Another problem with such a researcher's frame of reference of the power situation of a social context under study is that it can disguise cases, which do not follow the expected trend. For instance, although women are often regarded as oppressed, in certain cases they can be 'just as "patriarchal" as the patriarchs themselves' (Cornwall 1998, p.47). Such questions made me concentrate on images that people themselves had of their situation, basing my interpretation on their interpretation, and not just on observation of their actions. These actions could mean different things to the actors themselves. I took this position while being aware of the fact that, in literature, others have argued with the implication that, in certain situations, powerlessness cannot be understood from the actors themselves. For example, Kabeer (1999) has argued that power can emerge in the form of 'consent and complicity as well as through coercion and conflict'. Sen, similarly, argues that

> The hopeless underdog loses the courage to desire a better deal and learns to take pleasure in small mercies. The deprivations appear muffled and muted in the metric of utilities (Sen, 1997, p.512).

However, with this approach, of working through the images that people formed of their situation, pressures and influences were articulated either as direct forms of oppression, or as role conflicts they formed with those other actors within the society. In other words, it was clear that when they were negotiating from the other people's frames of reference, rather than from their own. The internal struggle could be seen from their behavior, as explained above. As a result, I was able to probe in various ways and came to a fair understanding of the nature of their engagement with NGOs or other community members in the context of NGO assistance. Therefore, I would not support the view that they were 'hopeless underdogs' in terms of images of their reality.

From this conceptual and methodological premise, in the following sections I reflect on the nature of negotiations that characterized the management of conflicts regarding the choice, management and quality of assistance. The power dimensions of the conflicts and their relationship to the activities, which were taking place in connection with those conflicts, reflected the strategies that the actors were using to advance their agency at the interface. It is also important to note that within the 'community' there were different forms of conflicts and hence power dynamics. In this connection, although I use conceptual categories such as the poor, committee members, women and traditional leaders, I use them in more general terms rather than suggesting that they were the only configurations. Furthermore, the data showed that there were other agencies, besides the ones on which the study was concentrated, which were interfacing significantly with both NGOs and the people under study (see Figure 8.1. below). For a proper drawing out of the themes emerging from the study, however, I concentrate on the NGO/Community interface, with reference to the wider contexts only in terms of implications that I perceive from my analysis of the data generated.

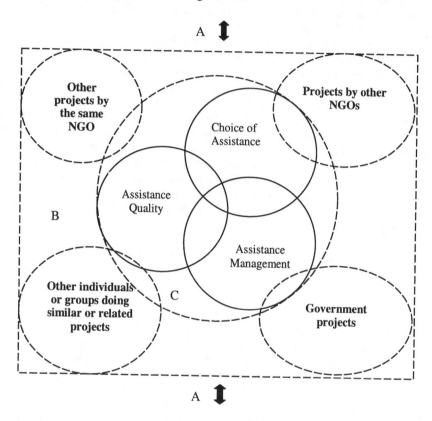

Figure 8.1 A conceptual map of the diversity of interfaces involved at the NGO/Community interactions

In the figure above, 'A' represents the wider environment within which projects studied were situated. Area 'B' represents a community in geographical terms, where each NGO provides assistance to different individuals and groups via projects. In the area of my study, each NGO was providing different forms of assistance through different projects, some of which were either similar to those that the government was supporting or people were doing on their own initiatives. At the same time, other NGOs were also working on the similar or related projects with the same community. Lastly, area 'C' stands for interface arenas that arise when an NGO and a community or group of people participate and negotiate for a particular project, such as a food security or small enterprise development project. Dotted lines signify the porosity of each boundary; no social interaction can be sealed-off from other interactions in the environment. In essence, any discussions that focus on the NGO/community interface should be understood in the context of the broader view that these interactions and interfaces imply. Such an understanding will enable us to avoid developing laboratory type of working frameworks that are practically irrelevant. In the following sections, I discuss the inner circle issues in more depth.

Negotiation: Choice of Assistance

The discussion on project appraisal, in chapter six, showed that there was a bargain of images in the decisions regarding the appropriate assistance for improving people's livelihoods with NGO assistance. This bargain was informed from image-conflicts of the role of NGO assistance in people's livelihoods. Negotiations between people and NGOs, for necessary assistance to form a project in this situation, were enacted through the interrelated processes of 'identification' and 'categorization'. This refers to the way both people and NGOs characterized themselves, and how they did the same to each other[3] (Jenkins, 2000). These processes were in turn mediated in the power of knowledge, resources and reputation, as understood from Dowding's (1992, 1996) conceptualization of power.

Power of Knowledge

The study results have shown that image-conflicts regarding the role of NGO assistance in people's livelihoods emerged in situations where people provided or shared information on their livelihood condition with NGOs. This 'sharing' was either directly or through traditional leaders. This process was where NGOs mapped out the intensity of the problems in the community and formed categories of 'the concerned' people based on their technical knowledge and that of the people, which was regarded as local knowledge. However, it has also been noted that people were not identifying genuinely with those categories, except to enable them to gain access to NGO assistance for use in their own purpose. This means that their local knowledge was selectively used to match with the expert knowledge in order to access assistance. On the one hand, this shows that NGOs indirectly exercised the power of their knowledge in defining both problems and solutions (Hobart, 1993; Escobar, 1999; White, 1999; Arce, 2000). They effectively acted on this power, as a form of agency in achieving their objectives.

On the other hand, however, the lack of genuine identities of the people and their selective use of local knowledge to access assistance suggests that they also effectively categorized NGOs, as part of their negotiation. Therefore, the NGO's discursive use of knowledge was of power only in situations where it fitted the categorization, which people made of NGOs. This should explain why people could not regard NGO training on its own as a form of assistance (see page 97). Similarly, people did not have conflicts with the idea of loan repayments, as a concept, except when loans were used as assistance from NGOs. This means that the role conflict was based on the categorization that people formed of NGOs, as different from the government and their colleagues. Therefore, the categorization process was based on the resonance between the two forms of image categorization, involving NGOs and the people. In this case, NGOs were using their technical knowledge while people were using their knowledge of NGOs in order to categorize the people and NGOs, respectively. As a result, this form of negotiation was also evident when observed from the use of the way people used NGO popularity or reputation in their choice of the different forms of assistance.

Popular Image/Reputation

NGO popularity or reputation was associated with images of 'Construction NGO' and 'Community assistance' (see page 96). These images were conflicting with the way in which the NGOs defined themselves and their assistance. However, they show us how people aligned their negotiations with the kind of assistance that a particular NGO was known to provide. The fact that they focused on 'availability', 'employment creation', 'cure' and 'socially-situated' purposes (chapter seven), means that they identified with their own problems rather than NGO problem categories. In essence, NGO categorization of the people was also effective for implementing projects as it resonated with the people's way of categorizing of NGOs. In this they categorized NGOs as providers of the assistance that could be used for purposes, which were different from those stipulated in the project design.

In this case, the power of 'reputation' or popularity of NGO was also only effective as it resonated with the way people, in their images of the role of NGO assistance, categorized these NGOs. As a result, it just mediated the actions of NGOs and the people at the interface. The case of fieldworkers using access to home craft classes or loans as 'fringe benefits' for encouraging women to attend literacy classes is a good example (see page 129). Women, in this case, attended classes because they had the image of NGO literacy classes leading to homecraft training sessions with provision of resources, which they could take home. This means that if resource prospects were not in their image of assistance, they could not have attended these classes. Their agency was in the form of ensuring access to resources and not achieving project objectives. In view of the situation of knowledge discussed above, this shows that the power of resources was another key mediator of these categorizations and identifications, as ways of negotiation.

Power of Resources

In the case of NGOs, the extra resources they provided had the 'incentive power' in enabling them to 'fill the gap' in their resources and move on to meet their livelihood objectives, as stated in the project design. The discussion above and the understanding that emerged in chapter seven (on understanding of change), however, show that these extra resources were incentives but not in the sense of filling the gap as construed by NGOs. This is because people concentrated on access and availability of NGO assistance and ended up using assistance on other purposes rather than those stated in the project design. In a way this also supports the argument made in chapter six that the involvement of people in establishing project priorities was not effective for developing the project focus as such. Instead, it was meant to facilitate access to resources for purposes, which already existed before these appraisal negotiations.

This form of negotiation, therefore, also shows that the power of resources was only evident in cases where the type of resource was supporting the purposes that both NGOs and the people had before face-to-face negotiations. The only difference with the power of knowledge and reputation could be in that resources are the underlying factor for the design and implementation of projects. In other words, projects naturally have to involve use of resources, and where external agencies are involved, they also bring in resources if their intervention has to be called a project. As a result, resources affect negotiations in many different ways. Since there are many uses to which they can be put, people always form images of the possibility of accessing them and improving their livelihoods somehow. As Menike, referring to the poor, points out,

> They don't reject or oppose them [*projects*] because, in their poverty, they feel some little benefit might eventually be derived from them (Menike, 1993, p.179).

However, it is this incentive power of resources that was associated with other forms of negotiation within the community, resulting in some people strategically accessing assistance, at the disadvantage of others. Since most people needed access to NGO resources for their own purposes, some people effectively reproduced the power of knowledge and reputation of NGOs within the community. This was done in order to fit the NGO expectations and succeeded in starting the project for their advantage. The case of the traditional leader, who effectively organized people for the goat project, based on his categorization of NGO assistance, is an example of this form of agency'. He changed the language from the provision of goats on loan to goats as 'free', when communicating to the members of his village and effectively enrolled as many people as the NGO wanted (see page 108). Similar negotiation strategies were used from the 'for the community' image, in order to cause the involvement of the very poor community members in projects that actually benefited the middle-poor and better off people. This shows how the concept of 'social capital', could be used to reinforce strategic negotiations within the community for the benefit of the powerful.

Ultimately, this shows how both NGOs and the people used categorizations and identities to bargain and ensure that projects were prepared and implemented, with minimal open conflicts. In this situation, the choice of assistance was not from nature of agency for enhancing the 'power within' and 'power to' for transformative change, because choices were framed within the expectation of the other actor. Otherwise as Dowding points out,

> Choice is only to be valued in itself in the sense that the process of choice or decision-making plays a part in our discovery of our own preferences (Dowding, 1992, p.301).

Therefore, the provision of extra resources does not necessarily fill the resource gap for people to improve their livelihoods as designed in a project. Instead, they become incentives for people to achieve their own purposes, which are different from the project and hence different from the providing NGO. Under the circumstances of strategic negotiations, this incentive situation usually ends up with some people choosing assistance they did not want. This is because other community members convince them of the possibility of accessing assistance for addressing their critical needs if they choose forms of assistance, which they know NGOs would accept. Participatory activities, such as PRA, do not show how different people are affected through such negotiation strategies. The assumption is that having made people participate, then they have chosen and decided according to what they wanted in the first place; neglecting the fact that this might not be the case with the people concerned.

However, the discussion has shown that the people were using different categorizations and identities as strategic mechanisms for convincing NGOs of their choices of assistance. This strategy was reproduced within the community to the disadvantage of others because of the incentive of extra resources. The same was the case with NGOs who, by categorizing people according to their needs while facilitating their choice of assistance, affected the people's set of alternatives from which they could choose. The categories formed were suggestive of the likely form of assistance from the NGO. For example, people could not expect water assistance from an NGO that put them under the low-income category. Therefore, people went ahead to choose assistance according to their given deprivation category, while focusing on access to NGO resources. This then shows that the forms of agency of the people and NGOs at the interface, with regard to choice of assistance, were in accordance with these categorizations and identities. In other words, the actions of the people, or where they were standing at the interface with NGOs, were dependent on the way they categorized the NGO in question and identified themselves and vice-versa.

In Figure 8.2 below, I have summarized the conceptual processes that help to see how choices come out in a negotiation context within a project. The figure illustrates how people and NGOs come into the negotiation sphere for choosing assistance. As conceptualized in chapter two (Figure2.1), this negotiation is in the form of participation and intervention. However, both NGOs and the people come in with different strategies, as mediated in the power of knowledge, resources and reputation. From this conceptual approach, we can also envisage a particular community or village as 'popular for participation' in certain forms of assistance. With this popularity, the community or village can draw in development assistance without much effort. Conversely, with unpopularity, even the most daring development agency might avoid assisting such a community.[4]

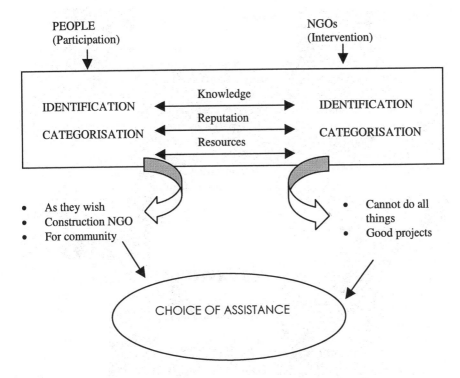

Figure 8.2 A conceptual overview of the process of choice of assistance

In the end, Figure 8.2 conceptualizes what emerges at the dialogue point for choosing assistance between NGOs and the people. At that point, there are images that emanate from identifications and categorizations, which effectively disguise the actual stand of both NGOs and the people. Their actual stand, which also motivates their actions, can only be understood when these images are analyzed for what they represent (in the rectangle). If this were to happen, we would expect a lot of open conflicts or withdrawal of participation from projects during project implementation. This is because we would expect that most of the impressions 'given' would give way to impressions 'given off'[5] (Goffman, 1969). In this case, people who were just enrolled into the projects of others in the first place would realize that the NGO's meanings of assistance are different from what was said at the beginning. Fieldworkers, on the other hand, would not continue with incentives as a way of offering NGO assistance because the business of the project is producing change in people's livelihoods and not offering performance incentives. In other words, NGOs would have to deliver on what they promised during initial project appraisal interactions with people. The discussion below, however, shows that this was not the reality in the cases studied. Whereas there were some open NGO-Community confrontations resulting from image-conflicts during project implementation, they were few because there were other ways of negotiation.

Negotiation: Assistance Management

In this section, I am primarily interested in discussing the nature of negotiations in situations of image-conflicts with regard to the handling of assistance. As presented in chapter six, these conflicts concerned conditions that NGOs set for providing assistance to the people against conditions that people also set. People set conditions (often not stated during open negotiations) as was fitting in their understanding of NGO assistance in their livelihoods. With image-conflicts occurring at the interface of these conditions, assistance was managed in the context of various forms of 'representations'.[6] In other words, it was through these representations that most of the latent conflicts did not come to the open and project implementation continued. These representations were enacted through the power signals of inclusiveness and control.

Inclusive Representations

This is where, in the communication and behavior of NGOs, people were given the impression of being part of the people who qualify for assistance, but the majority of these people were actually failing to access this assistance. They were failing because of the conditions that NGOs set for actual access to assistance, which were disguised in the image of inclusiveness at the start of projects. However, since the language of managing assistance was continually implying that people were part of the process, although the powerless could not access assistance during implementation, they kept participating. This was with the hope that they could still access assistance in some ways because they were part of the 'beneficiaries'. For example, when fieldworkers wrote people's names in their notebooks (registration) it had the representation of qualification for access to assistance according to the people (see page 108). Although most people failed to access assistance they continued to participate because their names were already on the assistance list. As was the case with categorizations and identifications, these representations of inclusion were replicated in some discursive ways within the community to the disadvantage of the powerless.

Within the community there were actors who were involved in managing assistance, both as representatives of others, mostly as committee members or traditional leaders, and as direct or potential beneficiaries themselves. Since NGO conditions for providing assistance were focused on the community or group rather than individuals, these actors used inclusive representations to organize either groups, or the whole community. In essence, it ensured access to resources for them as representatives and as members of some of these groups. As representatives, they had opportunities to attend training sessions during project implementation, where some NGOs provided allowances. In this context replicating images such as 'for the community', implying that assistance was good for the whole community, was instrumental for access. This representation was effective because the image of 'free' assistance, with which this assistance was also associated, affected the 'ownership legitimacy' of NGO assistance in the community (Sen, 1981). Giving a contemporary life example, Sen points out,

I own bread. Why is this ownership accepted? Because I got it by exchange through paying some money I owned. Why is this ownership of money accepted? Because I got it by selling a bamboo umbrella owned by me. Why is my ownership of the bamboo umbrella accepted? Because I made it with my own labour using some bamboo from my own land. Why is my ownership of land accepted? Because I inherited it from my father and so forth (Sen, 1981, p.1-2).

However, in this context, the provision of 'free' assistance meant that the 'I' became 'We' based on potential to receive from the NGO, rather than struggling together to produce the resource in question (example on pages 114 and 115). This created a 'free-rider' inclusiveness, which was effective for the quick organization of people, as the NGOs wanted. In this case, even people who were not necessarily facing the problems, for which assistance was provided, were included.

The inclusive representations in the management of assistance, therefore, were the cause for drawing people to participate in the projects when they might not have participated in that way without these representations. We could argue that for NGOs, this was helpful, in keeping with the pressure for results, as discussed in chapter three. Within the community, these inclusive representations also affected the nature of agency of some members negatively. There was 'adverse incorporation' of the poor into projects that were presented as existing for improving their livelihoods (Wood, 2001). The adversity comes in because of the opportunity cost of the time used to attend meetings, which were believed to facilitate the inflow of assistance. This time could have been spent working in their fields, or household chores, as was evident in the images of the very poor group (see page 104). Therefore, through these inclusive representations, the powerless assumed the images of the powerful, where they were contributing to objectives of these powerful people. This nature of agency becomes clearer when we consider control representations.

Control Representations

Whereas inclusive representations are used to impress on other social actors that they are part of the agenda or project in question, control representations are used to impress on them that they are in control of the process. With such representations, projects in which their stake is not clear can still be implemented, because they assume a share of power among those involved. In the real sense, control is still centralized in certain strategic interface points, facilitating the achievement of purposes of those who make the fundamental decisions. This understanding emerges from the study of image-conflicts that emerged in view of assistance management. In this case representations had an appearance of the people being in total control, as owners of the development process, according to the NGO's development ideology. However, the movement towards implementation, through preparation of project proposals, introduces different forms of NGO control. These controls frame the extent to which people are in control of the process. The account of Manfred, the fieldworker is a good illustration of this changing nature of control representations from NGOs (see page 91). These changing representations appear in the image-conflicts associated with the qualitative changes in people's livelihoods.

In the case of image-conflicts that were observed with non-material changes, we find that NGOs understood specific process activities as necessary for investing in people's capacities. For instance, for capacity building, committees had to be elected and trained in project management (enhancing their management skills) before assistance was provided. Similarly, for empowerment, NGOs devised specific ways of letting people perform so that they get empowered. In this case, we can also see how Lwesya starts from representations of people in control of finances in the form of decision-making and activities for empowerment. We then see the different forms of control from the NGO, which were also the basis for further funding of projects (see page 123). This therefore demonstrates the nature of agency of NGOs that was useful for facilitating movement towards project objectives.

Therefore, although control over resources or process of development is a strong indicator of the kind of agency that is empowering (Kabeer, 1999), a different picture appears when we see control in the light of the changing representations. In this case, control is situated in some other 'controls', beyond the actor's existing sphere of influence. This is true of any real life situation, because we cannot expect people to have a complete 'free will', which is individualism. However, where these external controls are not clear and hence not anticipated, it affects the exercise of decision-making, especially where this is tied to conditions for the inflow of resources. This should be the case, because the actor is not sure which decision might negatively affect the funding decisions on which he/she has no control. In the study, this was evident from image-conflicts that were observed with respect to NGO inconsistencies in the conditions of handling of assistance and the fieldworker's frequent reference to policy (see page 128). As one leader expressed it, 'they tell us it is policy and they change the way of doing things but we cannot sue them because we have nowhere to do that, we are uneducated!' These people's decision-making abilities were constrained, which implies that it was the agency of NGOs that shaped or 'framed' the participation of the people (Craig and Porter, 1997).

The kind of representations that were operational within the community, however, support the theory that agency can be constrained but not contained. Findings have clearly shown the control representations that the people found useful for facilitating their access to NGO resources. The study has shown that community members did not have problems with the formation of organizations that NGOs wanted for managing assistance. They, however, formed conflicting images of the role and purpose of these organizations. As a result these organizations could disband as soon as NGO assistance was over (see Mateyu's case, page 121). In this example, Mateyu compares the situation to the church and argues, 'If the pastor is not visiting you, even church services go down'. This means that the purpose of the church is linked to the pastor rather than to the purposes that members construe of the church in their lives. This just supports the understanding that representations of project control within the community were 'agentative' for accessing NGO resources rather than project purposes. Furthermore, these community-based organizations were more accountable to the NGOs than to the people they represented. As noted earlier, these organizations were even frequently called by the name of the NGO that was assisting and yet with role-conflicts, as shown in chapter six.

Looking at the nature of agency of the people and NGOs as regards assistance management, therefore, we notice that representations of inclusion and control were used to affect each other's engagements and actions. This affected the achievement of project objectives, especially with regard to transformational outcomes. However, the analysis of role conflicts, presented in chapter six showed that there were cases where these conflicts were not in terms of management of assistance *per se*. There were image-conflicts that had to do with the definition of assistance itself, in the context of NGOs. With such conflicts, we can only understand the nature of agency if we delve into how NGOs and the people were negotiating in the context of image-conflicts regarding change expected or experienced with assistance. As discussed in chapter seven, this had to do with quality of assistance.

Negotiation: Quality of Assistance

Looking at the image-conflicts that have been observed in the study in relation to the quality of assistance, it can be seen that they were negotiated through the meanings that people and NGOs formed of inputs and outputs for a specific project. In this case, these meanings informed the images they formed of the nature of change that would result from using specific project inputs to produce certain outputs. In which case, both inputs and outputs derived their value from this social-construction, rather than from their implicit values as could be technically defined. In other words, as Ingold rightly argues,

> Objects do not, in themselves, prescribe the nature or the context of their uses*; they become use values only through a system of signification which links each object to an idea or representation in the mind of a cultural subject.* This representation, furnished by an expectation of how the object will be used or consumed, *both precedes and motivates the act of its production* (Ingold, 1992, p.49, emphasis mine).

In this case resources, including money, labor, time and knowledge, were given value, in terms of the change they could potentially bring to a livelihood situation, by the cultural meanings that were held by both the NGOs and the people. In which case, image-conflicts were implicit in the value framework that both NGOs and the people brought to the inputs and outputs that were included in the project design. These outputs were meant to enable the achievement of specific project purposes or changes in people's livelihoods, also part of the project design. As evident in several ways in the study findings, these 'use-values' then formed the basis for strategic negotiations for both people and NGOs. In other words, because the actual uses of assistance could easily be disguised, some people could mention things for the purpose of ensuring that they have access to NGO assistance. In a real sense, however, they used assistance on other things. This was, therefore, their form of agency in negotiating assistance with NGOs, in terms of quality.

It was in this context that the findings show that NGOs looked at the available material possessions of the people as assets of the people of a certain value, while people saw them differently (see page 81). The same applied to the NGO's understanding of labor and time availability for local people, which was different from images people formed of these resources. This affected the design of projects because NGOs then decided which materials required procurement from funding in order to 'fill the gap', with a corresponding formation of images of the 'locally available resources'. This shows that NGOs negotiated image-conflicts regarding the quality of assistance through use-values of the different forms of assistance, as noted in their construction of these uses. In other words, they were use-values constructed, based on 'what goods can do for people', where the 'doing' is defined by NGOs themselves (Sen, 1997, p.510). This was the nature of agency of NGOs at the negotiation interface. In this context, the people had the nature of agency that was instrumental for access to assistance, as also noted in the sections above.

The people's construction of use-values was related to the critical needs, experiences and pressures that they were facing in their social, economic and political livelihoods, with aspects of 'subjective' realities (Edwards and Sen, 2000). However, knowing that the 'use-values' used at the interface with NGOs related to their command of resource inflows, people emphasized resource availability. With their emphasis on resource availability, people could easily fit into the NGO's technical understanding of project outputs. For example, that they needed to grow vegetables in order to improve their nutritional status was not difficult for them, and NGOs quickly agreed. However, people knew that they could sell the vegetables and gain some money for different purposes rather than food. As discussed in chapter seven, the emphasis on availability, rather than actual uses, has mostly been regarded as the appropriate approach to loan provision (Wright, 1999; Rutherford, 2000). The findings from this study, therefore, imply that the same understanding, of loan assistance, could be used in providing other forms of assistance as well, because this is the nature of agency of the people.

However, such an approach ignores the fact that within the community, this agency can be instrumental for the inclusion of most people into the projects by others. In my view, from analysis of data from this study, the forms of mediation that are operational in the community are in certain cases subtler than at the interface with NGOs. This is because people know each other very well and can use different forms of societal power to negotiate for their projects within the community. This will be seen as a 'community idea' at the interface with NGOs. For example, the idea of construction of school buildings first, before attending to other forms of poverty, was construed as a community view in Mpira (see page 126). In this case, the very poor people did not articulate change in that way but were effectively included in school projects and had to contribute their labor and time. These resources were vital aspects of their social power (Friedman, 1992). Therefore, there is need for analyzing 'availability' rather than just accepting it as a way to provide assistance to the poor, especially for public goods. The analysis in this case should focus on use-values as negotiated within the community. In other words, we should seek to understand the agency of the people, as 'situated agents' within their societies.

Ultimately, therefore, there were various forms of strategic negotiations between NGOs and the people regarding the choice, management and quality of assistance. In each case, these negotiations were mediated in such a way that image-conflicts were observed more in a latent than in an obvious sense. As a result, open confrontations were minimal, but still affecting the nature of agency of the people and NGOs. This agency was used through different forms of identification and categorization, different representations of inclusion and control and finally, use-values of products of NGO project activity. This supports the deconstructed understanding of the project design processes for achieving empowerment-based transformation, as discussed in chapter three. Therefore, it is important to re-conceptualize this design process in terms of what it might look like in a negotiation framework. This is where thinking in terms of the nature of agency of stakeholders is an important point of reference.

Project Design and Implementation: a Negotiation Framework

The foregoing analysis of has shown that interface image-conflicts were negotiated through categorizations and identifications, use-values and representations, for choice, quality and management of assistance, respectively. These negotiations were with regard to image-conflicts that occurred at interfaces, both between NGOs and the different communities and among different people within these communities. Therefore, a project design and implementation process that has to be improved from an understanding the nature of agency of the involved stakeholders has to place negotiation analysis as its central activity. It has to be conducted as NGOs develop an understanding of livelihoods in a community, as they define problems and propose appropriate interventions with the people and as they implement projects. In which case, the development of project goals will be informed from this process. The exact form this negotiation analysis would take cannot be predetermined, because it will depend on the specific contextual issues. In the next chapter, I have developed a theoretical framework that could inform this negotiation analysis.

As a way of conceptualizing outcomes and impacts from a negotiation framework, my view is that there is need to focus on the changing nature of image-conflicts and negotiations. These changes will be the ones to be monitored alongside improvements in the tangible aspects of people's livelihoods, such as the increase in people's income levels. For instance, instead of only emphasizing on solidarity of groups, often observed in terms of how members of the group work together, the focus will also be on the nature of image-conflicts in the group. For example, when forming a group for loans some people might join just to participate in the NGO's 'free' assistance. They would hence be in purpose conflict (which could manifest into open conflicts) with those who joined the group to take advantage of the synergy of joint action. Later on, however, we might find that they have recognized the group advantage but that, instead, the conflict has shifted to the prices of goods or services. The conflict on prices reflects on the operations of the group rather than on the very purpose or goal of belonging to that group. If such a group disbanded, the NGO will not see it as a failure of capacity building. Instead, fieldworkers will help the people to form other strategic alliances where they agree on prices for selling their goods.

In this case, the changing nature of negotiations among the actors implies changes in the way these actors negotiate image-conflicts, which is the changing nature of agency. For example, at the start of the project the nature of negotiation of image-conflicts by a group of powerless women could be by pretending to the NGO that they are in control (so that they get assisted). In the real sense, husbands are in control from the background, through tuning their nature of dialogue with NGOs in advance (while at their homes). It could also be that a group of men are using them as part of their group or committee in order to reflect 'gender sensitivity', which will likely please the assisting NGOs.[7] All these different situations can be understood through negotiation analysis, as discussed above. If these same women are later on noted, from another negotiation analysis, to be able to negotiate from their independently formed decisions with these NGOs and other actors, the nature of negotiations will have changed. This is a form of agency that is theoretically implied in the definitions of empowerment, participation and capacity building discussed in chapter two.

Finally, such a design process implies that we conceptualize the environment, in terms of how stakeholders within a project are interfacing and negotiating with factors outside management control. In this negotiation, these factors, which include both the natural and human factors, influence the project negotiations and are themselves influenced in different ways. The natural factors relate to naturally occurring changes such as climate, which could be seen differently by the people and NGOs. Human factors, on the other hand, pertain to structures and processes that are part of the social organization of human activity. These factors have been well stipulated in a livelihood framework (Carney, 1998; Bebbington, 1999; DFID, 1999), which relates very well to NGO approaches to livelihoods (see page 72). Learning from the study, we could conceptualize the aspect of 'influence and access', as mechanisms for transforming structures and processes[8] (DFID, 1999) from a negotiation point of view. In this case, 'influence and access' are constructed from the nature of agency of those stakeholders whose improvement of livelihoods, through expansion of assets and control, is sought.

The various structures and processes influencing the nature of agency in a particular project will be identified through the same interface analysis, with emphasis on the representations, use-values and categorizations that are being used. This approach is different from the 'roles and responsibilities' approach that is proposed for analyzing structures. It is also different from the 'participation approach', which has been conceptualized for analyzing livelihood processes (ibid., 1999). The interface analysis could be used to reveal the forms of negotiation outside the direct NGO/Community interface. This is where interfaces with the state and market come into the analysis. In the study, people in the two communities (see Figure 5.1) reflected most of these kinds of interfaces in their construction of livelihoods. For example, the prevalence of diseases was seen as due to lack of drugs in the government hospitals and lack of cash income to purchase these drugs from shops, or to pay for treatment in private hospitals. In this case, the government changed its financial controls to the cash budget system for its public operations, which was part of the World Bank influenced restructuring process. This restructuring process came with a representation of the State giving room for participation of the private sector in order to improve efficiency in the delivery of services.

In my view, understanding structures and processes from the interface approach, therefore, has the advantage of enabling NGOs to understand how people in a certain locality locate the different relations and influences to their livelihoods. NGOs would then understand how external representations, from the different pressures for performance and their own (see Figure 3.1), affect the people in a project. This is where the nature and effect of the donor development fashions, which do not have the positive impact that they claim to have on the people, could be understood (Mawdsley et al. 2002). NGOs would also understand how people perceive their role and purpose in supporting them in their struggle to face such negative situations. On the whole, I find this conceptualization of the project environment as enriching the design and implementation of transformational projects.

Conclusion

This chapter has shown that it is possible to gain understanding into the nature of agency at the interface between NGOs and the different communities and among the different people in these communities, in a project context. It has further been demonstrated that how these project specific interfaces are influenced, and influence interfaces outside the control of project management, can also be understood. These insights when taken together and put into the understanding of project objectives, progress indicators and the project environment, represent a paradigm shift in the theory of project designing and implementation. The paradigm shift has its main methodological premise on the ability to identify image-conflicts and understand how negotiations are mediated in these conflict situations. In doing so, we will have considered the spaces that are created for the poor in programs and projects, and how they construe those spaces (cf. Cornwall, 2002). Furthermore, we have paid attention to how the poor negotiate the achievement of their critical livelihood goals among other actors who are actively pursuing their agendas at the same program or project interface, including the intervening NGOs. In the next chapter, I discuss an image-sensitive approach to project designing and implementation, so as to share how I perceive the practicality of this conceptual thinking.

Notes

[1]　'We do negotiate even when we don't know that we are negotiating ... negotiation is not just some kind of compromise or "selling out" which people too easily understand it to be' (Bhabha, 1990: 216 cited in Tucker 1999 p.17).

[2]　In many instances these images of power relations were not understood from just one answer but a whole interaction, as the interviewee provided more information, through comparing and contrasting different life situations. I also had to be sensitive to changes in tone of voice and perhaps the interviewee looking down when speaking about a certain actor in relation to something else in the project. I did not quickly conclude that this was power, but it gave me clues as to where to ask more questions either immediately or later during the interaction, until I became convinced that I saw it the way people saw the issue, with their confirmation.

[3]　According to Jenkins (2000), the process by which social actors applies their frame of reference to characterize the other actors is 'categorization', while the meanings that the actors hold in characterizing who they are by themselves, is their 'identification'.

[4]　This could explain the situation where the number of development agencies working in Mpira was more than double the number that was working in Zabwe. As discussed in chapter one, Zabwe was less than 10 Kilometers from the district headquarters and was socio-economically poorer than Mpira. However, the results of this study have show that Zabwe community had more conflicts with NGOs than Mpira

[5]　Goffman (1969) refers to impressions as 'given' when actors assume roles that are expected by those watching them but then as time goes they start showing their true characters, thus give out impressions as 'given-off'. In other words, they cannot continue pretending.

[6]　According to Mohan (2001), representation stands for '... "speaking of" – constructing accounts and written texts – or it can mean "speaking for" – advocating and mediating' (page 157). In this context I use it for both meanings but I am mostly inclined to the former, where some actors strategically use the popular discourse in order to advance their purposes.

[7]　During my fieldwork I came across a bee-keeping group in Zabwe, which had eight members, four of which were women. In my analysis of their images of assistance, where belonging to the group was part of the issues discussed, it emerged that the four women were in the group but were not taking part in the group activities. The men said that these women were afraid of bees because they were women. In the interaction I came to know that these women were kept in the group for the sake of showing to visitors that the group included women. I later on further discovered that three of these women were wives of men in the group, who must have been coerced to be part of the group for external etiquette.

[8]　In DFID (1999), structures are defined as 'the hardware' including organizations of public and private nature, which formulate and enact policies, trade and provide services to the people. Processes are 'the software', showing how the operations and relationships among the structures and individuals in the provision or trading of their services (section 2.4).

Chapter 9

Towards an Image-sensitive Approach

Introduction

The main puzzle that I have tried to contend with in this thesis is why there is lack of clarity in the outcomes of NGO interventions aimed at social transformation, despite objectives that appear very promising for the poor. In the thesis introduction, I argued that the problem should be in that the way people and NGOs accommodate each other in a project, against the background of other influences that they both face, is not properly understood. This was then put into a research proposition in which theoretical gaps were identified, through conceptual debates that were advanced in chapters two and three. Looking at the findings from the empirical study and their implications on the design and implementation of social transformation projects, the initial argument for the research holds. This chapter focuses on the conceptualization of an image-sensitive approach, as a proposition for improving the design and implementation of the NGO's social transformation projects.

The chapter starts with a reflection on the initial research argument, based on the major insights from research findings. It is from this reflection that the need for an image-sensitive approach to the design and implementation of social transformation projects is justified, and its theoretical foundations are defined. I then go on to elucidate how this approach is conceptualized within the anthropological and participatory approaches to project designing. The chapter concludes with what I consider as the potential applications and limitations of the image-sensitive approach. On the whole, since this approach emanates from a single study, it should be treated as a thought provoking construction, requiring further research and debates.

Approach Justification

A proposal for a new approach is only justifiable to the extent that it fundamentally shifts or adds to approaches that are currently in use, in providing answers to the prevailing research puzzles or problems in practice. The findings of this study have shown that it is possible to analytically understand the accommodation process between people and NGOs in an NGO assisted project. This is possible through the development of an analytical approach that has an in-built sensitivity to interface image-conflicts and to how the different stakeholders involved negotiate them. The question then is not just about the 'stake' that stakeholders have in a project, but also about the way they are positioned and are acting in pursuit of that stake in relation to other stakeholders pursuing their stake through the same project. This then becomes the central part of designing and implementing transformational development projects.

In order to build this proposition, I largely draw on the findings of the research process, which have been discussed in chapters five, six, seven and eight. However, my past experience with NGO work in several Malawian communities also plays an important part. The experience helps me to always think of the real situations of life in rural communities. As a result, all theories and practices that I suggest are based on the image of an active project that is not just 'paved with good intentions' (Porter, Allen and Thompson, 1991). Instead, it takes into account the life situations of both NGOs and the people. This is important because, as Garber and Jenden (1993) point out,

> Development projects are about delivering resources, not about anthropological analysis; they have to deliver resources *and achieve definable outcomes and impacts from these resources* to exist (Garber and Jenden, 1993, p.68, italics mine).

Setting the Theoretical Premise

My construction of an image-sensitive[1] approach is that it is a way of conducting anthropological and/or participatory analysis in projects, which provides deliberate attention to the political interplay of different actor images that arise in the context of external assistance. This analytical ability is achieved by focusing on the way the different stakeholders negotiate image-conflicts in pursuit of their goals at the interface with others also pursuing their own goals, in view of external assistance. As such, it is primarily a mechanism for understanding the share that particular stakeholders have in the processes of designing and implementation of NGO assisted projects. The pertinent question to be kept in focus is; what is the nature of the share that a stakeholder takes in shaping the different aspects of this project? In other words, where do they stand in this process, which also involves various forms of actions by other actors? It is this aspect of the NGO/community relationship in a project that relates to empowerment-based transformation (details in chapter two and three). Since an image-sensitive approach is conceptualized within the anthropological and participatory practices that NGOs use for designing projects, I continually refer to these practices. In the process, I also attempt to make the contribution of the new approach clear.

The main theoretical premise of an image-sensitive approach is the negotiation of image-conflicts among the stakeholders in whom one is interested, in view of external assistance. The objective is to effectively use anthropological and participatory methods to identify these image-conflicts. Based on the known image-conflicts, we could devise appropriate negotiation strategies in order to create room for the particular stakeholder (e.g. women) to have their desired share in the shaping of the design and implementation of projects meant for them. This, however, does not mean that image-conflicts will deliberately be sustained.

Instead, the focus will be on the process of the resolution of these conflicts, rather than getting rid of the conflicts *per se*. In other words, questions of 'who' and 'how' conflicts are resolved will be central rather than going for forms of arbitration, which could impair the transforming agency of the people concerned. This is where this approach differs with the negotiation approaches proposed by proponents of negotiation approaches to development, such as Leeuwis (2000) and Warner (2001). These authors have a clear focus on conflicts, but their methodologies emphasize on building consensus in ways, which could disguise whose agency is behind 'the consensus'.

The theoretical proposition of an image-sensitive approach is developed based on the case of the community/NGO interface discussed in the study. Nevertheless, as the study has also shown, the other interface areas that have a bearing on the nature of interfaces in a particular project are also important.[2] They could form the next stage for developing and fine-tuning this approach. Considering the community/NGO interface, however, discussions in chapter eight point to the appropriate logic for developing the approach. In order to explain the nature of agency of actors in the choice of assistance, we have to focus our attention on the categorizations and identifications that actors use in order to negotiate their project priorities, with respect to the incoming assistance. For the quality of assistance we need to examine the 'use-values' of inputs and outputs that stakeholders form in the context of the assistance in question. Lastly, a focus on control and inclusive 'representations' will help to explain the nature of the engagement that actors have with regard to management of assistance. The problem however is; how does one methodologically look at these modes of negotiation of image-conflicts, in such cognitive forms? For example, how does one know which actor is identifying themselves with a certain category just to ensure access to a certain form of assistance, taking advantage over the other actors?

The discussion in chapter eight showed that people and fieldworkers negotiated interface image-conflicts in the form of language and behavior in different ways. For choice of assistance, they negotiated through image pre-dispositions. Regarding the management of assistance, people and NGOs negotiated through the different processes and ways of organizing for assistance. Lastly, in terms of quality of assistance, they articulated the use of particular project inputs to achieve certain outputs for achieving their livelihood purposes in different ways. Therefore, an analysis of pre-dispositional images, performance of project activities and conditions for providing/receiving assistance, should lead to the identification of image-conflicts. It should be possible with these identified image-conflicts to locate the specific aspects of NGO assistance where these conflicts occurred. This could then enable the analysis of how different actors negotiate these conflicts, especially the stakeholder of our interest (e.g. youths), their nature of agency. In this next section, therefore, I will demonstrate how these analytical processes could proceed as a consolidated approach, starting with the crucial aspect of identification of 'image-conflicts'.

Identification of Image-conflicts

This is a process of identifying conflicts in the images that different stakeholders form of particular forms of assistance. Some of these conflicts exist in disguised forms, because of their 'situatedness' in social constructs and power. Nevertheless, they can still be identified through active engagement with the actors involved. According to my experience with this study, there are two types of image-conflicts. The first type occurs when social actors within their own constructs, identify conflicts when reflecting on NGO assistance, in the context of other stakeholders. The second type of image-conflicts, are those where the social actor holds a particular meaning of NGO assistance, which is just different from that of the other actors. They also constitute conflicts, but in a potential sense, because they will only be revealed when situations arise where the actors perform in a particular act together. At that point, this second type of conflict becomes the first type because they will influence the nature of the actor's negotiations in a particular way. Therefore, they have to be included as components of the image-conflicts. It is from this theoretical framework that we could look at pre-dispositional images, images of performance of project activities and the conditions of assistance provision in order to identify image-conflicts.

Use of Image Pre-dispositions

These are the images that stakeholders form of the role and purpose of NGO assistance before face-to-face experiences and negotiations with NGOs and with each other. Learning from the study, these pre-dispositional images come from the development ideology that the NGO is using, the project design systems and the orientation of the individual fieldworkers. For these fieldworkers, it could also be because of their experience with other communities, where similar assistance was provided, and their distant experience of rural life. For the people, the study showed that pre-dispositional images were linked to the popular assistance, associated with specific NGOs. This could be because they, in the past, experienced projects that were similar to the one being proposed. It is also possible that they already have a similar project being implemented with assistance from another agency. As a result, the language and behavior of the people and fieldworkers is clad with a lot of such pre-dispositional images of the necessary forms of assistance to be chosen for a new project. Therefore, image-conflicts could effectively be identified through analysis of pre-dispositional images. In this case, PRA and social analysis activities can be conducted with the identification of both the existing and the potential image-conflicts in focus.

With an image-sensitive approach, NGO fieldworkers involved in project appraisal would have to focus their attention on how pre-dispositional image-conflicts emerge as they conduct PRAs or social analysis in a particular community. In such a situation, in their attendance at a village meeting or an organized PRA activity, fieldworkers should not assume that people do not have pre-dispositional images about NGO assistance. They will also not assume that mere explanation of which agencies they are, where they come from and how different they are from other agencies, although important, will have settled these pre-dispositional images. Instead, they will identify any conflicts within the groups or communities and with their pre-dispositions, as NGO representatives. Fieldworkers would have to look for the 'innovative speech'[3] of the poor in such meetings, including encounters that people have with them in order to identify these conflicts (Pottier, 1989). Image-conflicts could also be identified while conducting social analysis in the community. This is where fieldworkers carefully observe and listen to how people talk and behave in relating NGO projects to their own social, economic and political aspects of livelihoods. As discussed earlier in the study, they will have to be careful not to quickly jump to conclusions about these image-conflicts by actively checking what they are observing and hearing from the people.

The important operational principle for identifying image-conflicts is that, instead of pretending or assuming that these pre-dispositional images are not there or that somehow they can be avoided, we must start from acknowledging their existence. From that point we can then deliberately focus at the conflicts that arise at the various interface points in the process of designing projects, when certain pre-dispositional practices are in operation. Such sensitivity would enable fieldworkers to understand which and how the different stakeholders take their share in designing the project. Furthermore, the fieldworker's own pre-dispositional images that conflict with those of the people will also be identified and be made part of the analysis. From these different ways of focusing on pre-dispositional images of the people and NGOs, therefore, a broad range of image-conflicts could be identified. After identifying these image-conflicts, however, it will be noticed that still more image-conflicts emerge during project implementation. The study showed that it was during the performance of specific project activities (using specific inputs to produce outputs) that other image-conflicts emerged.

Use of Project Activities

This implies focusing on images that people form of the performance of different NGO assisted project activities in order to identify image-conflicts. As specific projects are implemented, both people and fieldworkers will talk and behave in accordance with their images of necessary inputs and outputs in the context of NGO assistance. Therefore, image-conflicts can be identified from this process. In the study, image-conflicts emerged in the people and fieldworker's accounts of the process of using specific forms of inputs to produce outputs. The use of inputs involved resources from both NGOs and the people and they formed specific images of which inputs constituted 'assistance' (see page 99). In my view, these image-conflicts can also be identified through PRA and social analysis. In this way, instead of waiting for the intended project to start, the project appraisal period could also be useful in identifying these image-conflicts.

During the project appraisal period, the analysis could be built into PRA or social analysis activities as part of understanding the past projects or those that are currently being implemented with assistance from other NGOs. This would be more useful where project activities are similar to those that are likely to take place in the new project with assistance from the new NGO. As people and NGOs talk about these old or ongoing project activities and also through their actions, which can be observed, image-conflicts relating to the performance of these activities will be identified. However, we have to consider the fact that the incoming NGO is different, which could create a different set of image-conflicts. Furthermore, there are changes in the community in the context of their interfaces with the local and wider socio-economic and political environments. This means that the context is different and, therefore, we cannot predetermine which image-conflicts could emerge with the new NGO or new project. We have to compare the images people form of assistance in the context of project activities with the incoming NGO or the new project. This is where, as Mosse (1998) rightly argues, starting with small levels of assistance, before scaling up, will be necessary.[4]

The kind of analysis that focuses on the use of inputs to produce outputs will assist in identifying image-conflicts that relate to the quality of NGO assistance. However, the study further showed that image-conflicts occurred in the way assistance from NGOs was managed as it flowed to meet particular needs among the people. These conflicts also significantly affected the nature of agency of the stakeholders in the projects. This was evident in the way people and NGOs behaved and talked about assistance in terms of the conditions they set for managing assistance. Therefore, we could analyze images that people and NGOs form of assistance in terms of conditions for managing assistance and identify image-conflicts.

Analysis of Conditions for Managing Assistance

It is clear from the study that assistance to communities is not just given or just received. There are set conditions, which although not fully discussed during project appraisal, take effect when implementation starts. For NGOs, it is part of their development ideology and systems for proper relationship to their donors; for example, the fact that loans should be provided only to people who are in a group because it is part of capacity building. Interestingly, the people also had set conditions for the way assistance from NGO needed to be provided if it was to be called assistance. The interface of such conditions from NGOs and the people resulted in image-conflicts, which were identified in the study. Therefore, we will effectively identify image-conflicts if we can focus on images that the stakeholders' form of conditions that NGOs set for providing assistance. My opinion is that, in terms of methods, it is also possible to use PRA activities and social analysis to identify these image-conflicts.

With PRA practices we could map out community configurations, through activities such as social mapping and Venn diagrams and show the relationships among the different forms of community management of projects alongside traditional structures. In the process of mapping out these structures or the actual process of deciding on the way in which projects should be managed with the people, people will articulate what they see of the different conditions NGOs set for providing assistance. Within this dialogue, image-conflicts of these different conditions will emerge from both NGOs and the people. However, in view of the possible 'depolitisation' of PRA activities (Stadler, 1995; Mosse, 1995), we would need to follow-up this analysis with social analysis activities. These would enable us to explore the nature of social relations among the project, traditional and other structures in the community as projects are being implemented (Mosse, 1995, 1998). However, relying purely on participant observation could lead to wrong judgments on meanings that people form of these structures because of externality problems (see page 38). Therefore, we would have to actively check our observations. This will include active interviewing of some members of the community.

In the final analysis, through use of pre-dispositional images, project activities and conditions set for assistance, we could identify the different forms of image-conflicts regarding a particular project, which is being designed. This theoretical proposition could be put into practice within the PRA and social analysis methods, now focused at identifying image-conflicts. If we stop at this point, however, we will have identified different forms of image-conflicts but not known how the actors involved are affected by these conflicts, in their agency. Since the objective is to understand the nature of agency of stakeholders with whom we are interested, so that something can be done in the way of designing the project better, the analysis needs to show the nature of that agency. This occurs through negotiation analysis. For this analysis to be possible, however, we need to identify the specific aspects of assistance where these image-conflicts occurred. I conceptualize these specific areas of assistance, where conflicts emerge, as 'interface-fields'.

Identification of Interface-fields

The study has shown that, although image-conflicts were identified in pre-dispositional images, project activities and conditions for managing assistance, it was not every pre-dispositional image that formed conflicts. Similarly, not all project activities and not all conditions of providing assistance to the people were associated with image-conflicts. Instead, these image-conflicts were associated with specific aspects of the process of project designing and implementation of projects. In this case, it was the specific area of 'priorities' that was the major issue with pre-dispositional images. In other words, it was in the process of 'coming-up with the priorities' of the people that image-conflicts with the people were identified. Otherwise, there were no image-conflicts identified in association with the holding of community meetings, in preparation for projects. As a result people attended these meetings when called upon by their traditional leaders, in response to requests from an NGO. Similarly, it was with particular ways of using inputs and particular kinds of inputs and outputs that conflicts emerged and not every other project input and output. The same was the case with conditions for managing assistance.

From this understanding, my theoretical position is that the process of identifying the specific areas of NGO assistance, where the identified image-conflicts occur, is necessary. This analysis will enable us to put these image-conflicts into a definable context rather than make generalizations covering all situations. With the identified interface fields on which to focus, the analysis will be faster and more useful for the project design process, where specificity adds to the quality of the design. Furthermore, it should be easier to take the analysis further to understand what the different actors were doing in those areas of conflicts. This is necessary because we have an interest in understanding how different actors are negotiating these image-conflicts, which shows us the nature of their agency. I conceptualize this analytical process as negotiation analysis.

Negotiation Analysis

This is a process of analyzing interface situations where image-conflicts between or among different stakeholders occur in order to establish what these actors are doing about these conflicts. As established in chapter three, the actions of stakeholders in those interface fields in the context of these conflicts show the nature of their agency. It is important to note that this does not foretell of the actions of the stakeholders, in terms of resolving these image-conflicts, but shows how they are acting in some ways despite image-conflicts. Some of the stakeholders might be strategically sustaining these image-conflicts; especially where they know that the other stakeholders do not fully understand the objectives of the project.[5] This is where the analysis emerges with categorizations and identifications, use-values and representations, which ultimately show the nature of agency of the different stakeholders involved in a project. Essentially, they are also part of the language and discourse that the different stakeholders use at the interface with others in a project. It is for the purpose of developing a proper understanding of these categorizations, use-values and representations that we have to approach them from image pre-dispositions, ways of defining project activities and the setting of conditions for managing assistance.

An image-sensitive approach, therefore, is based on the three aspects of analysis, which include the identification of image-conflicts, identification of interface fields and negotiation analysis. These forms of analysis cannot effectively be de-linked from each other into logistical steps. Instead, they are logical ways of organizing our thought processes while designing and implementing projects. In which case, the project manager or fieldworker should be thinking about identifying image-conflicts while alert to the identification of the specific areas of assistance where they are occurring and how they are being negotiated. The resulting picture, which should emerge, is the understanding of where the stakeholder of interest in the project stands in that aspect of project designing under consideration. This analytical logic has been summarized in Table 9.1 below.

Table 9.1(a) A conceptual map of the nature of analysis that will inform an image-sensitive approach

Type of Analysis	Major Categories of Image -conflicts		
Identification of Image-conflicts	Pre-dispositions	Project activities	Conditions of assistance
↓	↓	↓	↓
Identification of interface fields	Priorities	Inputs and outputs	Organizations
↓	↓	↓	↓
Negotiation analysis	Identifications/ Categorizations	Use-values	Representations

The first column in Table 9.1(a) above shows the main theoretical aspects of an image-sensitive approach to project designing and implementation of social transformation projects (hence in thick headed arrows). The other columns show the possible categories of image-conflicts that could emerge when an image-sensitive approach is used in a community such as those I studied in Malawi. They are also theoretical categories, and a different combination might emerge when the approach is used in another community. As theoretical categories, they are 'containers' of different forms of image-conflicts that could arise where different NGOs and communities, or people within the same community, are involved. This means that the nature of pre-dispositional images in one community might be different from those that could be found in another community, but they are all pre-dispositional images. The other important part to bear in mind in order to practice using this approach is the conceptualization of the use of participatory and anthropological methods. I summarize the way PRA and social analysis, conducted from an image-sensitive approach could be conceptualized in Table 9.1(b) below.

Table 9.1(b) A comparative conceptual view of PRA and social analysis when conducted conventionally and when conducted from an image-sensitive approach

Critical Interface Areas	PRA (conventional)	Social Analysis (conventional)	With an Image-sensitive Approach
Choice of assistance (with conflicting identifications and categorizations)	Let the poor analyze their livelihoods and devise appropriate interventions)	Social-cultural relevance of people's problems and priorities	Looking for image-conflicts in the participation of different stakeholders
Management of assistance (with conflicting inclusive and control representations)	Community choices of organizations (let people chose their own groups and representatives for the committees)	Social power-relations observed in relation to traditional structures and culture.	Locating image-conflicts in the conditions for assistance provision, which stakeholders are mentioning
Quality of assistance (with conflicting use-values)	Composite values of resources (the consensus views of the people on what resources they use and why)	Observed socially-constructed values (the way people use the materials in a project in their cultural life)	Identifying image-conflicts from the way stakeholders look at the performance of project activities

In Table 9.1(b) above, the first column shows the critical interface areas, which are the general areas in the NGO/Community interaction where conflicts in the images that stakeholders form of particular forms of assistance occur. Some of these conflicts exist in disguised forms, because of their 'situatedness' in social constructs and power. In order to identify them, we have to compare images of assistance as formed by the different stakeholders involved. This is how in the critical areas of choice, quality and management of assistance were identified. They are presented here as areas, which project managers would have to consider when conducting PRAs or social analysis as they design and implement projects. In essence, they will provide the working framework for the project design and implementation processes. The other two columns that follow show the nature of concerns, which the conventional way of conducting PRA and social analysis would have (explanations or concerns of each are in italics). My emphasis here is on demonstrating that while yielding valuable information for the project design process, they would fail to show the conflicts in the identifications and categorizations between people and NGOs and among the people themselves, inclusive representations and use-values of resources being mentioned. Image-conflicts in these areas are always implicit in the interactions between NGOs and the people, while they are conducting these exercises but they are not easily identified.

The last column, however, shows the concerns, which the PRA or social analysis activities conducted in a project community from an image-sensitive approach would also focus on. As discussed above, it is this information that will form the entry point into the analysis for interface fields and then negotiations so that the stakeholder's position (nature of agency) in these areas of assistance is understood. This proposition clearly shows that the way project managers manage the process will be crucial for the successful use of information in terms of the actual improvement of the design and implementation of social transformation projects.

Process Management

Process management is necessary because, as discussed earlier, these image-conflicts will not initially emerge as expected, because of the nature of image bargains that characterize the project appraisal, where choice of assistance is the main agenda. Secondly, even experiences with similar projects in the past cannot predetermine the nature of image-conflicts that could characterize the new projects. Most of these image-conflicts will, therefore, be seen when projects are in operation. The design and implementation approaches might require changing in order to ensure that project inputs are properly used to achieve the desired outputs. Changes will also be necessary in order to ensure that project outputs achieve the desired outcomes or purposes. The two aspects of the project design process are referred to as 'efficiency' and 'effectiveness', respectively (Fowler, 1997; Akroyd, 1999). In this case, both efficiency and effectiveness of the project intervention will improve incrementally as managers commit themselves to understand 'processes' rather than being limited to the 'means' and 'ends' thinking.

Potentials, Conditions and Limitations

In the discussion above I have concentrated on the grassroots practice. However, with this approach, there is potential to improve the effectiveness of NGO negotiations at other interfaces that have a bearing on the community or group they are assisting. The basic way to start conceptualizing these possibilities is by considering other interfaces as shown in Figure 8.1. In this case, we can think in terms of other NGOs working in the same community, or having a distant relationship to development activities in the community. The government is also likely to be supporting different development programs in the community through its various departments. We can also include other groups within the community, which are managing their own activities that are similar or have connections with those to which the NGO is providing assistance. We can then think in wider terms, to consider other distant activities, decisions, and inter-linkages that have a bearing on what is happening in the community.

An image-sensitive approach will help the NGO to analyze what is happening at these other interfaces strategically, so that appropriate action can be taken. I am thinking of appropriate action in negotiation terms, which means that the NGO will understand how actors at these interfaces are pursuing their objectives and affecting people whom the NGO is assisting. This understanding will help them either to pursue face-to-face negotiations with these other actors, or to build the capacity of the people to effectively take advantage of these interfaces. For example, if it is a business interface, should they develop alliances with more experienced middlemen or purchase storage facilities for their products, to be held until supplies from other businessmen have been depleted? In this case, their ability to analyze interface conflicts will be a political leverage for persuading the other actors to adopt policies that will support genuine poverty-focused strategies (Tembo, 2001b).

The possible limitation to an image-sensitive approach is that it will work best with NGO staff that are committed to reflexivity as a way of managing development. This is to understand themselves, doubt their actions and perceptions as they analyze other people's images of reality. However, as Chambers (1997a) has argued, the best reflexivity is personal commitment to change and to know that there is mutual benefit to the process. Secondly, it can best be done from a commitment to participant observation rather than one that only relies on interviewing. This implies more time and money has to be spent at these interfaces in order to understand the images and critical interface areas. NGOs that are impatient for results and consider budgets purely in terms of quantitative deliverables might find this approach not acceptable.

Furthermore, I foresee the problem of lack of a built-in mechanism to protect the design process from use by some agencies to 'market' their ventures, as one of the weaknesses of the approach. In this case, they will know what the people want and yet develop strategies for winning them over to projects that are more for the agency's benefit than that of the people. However, such weaknesses point to the continuous challenge of dealing with the 'person' as a facilitator and as a social actor with personal objectives at the same time. Perhaps this is the reason that Chambers (1995b) has talked about 'the primacy of the personal'; against which we can hardly insulate ourselves.

Conclusion

In this chapter, I have proposed the image-sensitive approach to projects designed for social transformation, based on my research findings. The approach is pivoted on three interrelated analytical phases including the identification of image-conflicts, identification of interface fields and conducting a negotiation analysis. For these analytical processes to work well, project managers need to learn to manage projects as 'process', where the project design improves incrementally. Furthermore, the image-sensitive approach is a presentation or principles rather than a 'tool box', emphasizing thought processes that enable the person in action to ask the next questions and reflect on their own images of reality. In the next chapter, which forms the conclusion for this book, I summarize the major research outputs, based on the initial research questions. I also provide my key learning points and make suggestions for improving future practice in transformational development.

Notes

1 My understanding of 'sensitivity' in this case is that of 'having insight into and being able to give meaning to the events in data' (Strauss and Corbin, 1998, p.24). My emphasis here is on gaining this meaning as construed at the data source.

2 The mapping of the different interfaces that were identified in the study is shown in Figure 8.1.

3 Pottier (1989) distinguishes between 'set speech', which is ordered according to the norms of the group or society and often used by those in authority to exercise their power, and 'innovative speech', which the powerless in those situations use in order to communicate their true interests.

4 In the cases studied, there was an NGO, which had start-up funds (in what they called a 'seed project') for the first year or two. The seed project was meant for proper designing of the main projects.

5 We should also always bear in mind that the NGO itself is also among these stakeholders. Fieldworkers may act strategically in order to proceed with implementation of the project and use the project budget, as reflection on their performance.

Chapter 10

Conclusion

Introduction

In this chapter, I focus on the major issues that have been discussed in this book, reflecting mainly on how the study, on which the book is based, answered the initial research questions. This is followed by recommendations for NGO development policy and practice that can be drawn from the study. I then discuss the limitations of the study experience and conclude with areas that will require further research.

Major Outputs and Implications

The discussion in various chapters of this book point to the fact that the accommodation process, involving people and NGOs in a project, is mediated through images that both NGOs and the people form of each other and of the specific forms of assistance involved in the interaction. This process entails negotiation, as both NGOs and the people seek to achieve their (often not fully disclosed) purposes of participation in projects. The different forms of negotiation fundamentally affect the nature of agency that both NGOs and the people have at the various interfaces, which are created in a project. It is the nature of agency that affects the achievement of 'transformative' goals of a project, with respect a particular category of people on whom the NGO is focusing, such as women. To this effect, I have proposed an image sensitive approach, which could enable NGOs to understand the nature agency of the different actors (including themselves) at the interface.

The image-sensitive approach involves identifying image-conflicts and turning them into opportunities for understanding how social actors engage with each other in the different aspects of negotiation interfaces. This approach, therefore, forms another way of understanding participation of the people in projects, through which the local politics can be managed, in order to create room for the poor. In this case, the ways in which people interact with each other, their environment (external influences) and specific forms NGO assistance, will form the substance for understanding people. This is different from a situation where it is a list of 'needs' that drives action, in projects. In this case, the focus is on the value framework within which these needs are defined and the understanding of change that is construed, in view of external assistance. Accordingly, it provides a way of understanding development agencies, in this case NGOs, as not just intervening into the people's agenda, but also acting as interface negotiators, with their own cargo of knowledge and values.

Such a research output, although discussed primarily in terms of what happens at the community interface, has significant implications on how we could pursue the way in which the 'global and local transformations' are mediated; producing diverse responses within a rural community (Long, 2000). The case of the power of external discourses and cultures of development, and the detrimental effects they could have on the poor, in connection with development NGOs, has been made in literature (Tvedt, 1998; Mawdsley et al. 2002). In this connection, however, the study has pointed to specific ways through which such forms of knowledge and values are mediated as they work their way to specific rural communities in the world. The idea of the power of identification and categorization, representations, and resource use-values that have emerged from this study, provide some specific issues to look at when pursuing such realities.

This is where I also find the relevance of such an analysis to understanding the fourth position role of NGOs, as is being conceptualized at the moment (see chapter one). In this case, 'the negotiation', 'validation' and 'innovation' roles of NGOs will be based on the understanding of how other actors are pursuing their objectives. Otherwise, as argued elsewhere, NGOs could become agents of images of the state and the market at the interface with the people and enhance the 'new imperialism' (Tembo, 2001b). The new imperialism is based on 'cultural and ecological invasion' rather than direct political control. I am of this opinion because the future of NGOs has been conceptualized as in behaving as the state in 'pursuing public agenda', markets in 'surplus generation' and civil society in pursuit of value-based roles (Fowler, 2000b, p.598). However, this presupposes that NGOs would be in control of their behavior as they interface with these spheres. In view of the results of this study, I can see the danger of NGOs transferring most of the discourse and culture of these other spheres of operation to the interface with people in rural communities. This is because issues of these other actors (the state, market and other civil society organizations) negotiating through representations, categorizations and use values of their assistance, as they engage with NGOs might apply. NGOs might already be at a weaker standpoint because of having to raise funds from the same state or market channels, coupled with their legitimacy questions in civil society. This is where ideas from an image-sensitive approach, discussed in this study, might make a difference.

A further situation of the current development context, in which the results of this study would assist the practice of development NGOs, emerges when we consider the current neo-liberal development agenda. Mohan and Stokke (2000) have a point in this connection when they point to the institutional reforms and emphasis on social development and civil participation in this agenda, rather than the market alone. In the case of Malawi, for example, this is evident in the PRSP where the government seeks to develop the rural social infrastructure and empower rural communities (GOM, 2000). More interesting, however, is the argument that Mohan and Stokke (2000) advance; that the current neo-liberal position undertakes a top-down strategy for participation, where NGOs are being included as collaborators. In essence, NGOs are seen as promoters of the new participatory agenda. This agenda, however, according to Mohan and Stokke, does not have significant effects on the structural causes of poverty, which the notion of empowerment from bottom-up is meant to achieve. This shows, therefore, that in the current development agenda, NGOs can only protect the bottom-up participation and empowerment, for transformational development, if they can make a difference in the practice. This is where I also see the discussions in this study contributing, in seeking to engage with representations that adversely include of the poor into social development programs (Wood, 2001).

In discussing the people, however, this study has shown how they negotiate with NGOs through their own representations and categorizations, for their advantage. As a result, the initial intervention intentions of NGOs are not achieved as they were planned, but projects are still implemented. This observation supports the research arguments, which have been advanced in order to 'deconstruct planned interventions' and urged development agencies to appreciate the fact that there is no effective blue print to social interventions (Long, van der Ploeg, 1989, 1994; Arce, 2000). However, this study has shown that not all the people were in a position to change these interventions to their advantage. Within the community were ongoing social action processes, where some of the people were manipulating the ideas of others in order to access NGO assistance, for the advancement of their own goals. In the situation of poverty, even well recognized and respected cultural and social norms are challenged (Pottier, 1999). They can, therefore, be turned into instruments of political access to incoming resources, as demonstrated in this research. An image-sensitive approach would help to reveal who is gaining and losing from the development programs in these situations.

The methodology that was deployed in this study has shown that the use of Personal Construct Theory can be an effective tool for enabling the researcher to stand back from making hasty evaluative judgments during the research. At the same time, the researcher is urged to give people room to question what they think is expected in their interaction with outsiders, in this case the researcher and NGOs, and articulate their own understanding of life experiences. Such a research posture, however, demands continuous, active and analytical engagement with one's data. As a researcher, you can then re-position yourself in order to generate more data in areas, which are deficient and if required, change the strategy for approaching data sources. This is where I found the use of the NUDI*ST computer package a handy tool (see pages 67 and 68).

With NUDI*ST, one is able to organize data and interact with them from different angles in relation to the research questions. The use of memos, which permit you to insert dates, enables you to develop your own changing analytical thoughts about the data being generated in form of research diary. These different analytical ideas in the end become very helpful when developing themes necessary for answering research questions. The inbuilt flexibility of the index trees developed in NUDI*ST also enables you to develop different ways of looking at the same data and ideas and hence develop robust research results and discussions. The major challenge with the package, however, (from my experience) is that it demands a good working knowledge of the way it functions before starting on the main research. Otherwise, even the way the files are imported into the programme affects the way one will use the searching functions and hence the data results. I would, therefore, recommend sound familiarity with the programme before conducting the main research assignment. Similarly, if one decides to use PCT techniques in interviewing, such as using a repertory grid, practical experience in its use, even in a different context from the one in which the main study is to be conducted is desirable. I personally found the process of practicing some of these skills with my research colleagues before going to the field very useful.

The Main Conclusions

The ultimate conclusion for this book is that the transformational development process, which takes place in a situation involving rural actors and NGOs, is based on the nature of their engagement with each other and with the process itself. The exact transformation, or the lack of it, is difficult to externally comprehend, in terms of understanding its full dimensions. However, the different and changing images that development agencies and the people form of the same processes provide us with a window through which we could attempt to follow the process. This is in terms of being able to deliberately seek to understand the position of specific participants in a transformation agenda, pursed through projects. Are they the active agents, able to develop and negotiate their original ideas and visions or not? Is the positive change we are seeing in people's livelihood situation a result of their developing capabilities (agency), that are rooted in their 'cultural currency' (Muchie and Baca, 2001) or a successful external project that will become history after withdrawal of external support? Is there some change that is taking place in people's livelihoods that is significant to people but does not fit our (as external interveners) images of proper change and therefore is not being said or is said negatively? The discussions in this book enable the researcher, development facilitator, development worker, donor, program officer and any person involved in interventions and what they are meant to achieve to ask such searching questions.

The argument, for instance, is that there could be positive transformation as a result of NGO assistance in a certain livelihood situation, which most project evaluations are able to show. This, however, does not mean that certain actors of our concern (e.g. women, youths, the poor or children), who were involved along with the others, were actively engaged in that transformation. They might have been 'enrolled' into the process by others, as case studies discussed in this book have shown, and therefore it is not their empowerment project. Knowing where people are in such a process is crucial information for program managers, so that they can revisit and reshape the design and implementation of projects, for the benefit of those people on whom the projects are focused. They can also properly inform a local or wider advocacy programme from which people in the particular grassroots situations will benefit. For instance, advocacy on how a national food policy affects people in real local communities. Increasingly, it is the voices of the poor themselves or with the poor, rather than mere 'representing them' or 'speaking for' that will become the basis for NGO credibility in these advocacy endeavors. Unless the poor people's nature of agency is actively made the premise for such voices, however, the noise or lack of confidence in their voices will be evident. Otherwise they will perform no more than the parameters set by the supporting external agencies.

Lastly, commitment to understanding the 'agency' position of the powerless in development programming will certainly set us, the researchers, development workers and programme officers on a self-reflective 'pedagogy' (Chambers, 1997; Edwards, 1999). This is necessary because, as demonstrated in several chapters of this book, most of the power to define problems in people's livelihoods, to neatly categorize them and package them for Logical Frameworks, and to then monitor expected change, comes from our images of what should be and what should not be. This comes from our backgrounds, our organizational philosophies and the urge to protect if not increase our cash flows and indeed the security of our jobs. With an image-sensitive analysis helping us to ask appropriate questions, we will be left with a glaring choice of 'whose reality' and 'whose empowerment' we deal with and how. It is my hope most of the readers who interface, directly or indirectly, with the poor in development programming will make some difficult choices as each instance arises for the benefit of the poor.

Recommendations for Development Policy and Practice

The most necessary policy recommendation that emerges from this study is epistemological, a way of approaching reality, in this case, pro-poor development programming reality. The understanding of actor images at the different interface points in NGO assistance is central to programme or project designing. In this connection, I find adopting the framework developed by the Social Policy in Developing Contexts (SDPC) team at the University of Bath (Wood, 2001), a useful starting point. The framework, according to the Bath team, is based on four principles, which are tailored to support the 'meso' (middle) level institutional activity. These are activities meant to enhance the role of organizations of civil society, operating in between the individual household and the state or market, to provide livelihood security for the poor. These principles include,

- That only the poor will ultimately help themselves to the point of structural significance in relation to the basic terms of control over key societal resources;
- That the poor will act according to their perception of options, but that these perceptions can be enlarged by their own and others' actions to expand room for manoeuvre.
- That individual acts can be significant at the level of the graduating individual, but come up against the usual social mobility arguments in which only a few change status and only in steps rather than jumps.
- That collective action can be structurally significant for wider units of solidarity with many gains on the way to full structural re-formation (which may never be). [*Source*: Wood, 2001, p.12].

Most development NGOs have their development philosophies based on the first presumption, in the framework above. World Vision, for instance, defines transformational development as beginning with people (Myers, 1999). This presumption forms the basic epistemology of the theory of social transformation, focusing on the nature of agency of the social actors, as discussed in chapter three. In view of an image-sensitive approach, however, the second to fourth presumptions have to be construed, not in terms of preoccupation with creating organizations, such as project committees or forming loan groups as 'the means', but with a focus on formation of 'strategic alliances' (Edmunds and Wollenburg, 2001). As discussed in chapter nine, strategic alliances imply that people are engaged into joint action with others based on purpose rather than preserving the life of the group *per se*. The purpose of belonging to an organization or group will have to be negotiated in the people's images of their livelihoods goal in mind. This will avoid 'problematic inclusion' of the poor in organizations that do not benefit them (Wood, 2001). For this to happen, however, the way forward is to think more in terms of better 'organizing' rather than 'organizations' (Ostrom, 1995; Crowther, 2000). These authors rightly argue that the former is centered on the process while the later is centered on the end result, 'institutionalization'. This will likely produce a lot of diversity between programs and projects as people exercise their expanding choices within expanding spaces for participation. I concur with Rick Davies to argue that this should be celebrated as empowerment based on 'differences' (2001), as long as negotiations with other actors are properly managed.

This is not to suggest that projects should be based on 'non-interventionist' approaches to development but to argue for creation of space for the often referred to as the 'primary stakeholders' to articulate development from their images of reality. They have to be a position or space where they can put their perceptual meanings on the table with other stakeholders for negotiation and have the right support to reflect on the total picture of their livelihoods based on which they are making decisions and negotiating with external agencies. A total livelihoods picture does not present itself into neat boxes of food, water, education, income and health but a complex web that includes security from witchcraft and such kind of realities. As argued in this book, these realities have strong links to 'power from within' on which other forms of power including 'power to do' and 'power over' are based; all being forms of empowerment. The traditional participatory approaches while able to provide 'situations of empowerment', through allowing people to speak and draw, for instance, they do not provide an 'empowering situation' (Crawley, 1998). It is an empowering situation when there is political space, which the poor effectively use to articulate their livelihoods and organize themselves from meanings as embedded in their socio-cultural frameworks.

This approach has cost implications for the NGOs because they might have to patiently work with the poor as they organize themselves in different ways, including formation of committees that might disband, having accomplished their purpose. This breaking and formation of new associations and groups should be seen as part of the transformational outcomes rather than a negative indicator on capacity building. This implies, therefore, that the ideological understanding of transformational development has to be continually revisited, in response to the grassroots. This is necessary in order to put value where it is most helpful for the people. Looking at the results of this study, value should be a negotiable aspect of development, so that the people's priorities and the NGO's priorities can be properly built into the design process. As indicated elsewhere, the claim that projects are based on 'priorities' of the poor is a fallacy in the context of such a bargain of interfaces as those that occurred between NGOs and the people in the study (Tembo, 2001c). It is this value construction that should also be the basis for NGO negotiations at the interface with donors, market and the state. In this case it becomes the center for the NGOs' political leverage.

Informed from this study and Villarreal's (1992), I define political leverage as the advantage that an actor has over others, which enables him/her to achieve his/her objectives, among other actors who are politically pursuing their objectives at the same interface. The use of advantage in this case does not suggest contained power in assets or popularity (ibid., 1992). In the case of NGOs it does not presuppose that they have power from the amount of funding that they have under their command. From this position they cannot make it with the market, the decentralizing state and the market working through bilateral and multilateral donors. Instead, the NGO advantage will be in their understanding of how specific communities interface with the various programs and the wider environment, showing examples of interventions are benefiting the people and the ones that are impoverishing them, as explained earlier. In my view, this political leverage could improve the effectiveness of NGOs in their negotiation with the state and donors on policy and programmatic issues. This will be a useful policy approach in working for example, with the European Union. The European Union has provided room for non-state actors, including NGOs, to participate in development policy dialogue, planning and programming, and evaluation and review of the development cooperation objectives (ECDPM, 2001) With the many non-state actors involved with different agendas, NGOs could promote pro-poor development cooperation through their analytical abilities that shows how poor people are benefiting.

Limitations of the Research Approach that was used in the Study

The research approach that was used in this study has two limitations that could be considered for future research. The first limitation is the use of categories, such as 'poor', 'traditional leaders' and 'committee members' in generating and analyzing information for the study. These categories, while useful, are not representative of the actual occurrence of images people formed of assistance in these communities. In other words, it should not be claimed that committee members in Zabwe or Mpira were of a certain image while people outside committees were of the other type. Instead, it should be seen as saying that a particular image of assistance was noted, for instance, among committee members rather than among non-committee members. In which case, this categorization cannot form an adequate basis for generalizing results to the community, in order for project designing and implementation processes to be properly informed. For an actual project design process, the researcher should characterize the community based on variations in the nature of images, while continuing with data generation. The resulting categorizations might not follow the conventions indicated above. The NGO researcher can then conduct a quantitative research design and generalize to the population that is involved in the program or project.

The second limitation is that the other interfaces were not studied in depth. For example, within the NGO, the study was more focused in the field but not adequately followed through to the regional and national levels. Similarly, the study of the interface with the government and other NGOs working in those communities, that had an influence on the NGO and community interface, was not adequately explored. I was not able to conduct such a study because of lack of time and the need to get the study focused in order to generate more concretized findings.

For further research, therefore, case studies of other interface areas, especially between NGOs and the state, between NGOs and other NGOs working in similar fields, and between NGOs and donor institutions related to NGO development work would be a worthwhile endeavor. This would generate other theoretical explanations that will assist in building better relationships in development cooperation of the 21st century for the benefit of the poor.

Bibliography

Ackroyd, S. and Hughes, J. (1992), *Data Collection In Context (Second Edition),* Longman, London.

Adler, P.A. and Adler, P. (1994), 'Observation Techniques', in N.K. Denzin and Y.S. Lincoln (eds), *Handbook of Qualitative Research,* Sage, Thousand Oaks, pp. 337-397.

Akroyd, D. (1999), 'Logical Framework Approach to Project Planning, Socio-Economic Analysis to Monitoring and Evaluation Services: A Smallholder Rice Project', *Project Appraisal,* Vol. 17(1), pp.54-66.

Arce, A. (2000), 'Creating or Regulating Development: Representing Modernities Through Language and Discourse', in A. Arce and N. Long (eds), *Anthropology, Development and Modernities: Exploring Discourses, Counter-tendencies and Violence,* Routledge, London and New York, pp. 32-51.

Arce, A. and Long, N. (1993), 'Bridging The Two Worlds: An Ethnography of Bureaucrat-Peasant Relations in Western Mexico', in M.Hobart (ed.), *An Anthropological Critique of Development: The Growth of Ignorance,* Routledge, London and New York, pp. 179-208.

Arce, A. and Long, N. (2000), 'Reconfiguring Modernity and Development from an Anthropological Perspective', in A. Arce and N. Long (eds), *Anthropology, Development and Modernities: Exploring Discourses, Counter-tendencies and Violence,* Routledge, London and New York, pp.1-31.

Atkinson, P. and Coffey, A. (1997), 'Analyzing Documentary Realities', in D. Silverman (ed.), *Qualitative Research: Theory, Method and Practice,* Sage, Thousand Oaks, pp. 45-62.

Atkinson, P. and Hammesley, M. (1998), 'Ethnography and Participant Observation', in N. Denzin and Y. Lincoln (eds), *Strategies of Qualitative Inquiry,* Sage, Thousand Oaks, pp.110-336.

Bates, R.H. (1981), *Markets and States in Tropical Africa: The Political Basis of Agricultural Policies,* University of California Press, Berkeley.

Bebbington, A. (1999), 'Capitals and Capabilities: A Framework for Analyzing Peasant Viability, Rural Livelihoods and Poverty', *World Development,* Vol.12, pp.2021-2044.

Bebbington, A. and Riddell, R. (1995), 'The Direct Funding of Southern NGOs by Donors: New Agendas and Old Problems, *Journal of International Development,* Vol.7(6), pp.879-893.

Becker, H. (1998), *Tricks of the Trade: How to Think About Your Research While You're Doing It,* University of Chicago Press, Chicago and London.

Berger, P. and Luckmann, T. (1984), *The Social Construction of Reality: A Treatise in the Sociology of Knowledge,* Pelican Books, London.

Bevan, P. (2000), 'Who's A Goody? Demythologizing The PRA Agenda', *Journal of International Development,* Vol. 12, pp.751-759.

Biggs, S. (1997), 'Rural Development: Livelihood, Coping and Influencing Strategies of Rural Development Personnel', *Project Appraisal,* Vol. 12(2), pp.101-106.

Booth, D. (ed.) (1994), '*Rethinking Social Development: Theory, Research and Practice,* Longman, Essex.

Bradshaw, B. (1993), *Bridging The Gap: Evangelism, Development and Shalom,* MARC, World Vision International, California.

Brinkerhoff, D.W. and Ingle, D.M. (1989), 'Integrating Blueprint and Process: A Structured Flexibility Approach to Development Management', *Public Administration and Development*, Vol. 9, pp.487-503.

Brown, D. (1991), 'Methodological Considerations in Evaluation of Social Development Programmes: An Alternative Approach', *Community Development Journal*, Vol. 26(4), pp.259-265.

Bryman, A. (1988), *Quantity and Quality in Social Research*, Routledge, London.

Bulmer, M. (1982), (ed.), *Social Research Ethics: An Examination of the Merits of Covert Participant Observation*, Holmes & Meir, New York.

Burkey, S. (1993), *People First: A Guide to Self-Reliant Participatory Rural Development*, Zedbooks, London and New Jersey.

Burns, T. (1992), *Erving Goffman*, Routledge, London and New York.

Buston, K. (1997), 'NUDIST in Action: Its Use and Its Usefulness in a Study of Chronic Illness in Young People', *Sociological Research Online*, Vol. 2(3), http://www.socreonline.org.uk/socreonline/2/3/6.html.

Carney, D. (ed.) (1998), *Sustainable Livelihoods: What Contribution Can We Make?* DFID, London.

Catteral, M. and Maclaran, P. (1997), 'Focus Group Data and Qualitative Analysis Programs: coding the moving picture as well as the snapshots', *Sociological Research Online*, Vol. 2(1), http://www.socreonline.org.uk/socreonline/2/1/6.html.

Cernea, M. (1991), 'Using Knowledge from Social Science in Development Projects', *World Bank Discussion Paper No. 114*, The World Bank, Washington.

Chambers, R. (1993), *Challenging the Professions: Frontiers for Rural Development*, Intermediate Technology Publications, London.

Chambers, R. (1995), 'The Primacy of the Personal', in M. Edwards and D. Hulme (eds) *NGO Performance and Accountability: Beyond the Magic Bullet*, Earthscan, London, pp.207-217.

Chambers, R. (1997a), 'Editorial: Responsible Well-Being – A Personal Agenda for Development', *World Development*, Vol. 25(11), pp.1734-1754.

Chambers, R. (1997b), *Whose Reality Counts? Putting the First Last*, Intermediate Technology, London.

Chambers, R. and Conway, G. (1992), 'Sustainable Rural Livelihoods: Practical Concepts for the 21st Century', *IDS Discussion Paper No. 296*, IDS, Brighton.

Charlton, R. and May, R. (1995), 'NGOs, Politics, Projects and Probity: A Policy Implementation Perspective', *Third World Quarterly*, Vol. 16(2), pp.237-255.

Chilowa, W. and Apthorpe, R. (1997), 'Towards a Malawian Human Development Report', in W. Chilowa (ed.) *Bwalo Vol.1*, Center for Social Research, Zomba, pp.1-9.

Chilowa W. and Chirwa, E. (1997), 'The Impact of Structural Adjustment Programs on Social and Human Development in Malawi', in W. Chilowa (ed) *Bwalo Vol. 1*, Center for Social Research, Zomba, pp.39-68.

Clark, J. (1991), *Democratizing Development: The Role of Voluntary Organizations*, Kumarian Press, West Hartford.

Clark, J. (1995), 'The State, Popular Participation and the Voluntary Sector', *World Development*, Vol. 23(4) pp.593-601.

Cleaver, F. (2001), 'Institutions, Agency and the Limitations of Participatory Approaches to Development', in B. Cooke and U. Kothari (eds) *Participation: The New Tyranny?* Zed Books, London and New York, pp.36-55.

Clegg, S.R. (1989), *Frameworks of Power*, Sage, London.

Cohen, P.S. (1968), *Modern Social Theory*, Heinemann, London.

Coleman, G. (1993), 'Evaluating the Health Impact of Water and Sanitation Projects: It Ain't Necessarily Necessary', *Project Appraisal*, Vol. 8(4), pp.251-255.

Collins, P. (1998), 'Negotiating Selves: Reflections on "Unstructured Interviewing"', *Sociological Research Online*, Vol. 3(3), http://www.socreonline.org.org.uk/socreonline/3/3/2.html.

CONGOMA (1996), *The Directory of Non-Governmental Organizations in Malawi*, Rami Agency, Blantyre.

CONGOMA (1997), NGO Code of Conduct for Malawi, CONGOMA, Blantyre.

CONGOMA/NDI (1997), NGO Policy and Legislation: Southern Africa Regional Workshop Report: CONGOMA/NDI, Blantyre.

Cooke, B. and Kothari, U. (eds) (2001), *Participation: The New Tyranny?* Zed Books, London and New York.

Cornwall, A. (1998), 'Gender, Participation and the Politics of Difference', in I. Guijt and M.K. Shah (eds) *The Myth of Community: Gender Issues in Participatory Development*, Intermediate Technology, London, pp.46-57.

Cornwall, A. (2002), 'Locating Citizen Participation', *IDS Bulletin*, 33 (2), pp. 49-58.

Cotterill, P. and Letherby, G. (1994), 'The Person in the Researcher', in R. Burgess (ed.) *Studies in Qualitative Methodology: Issues in Qualitative Research*, Jai Press, London, pp.107-136.

Cracknell, B.E. (2000), *Evaluating Development Aid: Issues, Problems and Solutions*, Thousand Oaks, Sage.

Craig, D. and Porter, D. (1997), 'Framing Participation: Development Projects, Professionals and Organizations', *Development in Practice*, 7(3), pp.229-236.

Crawley, H. (1998), 'Living Up to the Empowerment Claim? The Potential of PRA', in I.Guijt and M.K. Shah (eds) *The Myth of Community: Gender Issues in Participatory Development*, Intermediate Technology, London, pp.24-34.

Croll, E. and Parkin, D. (1992), 'Cultural Understandings of the Environment', in E. Croll and D. Parkin (eds) *Bush Base: Forest Farm: Culture, Environment and* Development, Routledge, London, pp.11-36

Crowther, S. (2000), 'NGOs and Local Organizations: A Mismatch of Goals and Practice? In D. Lewis and T. Wallace (eds) *New Roles and Relevance: Development NGOs and the Challenge of Change*, Kumarian, Connecticut, pp.165-175.

Curtis, D. (1991), *Beyond Government: Organisations for Common Benefit*, Macmillan, London.

Curtis, D. (1995), 'Power to the People: Rethinking Community Development', in N. Nelson and S. Wright (eds) *Power and Participatory Development: Theory and Practice*, Intermediate Technology Publications, London, pp.115-132.

Cusworth, J.W. and Franks, T.R. (eds) (1993), *Managing Projects in Developing Countries*, Addison Wesley Longman, Harlow, Essex.

Dalton, P. and Dunnett, G. (1992), *A Psychology for Living: Personal Construct Theory for Professionals and Clients*, John Wiley and Sons, New York.

Davies, R. (2001), 'Does Empowerment Start At Home? And If So How Will We Recognise It? In P. Oakley (ed.) *Evaluating Empowerment: Reviewing the Concept and Practice*, INTRAC, Oxford, pp.128-137.

Denzin, N.K. and Lincoln, Y.S. (eds) (1994), *Handbook of Qualitative Research*, Sage, Thousand Oaks.

Devereux, S. (1993), *Theories of Famine*, Harvester Wheatsheaf, Hemel Hempstead.

Devereux, S. (1997), 'Household Food Security in Malawi', *IDS Discussion Paper No. 362*, IDS, Brighton.

DFID (1999), *Sustainable Livelihoods Guidance Sheets*, DFID, London.

Digest, R.S. (ed.) (1987) *Reader's Digest Universal Dictionary*, The Reader's Association Limited, London.

Dingwall, R. (1997), 'Methodological Issues in Qualitative Research', in G. Miller and R. Dingwall (eds) *Context and Method in Qualitative Research*, Sage, Thousand Oaks, pp.51-65.

Dowding, K. (1991), *Rational Choice and Political Power*, Edward Elgar Publishing Ltd, Aldershot.

Dowding, K. (1992), 'Choice: Its Increase and its Value', *British Journal of Political Science*, Vol. 22, pp.301-314.

Dowding, K. (1996), *Power*, Open University, Buckingham.

Drinkwater, M. (1992), 'Visible Actors and Visible Researchers: Critical Hermeneutics in an Actor-Oriented Perspective', *Sociologia Ruralis*, xxxii (4), pp. 367-388.

Drinkwater, M. (1994), 'Knowledge, Consciousness and Prejudice: Adaptive Research in Zambia', in I.Scoones and J. Thompson (eds) *Beyond Farmer First: Rural People's Knowledge, Agricultural Research and Extension Practice*, Intermediate Technology, London, pp.88-93.

Dunn, E.S. (1984), 'The Nature of Social Learning', in D.C. Korten and R. Klauss (eds) *People-Centered Development: Contributions Towards Theory and Planning Frameworks*, Kumarian, Connecticut, pp.171-175.

Dusseldorp, D.V. (1990), 'Planned Development via Projects: Its Limitations and Possible Improvements', *Sociologia Ruralis*, Xxx (3/4), pp. 337-351.

Eade, D. (1997), *Capacity Building: An Approach to People-Centered Development*, Oxfam, Oxford.

ECDPM, (2001), *Cotonou Infokit: The New ACP-EU Partnership Agreement*, Maastricht, The Netherlands.

Edmunds, D. and Wollenberg, E. (2001), 'A Strategic Approach to Multi-Stakeholder Negotiations', *Development and Change*, (32), pp.231-253.

Edwards, M (1999), *Future Positive: International Cooperation in the 21st Century*, Earthscan, London.

Edwards, M. (2002), 'Does the doormat influence the boot? Critical thoughts on UK NGOs and international advocacy', in D. Eade (ed.), *Development and Advocacy*, introduced by Maria Teresa Diokno-Pascual, Oxfam, Oxford, pp.95-112.

Edwards, M. and Hulme, D. (eds) (1992), *Making a Difference: NGOs in a Changing World*, Earthscan, London.

Edwards, M. and Hulme, D. (eds) (1995), *NGOs Performance and Accountability: Beyond the Magic Bullet*, Earthscan, London.

Edwards, M, Hulme, D. and Wallace, T. (2000), 'Increasing Leverage for Development: Challenges for NGOs in a Global Future', in D. Lewis and T. Wallace (eds) *New Roles and Relevance: Development NGOs and the Challenge of Change*, Kumarian Press, Connecticut, pp.1-14.

Edwards, M. and Sen, G. (2000), 'NGOs, Social Change and Transformation of Human Relationships: a 21st Century Civic Agenda', *Third World Quarterly*, 21(4), pp.605-616.

Elwert, G. and Biesrchenk, T. (1988), 'Aid and Development: Special Issue', *Sociologia Ruralis*, Xxvii (2).

Epting, F.S., Prichard, S., Leitner, L.M. and Dunnett, G. (1996), 'Personal Constructions of the Social', in M. Walker and D. Kalekin-Fishman (eds) *The Construction of Group Realities: Culture, Society and Personal Construct Theory*, Krieger, Florida, pp.309-322.

Escobar, A. (1999), 'Discourse and Power in Development: Michael Foulcalt and the relevance of his work to the Third World', in T. Jacobson and J. Servaes (eds) *Theoretical Approaches to participatory Communication*, Hampton Press, New Jersey, pp.309-335.

Eyben, R. and Ladbury, S. (1995), 'Popular Participation in Aid-Assisted Projects: Why more in theory than practice? In N. Nelson and S. Wright (eds) *Power and Participatory Development: Theory and Practice*, Intermediate Technology, London, pp.192-200.

Farrington, J. and Bebbington, A. (eds) *Reluctant Partners? NGOs, The State and Sustainable Agriculture Development*, Routledge, London.

Fetterman, D.M. (1998), *Ethnography: Step by Step (2nd Edition)*, Sage, Thousand Oaks.

Fowler, A. (1988), 'Non-Governmental Organisations in Africa: Achieving Comparative Advantage in Relief and Micro-Development', *IDS Discussion Paper No. 249*, IDS, Brighton.

Fowler, A. (1996) 'Strengthening Civil Society in Transitional Economies- From Concept to Strategy: Mapping an Exit in a Maze of Mirrors', in A. Clayton (ed.) *NGOs, Civil Society and the State: Building Democracy in Transitional Societies*, INTRAC, Oxford.

Fowler, A. (1997), '*Striking a Balance: A Guide to Enhancing The Effectiveness of Non-Governmental Organisations in International Development*, Earthscan, London.

Fowler, A, (2000a), NGO Futures Beyond Aid: NGDO Values and The Fourth Position', *Third World Quarterly*, 21(4), pp.589-603.

Fowler, A. (2000b), 'Civil Society, NGDOs and Social Development: changing the rules of the game', *UNRISD Occasional Paper No. 1*, UNRISD, Geneva.

Fowler, A. and Biekart, B. (1996), 'Do Private Agencies Really Make A Difference? In D. Sogge with K. Biekart and J. Saxby (eds) *Compassion and Calculation: The Business of Private Foreign Aid*, Pluto Press, London and Chicago, pp.107-145.

Freire, P. (1972), *Pedagogy of the oppressed*, Penguin, London.

Friedmann, J. (1992), *Empowerment: The Politics of Alternative Development*, Blackwell, Cambridge and Oxford.

Fuglesang, A. (1982), *About Understanding: Ideas and Observations on Cross-Cultural Communication*, Dag Hammarkjold Foundation, Uppsla.

Garber, B. and Jenden, P. (1993), 'Anthropologists or Anthropology? The Band-Aid Perspective on Development Projects', in J. Pottier (ed.) *Practicing Development: Social Science Perspectives*, Routledge, London, pp.50-70.

Gaventa, J. (1980), *Power and Powerlessness: Quiescence and Rebellion in an Appalachian Valley*, Clarendon Press, Oxford.

Giddens, A. (1990), 'Structuration Theory and Sociological Analysis', in J. Clark, C. Modgil and S. Modgil (eds) *Anthony Giddens: Consensus and Controversy*, Farmer Press, pp. 47-56.

Glagow, M.H., Lowmann, H., Nickolmann, S., Paul, K., and Paul, S. (1997), *Non-Governmental Organizations in Malawi: their contribution to development and democratization*, Transaction Publishers, Hamburg.

Goffman, E. (1969), *Presentation of Self in Everyday Life*, Penguin Press, London.

GOM, (1987), *Statement of Development Policies 1987-1996*, Department of Economic Planning, Lilongwe.

GOM, (1994), *Food Security and Nutrition Bulletin*, 5(1), Ministry of Economic Planning, Lilongwe.

GOM, (1995), *Policy Framework for Poverty Alleviation Programme*, PAP Coordination Unit, Ministry of Economic Planning and Development, Lilongwe.

GOM, (2000), *Interim Poverty Reduction and Growth Strategy Paper - A Road Map*, Department of Economic Planning and Development, Lilongwe.

GOM, (n.d.) 'Local Governance and Development Management: Organization Flow Chart', Ministry of Economic Planning and Development, Lilongwe.

Gosling, L. and Edwards, M. (1995), *Toolkits: A Practical Guide to Assessment, Monitoring Review and Evaluation*, Save The Children, London.

Gueye, B. (1999), 'Whither Participation? Experience From Franchophone West Africa', *Programme Issue Paper No. 87*, IIED Drylands Programme.

Guijt, A, and Shah, M.K. (1998), 'Waking up to Power, Conflict and Process', in I. Guijt and M.K. Shah (eds) *The Myth of Community*, Intermediate Technology Publications, London, pp.1-23.

Gutie'rrez, G. (1988), *A Theology of Liberation: History, Politics and Salvation*, SCM Press, London.

Hamlyn, D.W. (1996), *Understanding Perception: The Concept and its Conditions*, Avebury, Aldershot.

Hammersley, M. (1995), *The Politics of Social Research*, Sage, London.

Hammersley, M. and Altkinson, P. (1995), *Ethnography Principles and Practice (Second Edition)*, Routledge, London.

Harvey, L. (1990), *Critical Social Research*, UNWIN Hyman, London.

Hentschel, J. (1999), 'Contextuality and Data Collection Methods: A Framework and Its Application to Health Service Utilization', *Journal of Development Studies*, 35(4), pp.64-94.

Hobart, M. (ed.) (1993), *An Anthropological Critique of Development: The Growth of Ignorance*, Routledge, London.

Holland, R. (1999), 'Reflexivity', *Human Relations*, 52(4), pp.463-484.

Honadle, G. and Rosengard, J. (1993), 'Putting 'Projectized' Development in Perspective, *Public Administration and Development*, 3(4), pp.299-305.

Hope, A. and Timmel, S. (1984), *Training for Transformation: A Handbook for Community Workers*, Mambo Press, Zimbabwe.

Hulme, D. and Edwards, M. (eds) (1997), *NGOs, States and Donors: Too Close For Comfort?* Macmillan Press, London.

Hulme, D. and Mosley, P. (1996), *Finance Against Poverty*, Routledge, London.

Hutson, S. and Liddiard, M. (1993), 'Agencies and Young People: Runaways and Young Homeless in Wales', in J. Pottier (ed.) *Practicing Development: Social Science Perspectives*, Routledge, London, pp. 34-49.

Ingold, T. (1992), 'Culture and The Perception of the Environment', in E. Croll and D. Parkin (eds) *Bush Base: Forest Farm: Culture, Environment and Development*, Routledge, London and New York, pp. 39-56.

Jenkins, R. (2000), 'Categorization, Identity, Social Process and Epistemology', *Current Sociology*, 48(3), pp. 7-25.

Kabeer, N. (1996), 'Agency, Well-Being and Inequality: Reflections on The Gender Dimensions of Poverty, *IDS Bulletin* 27 (1) pp. 11-21.

Kabeer, N. (1998), 'Money Can't Buy Me Love? Re-Evaluating Gender, Credit and Empowerment in Rural Bangladesh', *IDS Discussion Paper 363*, IDS, Brighton.

Kabeer, N. (1999), 'The Conditions and Consequences of Choice: Reflections on the Measurement of Women's Empowerment', *UNRISD Discussion Paper No. 108*, UNRISD, Geneva.

Kapambwe, T. (1995), 'World Vision's Goal- Mageria', *Vision Forum*, 2(6), pp.4.

Kaspin, D. (1995), 'The Politics of Ethnicity in Malawi's Democratic Transition', *Journal of Modern African Studies*, 33(4), pp.595-620.

Kincheloe, J.L. and Mclaren, P. (1994), 'Rethinking Critical Theory and Quantitative Research', in K. Denzin and Y.L. Lincoln (eds) *Handbook of Qualitative Research*, Sage, Thousand Oaks, pp.138-157.

Kishindo, P. (2001), 'The Malawi Social Action Fund and community development', *Community Development Journal*, 36 (4), 303-311.

Korten, D.C. (1990), *Getting to The 21st Century: Voluntary Action and The Global Agenda*, Kumarian, Connecticut

Korten, D.C. (1995), *When Corporations Rule The World*, Earthscan, London.

Krueger, R.A. (1994), *Focus Groups: A Practical Guide for Applied Research (2nd Edition)*, Sage, Thousand Oaks.

Kutengule, M. (1997), 'Resource Mobilization for Basic Education and Health Care', in W. Chilowa (ed.) *Bwalo Vol. 1*, Center for Social Research, Zomba.

Lakoff, G. and Johnson, M. (1986), *Metaphors We Live By*, Chicago University Press, London and Chicago.

Lecomte, B. (1986), *Project Aid: Limitations and Alternatives*, QECD, Paris.

Leeuwis, C. (2000), 'Reconceptualising Participation for Development: Towards a Negotiation Approach', *Development and Change*, 31(5), pp.931-959.

Leitner, L.M., Begley, E.A. and Faidley, A.J. (1996), 'Cultural Construing and Marginalized Persons: Role Relationships and ROLE Relationships', in B.M. Walker and D. Kalekin-Fishman (eds) *The Construction of Group Realities: Culture, Society and Personal Construct Theory*. Krieger, Florida, pp.323-340.

Lewis, D. and Wallace, T. (eds) (2000), *New Roles and Relevance: Development NGOs and the Challenge of Change*, Kumarian, Connecticut.

Long, N. (1977), *An Introduction to the Sociology of Rural Development*, Tavistock/Westview Press, London.

Long, N. (ed.) (1989) *Encounters At The Interface: A Perspective on Social Discontinuities in Rural Development*, Wageningen Studies in Sociology, Wageningen.

Long, N. (1997), 'Agency and Constraints, Perceptions and Practice: A Theoretical Position', in H. de Haan and N. Long (eds) *Images and Realities of Rural Life: Wageningen Perspectives on Rural Transformation*, Van Gorcum, Netherlands, pp.1-20.

Long, N. (2000), 'Exploring Local/Global Transformations: A View from Anthropology', in A. Arce and N. Long (eds) *Anthropology, Development and Modernities: Exploring Discourses, Counter-tendencies and Violence*, Routledge, London, pp.184-201.

Long, N. and van der Ploeg, J.D. (1989), 'Demythologizing Planned Intervention: An Actor Perspective, *Sociologia Ruralis*, Xxix (3/4), pp.226-249.

Long, N. and van der Ploeg, (1994), 'Heterogeneity, Agency and Structure: towards a reconstitution of the concept of structure', in D. Booth (ed.) *Rethinking Social Development: Theory, Research and Practice*, Longman, Harlow, pp.62-89.

Long, N. and Villareal, M. (1994), 'The Interweaving of Knowledge and Power in Development Interfaces', in I. Scoones and J. Thompson (eds) *Beyond Farmer First: Rural People's Knowledge, Agricultural Research and Extension Practice*, Intermediate Technology, London, pp.41-52.

Lucey, T. (1991), *Management Information Systems*, DP Publications, London.

Lukes, S. (1974), *Power: A Radical Review*, Macmillan, London.

Lyon, G. (1999), 'Language and Perceptual Experience', *Philosophy*, 74(290), pp.515-534.

MRCS, (1996), 'Community-Based Health Development Program (1997- 2001) in Karonga, Dedza and Machinga', MRCS, Blantyre.

Marsden, D., Oakley, P. and Pratt, B. (eds) (1994) *Measuring Process: Guidelines for Evaluating Social Development*, INTRAC, Oxford.

MASAF, (1998), 'MASAF Fact File: Total Projects Approved as at July, 1998', MASAF, Blantyre.

MASAF, (1999), 'Getting Acquainted with MASAF: An Orientation Booklet for Stakeholders in the Malawi Social Action Fund', MASAF, Lilongwe.

Mason, J. (1996), *Qualitative Researching*, Sage, London.

Mawdsley, E., Townsend, J.G., Porter, G. and Oakley, P. (2002), *Knowledge, Power and Development Agendas: NGOs North and South*, INTRAC, Oxford.

Maxwell, D. and Wiebe, K. (1999), 'Land Tenure and Food Security: exploring dynamic linkages', *Development and Change*, 30(4), pp.825-849.

Maxwell, J.A. (1992), 'Understanding Validity in Qualitative Research', *Harvard Education Review*, (62), pp.279-300.

Maxwell, J.A. (1998), 'Designing A Qualitative Study', in L. Bickman and R. Rog (eds) *Handbook of Applied Social Research Methods*, Sage, Thousand Oaks, pp.69-100.

Mayoux, L. (2001), 'Participatory Programme Learning for Women's Empowerment in Micro-Finance Programmes: Negotiating Complexity, Conflict and Change', in P. Oakley (ed.), *Evaluating Empowerment: Reviewing the Concept and Practice*, INTRAC, Oxford, pp.152-167.

Menike, K. (1997), 'People's Empowerment from the People's Perspective', in D. Eade (ed.) *Development Patronage: Selected Articles from Development in Practice*, Oxfam, Oxford, pp.25-30.

Middleton, N. and O'Keefe, P. (2001), *Redefining Sustainable Development*, Pluto Press, London.

Miles, M.B. and Huberman, M. (1994), *Qualitative Data Analysis: An Expanded Sourcebook*, Sage, Thousand Oaks.

Mohan, G. and Stokke, K. (2000), 'Participatory Development and Empowerment: The Dangers of Localism', *Third World Quarterly*, 21(2), pp. 247-268.

Mohan, G. (2001), 'Beyond Participation: Strategies for Deeper Empowerment', in B. Cooke and U. Kothari (eds) *Participation: The New Tyranny?* Zed Books, London and New York, pp. 153-167.

Morgan, D.L. (1998), *The Focus Group Guide Book: Focus Group Kit 1*, Sage, Thousand Oaks.

Morse, D. (1995), 'Designing Funded Qualitative Research', in N. Denzin and Y. Lincoln (eds) *Strategies of Qualitative Inquiry*, sage, Thousand Oaks, pp.56-85.

Mosse, D. (1995), 'People's Knowledge in Project Planning: The Limits and Social Conditions of Participation in Planning Agricultural Development', *ODI Agricultural Research and Extension Network Paper No. 58*, ODI, London.

Mosse, D. (1998), Process-Oriented Approaches to Development Practice and Social Research', in D. Mosse, J. Farrington and A. Rews (eds) *Development as Process: Concepts and Methods for Working with Complexity*, Routledge, London, pp.3-20.

Muchie, M. and Baca, S. (2001), 'The Distinction between Self-organizing Local Civil Society and the Global Constitution of Civil Society in Africa', Paper presented at the Second ISTR Africa Region Conference, Nairobi, Kenya.

Mukherjee, S. and Benson, T. (2003), 'The Determinants of Poverty in Malawi, 1998' *World Development*, 31 (2), pp.339-358.

Mushota, L. (1995), 'The Case of Women and Law Approach to Development in Zambia', in V. Titi and N. Singh (eds) *Empowerment for Sustainable Development: Towards Operational Strategies*, Fernwood, London.

Myers, B.L. (1999), *Walking with the Poor: Principles and Practices of Transformational Development*, Orbis Books, New York.

Myers, B.L. and Bradshaw, B. (1996), 'Introducing the Spiritual Dimension into Participatory Community Appraisals: Going Beyond Physical Needs for Transformational Development', *World Vision Staff Working Paper No. 21*.

Najam, A. (1996), 'NGO Accountability: A Conceptual Framework', *Development Policy Review*, 14(4), pp.339-353.

Narayan, D. (2002), *Empowerment and Poverty Reduction: A Source Book*, The World Bank, Washington DC.

Nelson, N. and Wright, S. (eds) (1995), *Power and Participatory Development*, Intermediate Technology Publications, London.

New, C. (1994), 'Structure, Agency and Social Transformation', *Journal for the Theory of Social Behaviour*, 24(3), pp.187-205.

Oakley, P. (1995), *People's Participation in Development Projects: A Critical Review of Current Theory and Practice*, INTRAC, Oxford.

Oakley, P. (ed.) (2001), *Evaluating Empowerment: Reviewing the Concept and Practice*, INTRAC, Oxford.

Oakley, P. and Marsden, D. (1984), *Approaches to Participation in Rural Development*, ILO, Geneva.

Oakley, P. and Marsden, D. (1991), *Projects with People: The Practice of Participation in Rural Development*, ILO, Geneva.

Ostrom, E. (1990), *Governing the Commons: The Evolution of Institutions for Collective Action*, Cambridge University Press, London.

Ostrom, E. (1995), 'Constituting Social Capital and Collective Action', in R. Keohane and E. Ostrom (eds) *Local Commons and Global Interdependence: heterogeneity and cooperation in two domains*, Sage, London, pp.125-160.

Peters. P. (1996), 'Failed Magic or Social Context? Market Liberalization and the Poor in Malawi', *Development Discussion Paper No. 562*, Institute for International Development, Harvard.

Pope, M. and Denicolo, P. (1993), 'Personal Psychology - Theory and Practice: The Art and Science of Constructivist Research in Teacher Thinking', *Teachers and Teacher Education*, 9 (5/6), pp.529-596.

Porter, D.; Allen, B. and Thompson, G. (1991), *Development in Practice: Paved With Good Intentions*, Routledge, London.

Pottier, J. (1989) 'Debating Styles in Rwanda Cooperatives: reflections on language, policy and gender', in R. Grillo (ed.) *Social Anthropology and the Politics of Language*, Routledge, London and New York, pp. 41- 60.

Pottier, J. (1999), *Anthropology of Food: The Social Dynamics of Food Security*, Polity Press, Cambridge.

Punch, K. (1998), *Introduction to Social Research: Quantitative and Qualitative Research Approaches*, Sage, London.

Quisumbing, A. (1996), 'Male-Female Differences in Agricultural Productivity: Methodological Issues and Empirical Evidence', *World Development*, 24(10), pp.1579-1595.

Rakodi, C. (1999), 'A Capital Assets Framework for Analyzing Household Livelihood Strategies: Implications for Policy', *Development Policy Review*, 17(3), pp.315-342.

Ravazi, S. (1999), 'Gendered Poverty and Well-Being: Introduction', *Development and Change*, 30(3), pp.409-433.

Reiss, G. (1992), *Project Management Demystified: Today's Tools and Techniques*, E. & F. N. Spon, London.

Richards, P. (1993), 'Cultivation: Knowledge or Performance? In M. Hobart (ed.) *An Anthropological Critique of Development: The Growth of Ignorance*, Routledge, London and New York, pp.61-78.

Rogers, A. (2000), 'Literacy Comes Second: Working with Groups in Developing Societies', *Development in Practice*, 10(2), pp.236-239.

Rogge, T. (1997), 'A Brief Overview of the NGO Sector in Malawi: Options for CIDA Programming', INTRAC, Oxford.

Rondinelli, D. (1983), 'Projects as Instruments of Development Administration: A Qualified Defense and Suggestions for Improvement', *Public Administration and Development*, 3, pp.307-327.

Rondinelli, D. (1993), *Development Projects as Policy Experiments: An Adaptive Approach to Development Administration*, Routledge, London and New York.

Rowlands, J. (1995), 'Empowerment Examined', *Development in Practice*, 5(2), pp.101-106.

Rutherford, S. (2000), 'Raising the Curtain on the Micro-Financial Services Era', *Small Enterprise Development*, 11(1), pp.13-25.

Sayer, A. (1992), *Method in Social Science: A Realist Approach*, Routledge, London.

Schneider, H. (1999), 'Participatory Governance for Poverty Reduction', *Journal of International Development*, 11, pp.521-534.

Schroeder, L. (2000), 'Social Funds and Local Government: The Case of Malawi', *Public Administration and Development*, 11, pp.521-534.

Schuurman, F.J. (ed.) (1993) *Beyond the Impasse: New Directions in Development Theory*, Zed Books, London.

Scoones, I. (1998), 'Sustainable Rural Livelihoods: A Framework for Analysis', *IDS Working Paper No. 72*, IDS, Brighton.

Scoones, I. and Thompson, J. (eds) (1994), *Beyond Farmer First: Rural People's Knowledge, Agricultural Research and Extension Practice*, Intermediate Technology Publications, London.

Scott, J.C. (1985), *Weapons Of The Weak: Everyday Forms of Peasant Resistance*, Yale University Press, New Haven and London.

Sen, A. (1981), *Poverty and Famines: An Essay on Entitlement and Deprivation*, Clarendon Press, Oxford.

Sen, A. (1997), *Resources, Values and Development*, Harvard University Press, Cambridge.

Seur, H. (1992), 'The Engagement of Researcher and Local Actors in the Construction of Case Studies and Research Themes: Exploring Methods of Restudy', in A. Long and N. Long (eds) *Battlefields of Knowledge: The Interlocking of Theory and Practice in Social Research and Development*, Routledge, London, pp.115-143.

Shields, D. (1993), 'What is a Logical Framework? A Step by Step User's Guide', *The Rural Extension Bulletin 1*, AERDD, University of Reading, pp.15-20.

Shorthall, S. (1992), 'Power Analysis and Farm Wives: An Empirical Study of the Power Relationships Affecting Women on Irish Farms', *Sociologia Ruralis*, Xxxii, (4), pp.431-451.

Silverman, D. (1997), 'Validity and Credibility in Qualitative Research', in G. Miller and R. Dingwall (eds) *Context and Method in Qualitative Research*, Sage, London, pp.12-25.

Smiller, K.R. (1994), 'Rural Poverty and Income Sources of Smallholder Farmers: A Household Economics Analysis with Panel Data from Northern Malawi', Unpublished PhD Thesis, Cornell University.

Smillie, I. (1997), 'NGOs and Development Assistance: A Change in Mind-Set? *Third World Quarterly*, 18(3), pp.563-577.

So, A.J. (1990), '*Social Change and Development: Modernization, Dependency and World Systems Theories*, Sage, London.

Squire, L. (2001), 'The World Development Report and the Global Network', *Journal of International Development*, 13, pp.813-821.

Srinivasan, L. (1990), *Tools For Community Participation: A Manual For Training Trainers in Participatory Techniques*, Prowess/UNDP, New York.

Stadler, J. (1995), 'Development, Research and Participation: Towards a Critique of Participatory Rural Appraisal Methods', *Development Southern Africa*, 12(6), pp.805-814.

Stake, R.E. (1995), *The Art of Case Study Research*, Sage, Thousand Oaks.

Stake, R.E. (1998), 'Case Studies' in N. Denzin and Rain Y. Lincoln (eds) *Strategies of Qualitative Research*, Sage, Thousand Oaks, pp.86-109.

Strauss, A. and Corbin, J. (1998), *Basics of Qualitative Research: Techniques And Procedures For Developing Grounded Theory*, Sage, Thousand Oaks.

Tembo, F. (2001a), 'Understanding 'Agency' Through Interface Image-conflicts for Improving the Design of NGO's Social Transformation Projects: case studies from Malawi', Unpublished PhD Thesis, IRDD, The University of Reading.

Tembo, F. (2001b), 'Conflicting Images Underlying Assistance Negotiation: The Case of NGDOs Working with Rural Communities in Malawi', Paper presented at the CGPE Conference on "The Global Constitution of Failed States: Consequences of a New Imperialism?" University of Sussex.

Tembo, F. (2001c), 'Deconstructing The Role of NGO Assistance in People's Livelihoods at the NGO/Community Interface: Case Studies from Malawi', Paper presented at the DSA Annual Conference, SOAS, London.

Titi, V. and Singh, N. (eds) (1995), *Empowerment for Sustainable Development: Towards Operational Strategies*, Fernwood, London.

Townsend, J. G., Zapata, E., Rowlands, J., Alberti, P. and Melcado M. (1999), *Women and Power: Fighting Patriarchies and Poverty*, Zed Books, London.

Tucker, V. (1999), 'The Myth of Development: A Critique of Eurocentric Discourse', in R.Munch and D. O'Hearn (eds) *Critical Development Theory: Contributions to a New Paradigm*, Zed Books, London and New Jersey, pp.113-134.

Turner, M. and Hulme, D. (1997), *Governance, Administration and Development: Making The State Work*, Macmillan Press, Houndmills.

Tvedt, T. (1998), *Angels of Mercy or Development Diplomats? NGOs and Foreign Aid*, Africa World Press, Trenton.

Vakil, A.C. (1997), 'Confronting The Classification Problem: Toward A Taxonomy of NGOs', *World Development*, 25(12), pp.2057-2070.

Vilarreal, M. (1992), 'The Poverty of Practice: Power, Gender and Intervention From an Actor-Oriented Perspective', in N. Long and A. Long (eds) *Battlefields of Knowledge: The Interlocking of Theory and Practice in Social Research and Development*, Routledge, London and New York, pp.247-267.

Walker, B.M. (1996), 'A Psychology For Adventures: An Introduction To Personal Construct Psychology From A Social Perspective', in B.M. Walker and D. Kalekin-Fishman (eds) *The Construction of Group Realities: Culture, Society and Personal Construct Theory*, Krieger, Florida, pp.7-23.

Warner, M. (2001), *Complex Problems, Negotiated Solutions: Tools to Reduce Conflict in Community Development*, ITDG Publishing, London.

wa Thiong'o, N. (1997), *Writers in Politics: A Re-Engagement with Issues of Literature and Society (A Revised and Enlarged Edition)*, James Curry, Oxford.

White, K. (1999), 'Importance of Sensitivity to Culture in Development Work', in T. Jacobson and J. Servaes (eds) *Theoretical Approaches to Participatory Communication*, Hampton Press, New Jersey, pp.17-49.

White, S. (1996), 'Depoliticising Development: The Uses and Abuses of Participation', *Development and Change*, 6(1), pp.6-15.

Weild, S. (1992), 'Unemployment and Making a Living', in T. Allen and A. Thomas (eds) *Poverty and Development in the 1990s*, Oxford University Press, Oxford, pp.55-77.

Wiggins, S. and Shields, D. (1995), 'Clarifying the 'Logical Framework' as a Tool for Planning and Managing Development Projects, *Project Appraisal*, 10(1), pp.2-12.

Willutzki, U. and Duda, L. (1996), 'The Social Construction of Powerfulness and Powerlessness', in B.M. Walker and D. Kalekin-Fishman (eds) *The Construction of Group Realities: Culture, Society and Personal Construct Theory*, Krieger, 341-362.

Wilmott, R. (1997), 'Structure, Culture and Agency: Rejecting The Current Orthodoxy of Organization Theory', *Journal of The Theory of Social Behaviour*, 27(1), pp.93-123.

Wood, G. (2001), 'Governance and The Common Man: Embedding Social Policy in Search For Security', Paper prepared for the SDPC, University of Bath Workshop.

World Bank, (1995), *'Malawi Agricultural Sector Memorandum: Strategy and Options in the 1990s (Volume 2)'*, The World Bank, Washington DC.

Wright, G. (1999), 'Examining The Impact of Micro-Finance Services: Increasing Income or Reducing Poverty? *Small Enterprise Development*, 10(1), pp.38-47.

WVI, (1991), 'Mission Statement For World Vision', World Vision International Partnership Office, California.

WVM, (1988), 'Training Manual No.1: History of World Vision', World Vision Malawi, Blantyre.

WVM, (1991), 'The Area Programme Approach', World Vision Malawi, Blantyre.

WVM, (1995), 'Strategic Directions: FY95 – FY 97', World Vision Malawi, Blantyre.

WVSA, (2000), 'ADP 2000 Initiative: Level 1 Report', World Vision Southern Africa Sub-Region, Johannesburg.

Yin, J. (1998), 'The Abridged Version of Case Study Research: Design and Method', in L. Bickman and D.J. Rog (eds) *Handbook of Applied Social Research Methods*, Sage, Thousand Oaks, pp.229-259.

Yin, J. (1994), *Case Study Research: Design and Methods*, Sage, Thousand Oaks.

Index